STUDIES IN AFRICAN AMERICAN HISTORY AND CULTURE

Edited By
Graham Russell Hodges
Colgate University

A ROUTLEDGE SERIES

STUDIES IN AFRICAN AMERICAN HISTORY AND CULTURE
GRAHAM RUSSELL HODGES, *General Editor*

ERADICATING THIS EVIL
Women in the American Anti-Lynching Movement, 1892–1940
Mary Jane Brown

PROPHETS OF RAGE
The Black Freedom Struggle in San Francisco, 1945–1969
Daniel Crowe

AN UNDERGROWTH OF FOLLY
Public Order, Race Anxiety, and the 1903 Evansville, Indiana Riot
Brian Butler

UPLIFTING THE WOMEN AND THE RACE
The Educational Philosophies and Social Activism of Anna Julia Cooper and Nannie Helen Burroughs
Karen A. Johnson

GRASS ROOTS REFORM IN THE BURNED-OVER DISTRICT OF NEW YORK
Religion, Abolitionism, and Democracy
Judith Wellman

W. E. B. DUBOIS
The Quest for the Abolition of the Color Line
Zhang Juguo

AFRICANS AND INDIANS
An Afrocentric Analysis of Contacts Between Africans and Indians in Colonial Virginia
Barbara A. Faggins

NEW YORK'S BLACK REGIMENTS DURING THE CIVIL WAR
William Seraile

JESUIT SLAVEHOLDING IN MARYLAND, 1717–1838
Thomas Murphy, S.J.

"WHITE" AMERICANS IN "BLACK" AFRICA
Black and White American Methodist Missionaries in Liberia, 1820–1875
Eunjin Park

THE ORIGINS OF THE AFRICAN AMERICAN CIVIL RIGHTS MOVEMENT, 1865–1956
Aimin Zhang

RELIGIOSITY, COSMOLOGY, AND FOLKLORE
The African Influence in the Novels of Toni Morrison
Therese E. Higgins

SOMETHING BETTER FOR OUR CHILDREN
Black Organizing in Chicago Public Schools, 1963–1971
Dionne Danns

TEACH THE NATION
Public School, Racial Uplift, and Women's Writing in the 1890s
Anne-Elizabeth Murdy

THE ART OF THE BLACK ESSAY
From Meditation to Transcendence
Cheryl B. Butler

EMERGING AFRIKAN SURVIVALS
An Afrocentric Critical Theory
Kamau Kemayó

SLAVERY IN THE CHEROKEE NATION
The Keetoowah Society and the Defining of a People, 1855–1867
Patrick N. Minges

TROUBLING BEGINNINGS
Trans(per)forming African American History and Identity
Maurice E. Stevens

GIVING A VOICE TO THE VOICELESS
Four Pioneering Black Women Journalists

Jinx Coleman Broussard

Routledge
New York & London

Published in 2004 by
Routledge
29 West 35th Street
New York, NY 10001
www.routledge-ny.com

Published in Great Britain by
Routledge
11 New Fetter Lane
London EC4P 4EE
www.routledge.co.uk

Copyright © 2004 by Taylor & Francis Books, Inc.

Routledge is an imprint of the Taylor & Francis Group
Printed in the United States of America on acid-free paper

All rights reserved. No part of this book may be reprinted or reproduced or utilized in any form or by any electronic, mechanical, or other means, now known or hereafter invented, including photocopying and recording, or in any information storage or retrieval system, without permission in writing from the publisher.

10 9 8 7 6 5 4 3 2

Library of Congress Cataloging-in-Publication Data

Broussard, Jinx C. (Jinx Coleman), 1949–
  Giving a voice to the voiceless : four pioneering Black women journalists / Jinx Coleman Broussard.
    p. cm. — (Studies in African American history and culture)
  ISBN 0-415-94717-0 (Hardcover : alk. paper)
  1. African American women journalists—Biography. I. Title. II. Series.
  PN4872.B76 2003
  070.92'273—dc21
                                                                  2003010320

To my husband, Robert Broussard Sr.,
for his constant encouragement and unconditional love and support . . .
my children, Robert Jr., Dana, and Erica, who cheered me on . . .
and my parents, Warren Coleman Sr. and the late Leona Sorrell Coleman,
who taught me to dream, to explore, and to always go the extra mile.

Contents

ACKNOWLEDGMENTS	ix
PREFACE	xi
CHAPTER ONE Introduction	1
CHAPTER TWO Ida B. Wells-Barnett: Militant Muckraker	25
CHAPTER THREE Mary Church Terrell: Captivating Crusader	55
CHAPTER FOUR Alice Dunbar-Nelson: Writing During the Jim Crow Era	83
CHAPTER FIVE Amy Jacques Garvey: Mouthpiece for a Movement	105
CHAPTER SIX Synthesis	135
NOTES	151
BIBLIOGRAPHY	191
INDEX	213

Acknowledgments

I would like to express my gratitude to members of my doctoral committee at the University of Southern Mississippi, Dr. Arthur Kaul, Dr. Gene Wiggins, Dr. David Davies, and Dr. Mazhural Haque, for their guidance and support throughout this project. David rekindled in me an appreciation of history and left me eager to continue investigating individuals, events, and aspects of the press which have received marginal exposure.

I am indebted to Dr. Gloria Wade-Gayles, an eminent professor at Dillard University in New Orleans, Louisiana, at the time I embarked on doctoral study. Gloria suggested I examine the lives, works, and contributions of nineteenth century black women journalists who are virtually obscure in journalism history. She figuratively introduced me to some of these women.

The librarians at Dillard University, Venloa Jones, Beverly Harris, Annie Payton, and Charles Dunn, provided guidance and assistance during my search for sources, and they processed my many interlibrary loan requests. To them, I am immensely grateful. Special thanks goes to the special collections librarians at Fisk University in Nashville, Tennessee, and Howard University in Washington, D.C., for providing assistance during and after my visits. I owe a debt of gratitude to the Dillard University administration for both moral and financial support; to my friends, Stephanie Thomson and Kathy Lee Torregano, who were my proofreaders and sounding boards; and to my siblings, who were my cheerleaders.

Preface

This book describes and analyzes the journalism careers of four black women within the context of the period in which they lived and worked. Ida B. Wells-Barnett, Mary Church Terrell, Alice Dunbar-Nelson, and Amy Jacques Garvey were among a group of approximately twenty black women journalists who wrote for newspapers, magazines, and other media during the late nineteenth century and early twentieth century. Despite journalism careers that spanned decades, the women are obscure in journalism history. The four women journalists called attention to the failure of American society to recognize the rights of African Americans during a time when they were struggling to gain a foothold in society. Collectively, the women worked for dozens of black publications, owned newspapers, and were editors, correspondents, columnists, and editorial writers. Some contributed to the mainstream press. Through their work as journalists, they informed, persuaded, entertained, and advocated as they sought to enlighten and elevate their race and gender. Significantly, the body of their journalism work advanced their activist agendas. However, literature about the history of the black and mainstream press rarely acknowledges them. With the goal of lifting the veil of obscurity and placing these women in journalism history, this project explores their lives, the publications for which they wrote, their audiences, and the themes in their writings. The ultimate aim of this research is to acknowledge and record the journalism careers and contributions of the four women.

CHAPTER ONE

Introduction

The history of the journalism profession has long been documented in hundreds of books, journals, television shows, movies, and speeches. In virtually every instance, the contributions of individuals to the field have been highlighted. Scholars have introduced men such as Benjamin Franklin, William Randolph Hearst, Joseph Pulitzer, and Lincoln Steffens to succeeding generations through textbooks and biographies. Likewise, the careers of women journalists Ida Tarbell and Nellie Bly are highlighted in journalism literature.[1] During the last thirty years, scholars have explored the black press with increasing frequency, giving most attention to the men who wrote for, edited, or owned black newspapers and other publications. However, investigators have given scant attention to the black women who worked as journalists during the formative years of that medium.

From the late 1890s to the 1930s, some twenty black women journalists used their writing and speaking abilities to present information aimed at calling attention to the ills in American society, championing causes, and enlightening and uplifting their race.[2] These women lectured extensively and wrote hundreds of articles for magazines, newspapers, and other publications during careers that spanned decades. Although they actively engaged in journalistic pursuits and received acclaim for their work at the time, these turn-of-the century black women journalists have remained virtually invisible in the literature about the history of the black press, the feminist, and the mainstream press. The historical experiences of the female journalists have received little attention and, likewise, neither have the issues they addressed.

This book, therefore, examines the lives, works, and practices of four late nineteenth-century and early twentieth-century black women journalists within the context of the period in which they lived. The journalists are Ida B. Wells-Barnett, Mary Church Terrell, Alice Dunbar-Nelson, and Amy Jacques Garvey.[3] By looking at these women, the publications for which they wrote, the themes they addressed, the audiences they reached, and their views on issues, this study provides insight into the breadth of their contributions to the journalism profession. The research also focuses on the extent to which the women accomplished their activism through journalism. Ultimately, the goal of this study is not only to describe the women and their journalism output, but also to fill a gap in the literature by placing these women into the pages of journalism history.

HISTORICAL CONTEXT

An oppressive, limiting, and dehumanizing society provided the backdrop through which these black women journalists picked up their pens and wrote. These late nineteenth and early twentieth century journalists wrote during a time when black people who had been freed after the Civil War were struggling to gain an economic foothold, equality, and access to opportunities that would allow them to do more than merely exist. Although slavery had been abolished, numerous written and unwritten rules assured that blacks would be relegated to the lower rungs of the economic and political ladder.[4] Writing in *The Colored American* magazine in 1908, W. R. Lawton described the status of blacks by calling their situation "peculiar."[5] Lawton said blacks needed the white man's help because, "the land is his, and the government is his."[6] Gloria Wade-Gayles used similar words a quarter century later when she asserted that blacks were freed from slavery and "delivered–with all deliberate speed–into a new-style [peculiar institution]."[7] Wade-Gayles wrote that the institution included ". . . Jim Crowism, disfranchisement, economic exploitation, lynching, rapes, and other institutionalized barbarities" that "sought to keep the race forever in a state of powerlessness."[8] Historian Harvard Sitkoff echoed those words when he explained that beginning in 1876, a "legal counter-revolution had occurred" in this country. Sitkoff observed that

> the Supreme Court legitimized the right of states to exclude blacks from jury service; to prohibit intermarriage; to segregate school children; to deny blacks equality in public accommodations; to permit the disfranchisement of Negroes; and finally to bar all interracial contact, however selective or voluntary.[9]

Historians characterize the late nineteenth century and early twentieth century as the "Nadir,"[10] a period of some forty years that reflected a low point for blacks in the United States. During that time race relations was volatile and racial conflict manifested itself through riots in the southern

Introduction 3

cities of New Orleans, Louisiana; Wilmington, North Carolina; Statesboro and Atlanta, Georgia; and Brownsville, Texas.[11] Moreover, racial segregation, misrepresentations of blacks, and lynching of black men and women were commonplace. Elaborating on the situation, Dorothy C. Salem pointed out that "blacks earned their living through domestic or personal services and agriculture" and "their children were less likely to attend schools and were six times more likely to be illiterate than their white counterparts."[12]

As the 1920s dawned, African Americans were further disillusioned with their country after having fought for freedom in Europe during World War I, and subsequently, denied rights at home when they returned. Lawrence W. Levine wrote that blacks who served "heroically" and with "devotion" believed that their "second emancipation" would come when they returned from the war.[13] According to Levine, their

> loyalty and hopes were rewarded by inferior treatment for black troops, by a hardening of the lines of discrimination by increased humiliation, and by the bloody summer of 1919 which saw major race riots in city after city. Blacks had played the game by the rules and discovered definitely that the rules simply did not apply to them.[14]

Blacks migrating to northern cities between 1910 and 1920 did not fare much better than their southern brethren.[15] The editors of *The Making of Black America* wrote:

> The Great Migration during and after World War I accelerated a trend toward greater segregation in northern cities, which had been evident for a number of years. By the 1920s Negroes were already barred from countless recreation centers, restaurants, and hotels. Many northern communities extended segregation in the schools.[16]

"In New York and Philadelphia," Salem explained, "the increasing number of attacks on blacks by crowds of white males demonstrated the racial hatreds of northern urban residents."[17] Sitkoff confirmed this, arguing that whites who viewed the arrival of blacks during the Great Migration as a threat to their jobs and the status quo, frequently attacked them.[18] He offered that most African Americans "found squalor, discrimination by labor unions and employees, decayed housing milked by white slum lords, and liquor and narcotics the only escape from despair."[19] Despite those conditions, "for millions of Afro-Americans, the Northern urban ghetto also meant surcease from permanent tenantry, poverty, disease, and ignorance."[20]

The early 1920s saw the flourishing of the Harlem Renaissance, a literary movement during which many African Americans believed their talents and contributions in art, music, literature, and drama were the means to gaining white America's respect and acceptance.[21] Providing further elaboration, Edward Peeks wrote, "the Roaring Twenties proved no exception to the rule of violence against Negroes, violence arising especially from the issues of jobs and homes in the North and from more general animosities in the South."[22] For years to come, dashed expectations and disappointment characterized black communities throughout the United States.[23]

A REVIEW OF EXTANT LITERATURE

BLACK WOMEN

Contemporary historians who have written during the last quarter century about African-American women argue that they faced the double burden of racial and gender discrimination because they were both black and women.[24] Like white women, black women were not allowed to exercise the franchise, thus they faced sexual discrimination. Like black men, African-American women faced discrimination in the woman suffrage movement and other areas because of their race.[25] Wade-Gayles stated that "according to nineteenth century racist definitions, black women were inferior members of the sex whom God himself had colored a distasteful hue and imbued with insatiable sexuality, phenomenal strength and limited intelligence."[26] Dorothy Sterling voiced a similar sentiment in 1984 when she wrote:

> To be a black woman in nineteenth-century America was to live in double jeopardy of belonging to an "inferior" sex of an "inferior" race. Yet 2 million slaves and 200,000 free women of that time possessed a tenacity of spirit, a gift of endurance, a steadfastness of aspiration that helped a whole population to survive.[27]

Black women, according to author Paula Giddings, struggled to define themselves and their world politically as they fought racial and sexual oppression.[28] Cynthia Neverdon-Morton asserted, "regardless of their social class, black women often suffered humiliation or physical harm simply because of their race."[29]

Scholars have begun to reclaim African-American women from marginalization.[30] Some professed that the women have been neglected and ignored largely because of racism and sexism.[31] Gerda Lerner noted,

> black women have been victimized by scholarly neglect and racist assumptions. Belonging as they do to two groups which have traditionally been treated as inferior by American society—blacks and

women—they have been doubly invisible. Their records lie buried, unread, infrequently noticed and even more seldom interpreted."[32]

Writing in *Black Foremothers: Three Lives*, Dorothy Sterling concurred. She suggested that "because of the nature of American history, and particularly because of the institutions of slavery and segregation, the names of black women leaders are all but unknown in American society."[33] Glenda Gilmore added that black women have disappeared from the historical record,[34] and Darlene Clark Hine maintained "race, class, and class status combined to consign the women to historical oblivion."[35]

Historians maintain that society viewed turn-of-the-century black women journalists as negatively as other African-American women of the time. Nevertheless, the women defied the odds, surmounted obstacles, and became social and political activists. Within the context of racism and sexism, the late nineteenth-century and early twentieth-century black women journalists picked up their pens and began to write. They gave a voice to the voiceless.

BLACK WOMEN JOURNALISTS

A review of the literature confirms that although nineteenth century black women journalists were very active during the period, their works and contributions are not widely chronicled by those who write journalism history. Publication of the autobiography of Ida B. Wells-Barnett almost a half century after the pioneering journalist died illustrates the historical disregard of African-American women. Wells-Barnett, who distinguished herself as a champion of the rights of blacks, women, and children, had almost finished the final pages of her life story when she died in 1931. However, the Wells-Barnett autobiography was not published until approximately forty years after her death.[36]

Two decades after publication of the autobiography, Roland E. Wolsely called attention to the historical neglect of black women journalists. In his history of the black press, Wolsely stated that "female editors and writers of the nineteenth century had been ignored as journalists by almost all who had written on black journalism before 1970."[37] Other writers acknowledged that while histories of the black press give early black women writers scant attention, apart from brief references to one or two pioneering black women journalists, the history of the mainstream or established press also does not acknowledge the existence of these women.[38] Some historians argued that scholarly neglect has rendered African-American women invisible, regardless of their class, status, or profession.[39]

Writing specifically about nineteenth century African-American women journalists, Rodger Streitmatter declared that because of "prejudice, injustice, and hatred . . . American historians have, until recent decades, largely ignored women of African descent."[40] Streitmatter maintained that "despite racial and sexual discrimination,"[41] black women journalists fought against racism and oppression. The author offered that they were "defiant, strong-minded, and independent,"[42] and they refused to be silent victims of their times. They became journalists and racial activists who advocated equality for their race, sisters, and for humankind.[43] Bernell Tripp stated that black women journalists before the advent of the Civil War "were the most visible and significant teachers, lecturers, and writers of the period—making their presence known in the classroom, in the public auditoriums, and in the newsroom."[44] Black women continued to wield influence after the war and into the new century.

Despite works by Tripp, Strietmatter, and other scholars that elevated African-American women journalists from the footnotes of history, most existing studies on journalism inadequately reflect the lives and contributions of the women. One critically acclaimed history describes the career of Ida B. Wells in less than ten lines and devotes even less space to several other black female journalists of the period.[45] Streitmatter pointed out that a major journalism textbook, although "generally sensitive to the contributions of women and minorities," had no mention of black women journalists.[46] Another widely used college text makes no mention of specific black women journalists in the chapter that highlighted the black press.[47] As recently as 1998, a history of the black press devoted only three pages to four nineteenth-century black women journalists.[48] The volume did not mention other turn-of-the century women journalists. Significantly, only three of the twenty women journalists I. Garland Penn named in his 1891 history are included in Gayle J. Hardy's 1993 reference, *American Women Civil Rights Activists, Biobibliographies of 68 Leaders, 1825–1992*.[49] Biographical sketches of some of the other women writers, columnists, reporters, and editors identify them as activists, teachers, and educators, but not as journalists.[50]

The lack of knowledge of late nineteenth and early twentieth century black women journalists and their work derives from a dearth of information about them. However, the existence of these women has long been known. Marion Marzolf noted:

> Women journalists by 1889 had made such an impact on the profession that the *Journalists*, professional journal in New York City, devoted its entire January 26 issue to profiles of 50 women editors and reporters, 10 of them black. The editor admitted his mistake in not devoting space to women workers in journalism previously and said he wished to disabuse the old fogies of the profession of the idea that a newspaperwoman is any less a woman because she earns her living by wielding a pencil instead of sewing buttons for the "lords of creation."[51]

Introduction

Two years after the article in the *Journalist*, Penn listed the names and contributions of approximately twenty black female journalists in his 1891 history of the Afro-American press. In a sixty-two-page chapter in his book, Penn wrote biographical sketches and highlighted contributions of eighteen women. The author also mentioned the names of five other women journalists, but provided no additional information about them.[52]

Existing literature confirmed that these journalists were part of a reform-minded group of women who sought to uplift their race, bring about racial and gender equality, and build communities.[53] Writing about women who wrote during the pre-Civil war period, Frankie Hutton, author of a book about the early black press, pointed out that they "were not stymied by the black editors or in the columns of the black press."[54] Other scholarship substantiated that view relative to women who wrote during the late nineteenth century and early twentieth century. In her article about southern black women journalists, Wade-Gayles asserted that this group consisted of "phenomenal women, impressive sojourners wielding pens of political militancy and social concern."[55] Writer Ruby O. Williams indicated that many of the female black journalists were also teachers because the profession provided a steady income for them. Williams added, "Other opportunities were not available to them as Black people, even though these hundreds of men and women could do many other things well."[56]

The nineteenth-century black women journalists about whom Penn wrote were:[57]

Josephine Turpin Washington
Mrs. C. C. Stumm
Mrs. N. F. Mossell
Ione E. Wood
Frances E. Harper
Mary V. Cook
Lavinia B. Sneed
Georgia Mabel DeBaptiste
Lillian A. Lewis

Alice E. McEwen
Miss A. L. Telgham
Ida B. Wells
Mary E. Britton
Mrs. A. E. Johnson
Victoria Earle Matthews
Lucretia Newman Coleman
Kate D. Chapman
Lucy Wilmot Smith

One hundred years after Penn's work, Wade-Gayles included Wells-Barnett, Mathews, Sneed, Strumm, Smith, and Washington in her article, and added to the list southerners Rosa Bowers, Mary Virginia Cook, Alice Ruth Dunbar, A. E. Johnson, Mary Church Terrell, and A. E. Tilghman.[58] Other early black women journalists are the focus of biographies, monographs, and other works. Armistead Pride and Clint C. Wilson's 1997 history of the black press indicated that Mary Ann Shadd-Cary, often called the first black woman journalist in North America, edited her own paper, the *Provincial Freeman*, from 1854 through 1858 and urged blacks to migrate to Canada.[59] An entry by Robert Skinner in *Notable Black American Women* pointed to the work of another pioneering journalist, Lucy Wilmot Smith. Not only did Smith write articles, she edited the women's department of *Our Women and Children*, an organ of the Baptist denomination and she wrote sketches on black women journalists for the *Journalist*, the precursor of *Editor and Publisher*.[60] Skinner wrote that after 1891, nothing about Lucy Smith's life or career is known and that the newspapers to which Smith contributed did not survive.

Penn's pioneering tome recognized another woman whom he called "impressive." Commenting on the promising work of Lavinia B. Sneed, Penn said she was "a regular and excellent writer."[61] Penn described Sneed's journalistic work as "not as great as others," but the historian stated, "she is indeed a writer for the populace in that she writes so that the meagerly educated may understand the purport of her articles."[62]

Of the women Penn included in his book, Ida B. Wells-Barnett has perhaps been given more visibility than any of the other early black women journalists. During the past thirty years, scholars and historians have written about the muckraking journalist, who has been called a brilliant investigative reporter.[63] Nonetheless, Wells-Barnett still gets only limited attention in major works that deal with both press and United States history.

Wells-Barnett was born on July 16, 1862, in Holly Springs, Mississippi, to slave parents, Elizabeth and James Wells. After her parents died of yellow fever, Wells-Barnett taught school from 1883 to 1884 to support her surviving brothers and sisters. She next moved to Memphis to teach school and attend LeMoyne Institute. Later, Wells-Barnett also studied at Fisk University in Nashville, Tennessee.

The years 1884 to 1891 saw Wells-Barnett embarking on a journalism career. She began writing for black newspapers across the country, and bought part interest in the *Free Speech and Headlight* weekly newspaper.[64] Wells-Barnett later purchased and ran the paper, changing its name to the Memphis *Free Speech*, until its office was destroyed because Wells-Barnett had written editorials castigating Memphis officials for tolerating and participating in lynching. Wells-Barnett moved to New York and, later, Chicago, where she continued to write and speak about lynching, suffrage, and other issues that affected her race and gender.

Penn wrote in 1891 that Wells-Barnett was called a "Princess of the Press," adding that she was "popular with all the journalists of Afro-American connection."[65] Sterling noted that Wells-Barnett reported on black life in Tennessee, and that her articles "were appearing in the most prestigious papers" in the country as well as "short-lived publications."[66] During her lifetime, Wells-Barnett wrote for the Negro Press Association and hundreds of newspapers and magazines, including the *New York Age*,

Introduction 9

the *Detroit Plaindealer*, the *Indianapolis World*, *Opportunity*, *Crisis*, *The Voice of the Negro*, and *Woman's Era*.

The pioneering journalist championed numerous causes, and was involved in creating organizations aimed at uplifting her race. In the introduction to the second edition of Sterling's *Black Foremothers: Three Lives*, Barbara Christian posited that Wells-Barnett was one of "the first to bring international attention to the unspeakable crime of lynching."[67] Gerda Lerner argued that Wells-Barnett waged "her solitary campaign against lynching by pamphleteering and lecturing on the subject."[68] Streitmatter submitted that Wells-Barnett launched "the first full-scale journalistic effort to report and counteract the atrocities" of lynching.[69] He added that she challenged "the myth behind which the lynch mob had hidden, speaking frankly about the most taboo subject in Victorian America: white women willingly engaging in sexual acts with black men."[70] In an Internet article, Clark Cook wrote that Wells-Barnett reported "in graphic detail, stunning many of her readers and listeners."[71] Cook continued by writing,

> Ida B. Wells' investigative reports made it clear that lynchings were terror tactics; fearsome reminders to black people of the status assigned to them and the apparent futility of resistance to that assignment. Her reports in all of the major black newspapers, in many white newspapers, in pamphlets that she published, and her speeches across the U.S. and in England focused the world's attention and condemnation on lynching in the U.S.[72]

Lerner added that "the work of black club women and the NAACP on lynching is a direct outgrowth of Ida B. Wells' persistent muckraking journalism, exposes, lectures and organization."[73] Christian maintained that "it was journalism that offered Ida Wells scope not only for her writing abilities, but for her dawning commitment to the advancement of her people."[74]

Like Wells-Barnett, Mary Church Terrell used her pen and her voice to address the ills of American society, to enlighten and elevate her race and sex, and to espouse causes. Terrell was born in 1863 to wealthy parents in Memphis, Tennessee. Terrell received a classical education from some of the country's most prestigious schools and even studied abroad. The woman could have lived a life of leisure, but she decided to become an advocate for blacks and women through her work as a journalist and activist.

Terrell worked as a writer, lecturer, and educator; she also became one of the foremost civil rights proponents of her day. She lectured extensively and wrote hundreds of articles for magazines, newspapers, and other publications during a career that spanned more than half a century. She exposed lynching, chain gangs, and the convict-lease system by writing about those issues and many others in a variety of newspapers and magazines through the beginning of integration in the United States.

It is significant to note that although Terrell was a journalist, she is remembered more for her contributions to the struggle for the rights of women of African descent.[75] Except for Gloria Wade-Gayles' article on southern black women journalists, none of the works on the history of journalism or the black press reviewed for this book mentioned Terrell as a journalist. When Terrell is highlighted in most biographies, she is not identified as a journalist. Instead, she is called a writer, lecturer, educator, and activist. For example, the entry in *Black Women in America* does not identify Terrell as a journalist, even though mention is made of her articles and short stories on lynching, chain gangs, and other realities of life for African Americans.[76] The authors of master's theses about various aspects of Terrell's life focused on her leadership role in the country, but did not call her a journalist.[77] Even Terrell may not have considered herself a journalist. In her autobiography, *A Colored Woman in a White World*, Terrell wrote that she contributed articles to various publications; however, she did not call herself a journalist.[78]

Nonetheless, Terrell wrote for many of the leading publications which she said were "published either by or in the interest of colored people."[79] Publications included the *Woman's Era*, a magazine published in Boston; the *Colored American*, a Washington, D.C. newspaper; the *New York Age*; the *Southern Workman; Crisis; Opportunity;* the *Indianapolis Freeman;* the *Baltimore Afro-American;* the *Washington Tribune;* the *Howard Magazine*, which was published by her brother;[80] and the *Norfolk (Virginia) Journal and Guide* during the 1920s. She also wrote about a variety of issues as a regular contributor to *The Voice of the Negro*.[81]

Like Terrell, Alice Dunbar-Nelson was another black woman who engaged in journalism as a means of accomplishing her activist goals. As is the case with Terrell, considerably more information exists about Alice Dunbar-Nelson's work and contributions in other capacities. During the past thirty years, scholars have explored Dunbar-Nelson's life and career from a literary perspective, and, as a result, Dunbar-Nelson has received acclaim as an author, poet, and dramatist.[82] Gloria Hull, who has written extensively about Dunbar-Nelson, devoted only one page of her book to Dunbar-Nelson's work as a journalist.[83] Ruby Williams, the author of a dissertation on Dunbar-Nelson, noted that while she has received acclaim as a literary figure, her work as a journalist has not been given recognition, nor has it been studied. Nonetheless, Williams devotes only three pages of her two hundred and seven-page work on Dunbar-Nelson to the woman as a journalist,[84] pointing out that it was as a journalist that Dunbar-Nelson received visibility during her time.[85]

Dunbar-Nelson's literary career began while she was a young woman in New Orleans. She wrote poetry and short stories, and also began what was possibly her first journalistic endeavor by editing the women's page of the *Journal of the Lodge*, the official organ of the local black fraternal order, the Knights of Pythias.

By 1913, she had begun to write for and assist with editing the *AME Church Review*, a publication of the African Methodist Episcopal denomination. Williams maintained that beginning in 1920 and continuing for the next decade, Dunbar-Nelson earned her living primarily as a journalist.[86] From 1920 to 1922, she co-edited and published the *Wilmington Advocate* newspaper in Delaware. Williams stated that this was "an excellent outlet" for Dunbar-Nelson because "she could be more than creative, and she would have a forum for some of her political and racial ideas."[87] Dunbar-Nelson reviewed novels, poetry, plays, and art. She also wrote editorials for the *Advocate*. Researchers noted that the newspaper ceased operations two years after its debut because the man the Nelsons had hired to manage it was ill-equipped to run it.[88]

The beginning of 1926 saw the debut of Dunbar-Nelson's column, "From A Woman's Point of View" (later called "Une Femme Dit") in the *Pittsburgh Courier*, a major black newspaper of the time. She later wrote for the *Washington Eagle*, a paper that her husband managed, and she contributed columns to the Associated Negro Press. Dunbar-Nelson also contributed to the *Messenger* that Spellman College published, as well as the *Journal of Negro History*, *The Negro History Bulletin*, and the Urban League's *Opportunity*. From the end of 1930 until her death in 1935, Dunbar-Nelson wrote a column, "Little Excursions Week by Week" for the black syndicated press.[89]

Just as Dunbar-Nelson is known in the literature as the widow of Paul Laurence Dunbar, another black woman journalist of the period is more widely known as the widow of a powerful black leader. Although Amy Jacques Garvey served as editor, managing editor, editorial writer, and woman's page editor of the *Negro World*, she is referred to more often in biographies and other reference works as the second wife of Black Nationalist Marcus Garvey (whose first wife was also named Amy). While the editors of *Black Women in America: An Historical Encyclopedia* pointed out that Jacques Garvey was a "journalist, Pan-Africanist, and historian,"[90] scholars have paid scarce attention to her career as a journalist. Other literature acknowledged that Jacques Garvey was the associate and managing editor of the *Negro World* and that after Marcus Garvey's death, Amy published her husband's books and wrote and published books of her own about her husband.[91] An Internet article pointed out that she "made sure that Garvey's name and work were not forgotten."[92]

Like Terrell and Dunbar-Nelson, Jacques Garvey did not refer to herself as a journalist. She saw herself more as an activist. She also referred to herself as the chronicler of the record of her husband and the Universal Negro Improvement Association (UNIA), the organization founded by Marcus Garvey in 1914 to advocate for black rights and economic independence, to foster black pride, and to encourage their repatriation to Africa.[93] In her personal papers, Jacques Garvey described herself first as the "widow of Marcus Mosiah Garvey–Jamaica's first national hero," and then as "the author of four books on the life and philosophy of this remarkable man."[94] She told *Ebony* magazine in 1971 that after her husband was sentenced to prison in 1925 for alleged mail fraud, "I took on the challenge of running the *Negro World*, Garvey's newspaper, and I roamed the country giving speeches and keeping the movement alive."[95]

Amy Euphemia Jacques was born in Kingston, Jamaica, on December 11, 1896. Her parents, George and Charlotte Jacques, were educated members of the country's middle class and saw to it that Amy was also educated. Because of ill health and a desire to further her education, Amy Jacques immigrated to the United States in 1917.[96] She joined the UNIA a year later, and four years after that, she married Marcus Garvey.

In his work about women in the Garvey Movement, scholar Tony Martin calls Jacques Garvey "an amazing woman" who ran the UNIA "almost singlehandedly when Garvey was imprisoned or otherwise unavailable."[97] The biographical reference in *Black Women in America: A Historical Encyclopedia* stated that Jacques Garvey's "three-tiered (writer, spokesperson, and archivist) activist nature evolved" during her husband's incarceration.[98] Not only did Jacques Garvey serve as editor of the woman's page column, "Our Women and What They Think," her papers indicated that she was the "editor" of the *Negro World* for four years.[99] Significantly, from February 1924 until April 30, 1927, Amy Jacques Garvey wrote more than 150 editorials in the *Negro World* that addressed Black Nationalism, the work of the UNIA and Marcus Garvey, his incarceration, and a host of topics that were on the national and international agenda. As other black women journalists of the period had done, Jacques Garvey challenged racism in America, and enlightened her readers on racial uplift and productivity, as well as the role that black women should play in their communities.[100] In addition to her editorials and columns, she wrote articles about world affairs, racial achievements, Christianity, woman suffrage, and other topics.

PUBLICATIONS FOR WHICH THE WOMEN WROTE

The nineteenth-century and early twentieth-century African American women journalists contributed to the early black press. Additionally, some

Introduction 13

of the females frequently supplied articles to the mainstream press. Church publications and periodicals produced by the black women's club movement were also organs for which the women wrote.

Of the black press, historians Pride and Wilson wrote:

> By and large, the majority of newspapers published for the Black community have followed the ideological course chartered by *Freedom's Journal* and its immediate successors, *Rights of All*, the *Weekly Advocate* and the *Colored American*—that is, to implement the drive for racial unity, full citizenship rights, and self-development, be it of the hand or the brain; in short, to serve as the agency or vehicle of a cause . . .[101]

Tripp offered that the early black press endeavored to uplift the race, to be a voice for blacks, and even to educate whites.[102] The medium had three broader journalistic objectives, Tripp maintained, that included countering anti-black prejudices among whites; developing a sense of black fraternity; and emphasizing the potential for intellectual and cultural achievement.[103] The quest to end violence was yet another goal of the black press throughout its history, according to Charles A. Simmons. The black press historian affirmed that over the years the medium also "fought for equal treatment of black soldiers, provided assistance through housing and job notices, offered guidance on where to obtain transportation and how to travel safely, and printed notices on family members and friends, whether they had gone North or were still in the South."[104] Wade-Gayles maintained that nineteenth century African-American women "chose to take on the demands of black journalism during the most difficult years of the black press."[105] During the last two decades of the nineteenth century, at least twelve women were writing, reporting, and editing articles and columns for the black press.[106] In addition to the black publications already identified herein, included among the hundreds of organs for which the women wrote are *The Virginia Star*, the *Industrial Herald*, the *New York Freeman*, the *Richmond Planet*, *Southern Workman*, and the *Washington Bee*. As noted, mainstream or establishment dailies included the *New York Times*, *New York Herald*, *New York Mail*, *The Earth*, and *Phonographic World*.[107]

Marzolf pointed out that the women often wrote for publications of religious origin.[108] Referring strictly to southern black women journalists, Wade-Gayles stated that most of the women became "journalists of consequence" by writing for black church publications.[109] Historians stated that through regularly published papers for which the women wrote and served as editors, the black church educated the community on matters relevant to black progress and achievement.[110] Those publications included the

American Baptist, the *AME* (African Methodist Episcopal) *Church Review*, and the *Baptist Journal*.

The African-American women also became journalists because of their work in the women club's movement during the middle and late nineteenth century. The women established, edited, and wrote for such club organs as the *Woman's Era*, begun in 1894 by Josephine St. Pierre Ruffin as the official publication of the National Association of Colored Women. Wade-Gayles stated, "as a paper dedicated to organizing 'colored women' of the country for systematic work for the uplifting of the race, the *Woman's Era* was a beckoning light for many women journalists."[111] Streitmatter added that the "national newspaper was published both by and for African-American women."[112] The author added that the paper was used "to document the achievements and showcase the strengths of African-American women."[113] The publication, later called the *National Association Notes*, carried the writings of African American women from around the nation. According to Wade-Gayles, those organs, along with another, *Our Women and Children*, "made journalistic careers possible for many Southern women who might otherwise have never entered the field."[114]

Writing for the various publications was not the only journalistic role the women undertook. Some were also editors, co-owners, publishers, and financiers.[115] Ida B. Wells was a part owner and editor of the *Memphis Free Speech*, and later held partial interest in the *New York Age*. Along with her husband, Dunbar-Nelson co-founded and co-owned the *Wilmington Advocate*, a newspaper in Delaware. Shirley J. Yee wrote that African-American women in the mid-nineteenth century raised money to help finance the *Liberator*, a Boston-based abolitionist newspaper.[116] Therefore, the women were engaged in a variety of journalistic activities for both the black and mainstream press.

THEMES AND ISSUES

Early nineteenth century black women journalists such as Mary Ann Shadd Cary and Frances W. W. Harper worked through their papers for social reform, including education, temperance, and "vindicating and uplifting the race."[117] Other scholarly interpretations corroborate that the women who wrote later that century addressed those topics as well as a multiplicity of others. Those themes included the "legal, economic and social conditions of African Americans."[118] Nora Hall classified the themes as gender, politics, status, class, African-American relationships to mainstream institutions, African-American history and literature, employment, and education.[119]

Because the women wrote primarily for the black press, they reinforced issues and themes advocated by that medium. Frederick Detweiler wrote that favorite themes of the black press included "race wrongs" and "race clashes," race progress, individual achievement, Jim Crow laws, race movement, and the right for men and women to vote.[120] Streitmatter asserted:

> Since the black press was founded in 1827, the African-American press has served to sustain the spirit of its readers as they have endured the heavy burden of racial oppression. African-American journalists have chronicled instances of physical and psychological abuse, interpreted policies that have veiled discrimination in housing and employment, and represented the conscience of the black community.[121]

Historians submit that the early black press also saw as its mission fulfilling the role of uplifting and vindicating people of color in the true spirit of American democracy.[122] Pride and Wilson pointed out that themes in *Freedom's Journal*, the first newspaper published by blacks, included offsetting the misrepresentations of blacks in publications, providing African Americans with their own forum to "plead their own causes," and portraying blacks "as useful members of society."[123] The women journalists picked up those themes.

They also used their columns "to expand reader awareness of racial and gender issues."[124] According to Wade-Gayles, they "knew that they were significant journalists and that their work was indispensable to the black struggle."[125] Streitmatter observed that the early women writers addressed causes and ills that they believed were visited upon blacks and females by a society characterized by racism and sexism.[126] Rosalyn Terborg-Penn wrote that "by the 1890s, the growth in the number of black women journalists with feminine perspectives writing for black newspapers had become more evident."[127]

Scholars and writers maintained that lynching was another major theme that some of the female journalists addressed. C. A. Simmons stated that "the black press fought for an end to lynching and violence against blacks."[128] Both Wells-Barnett and Terrell wrote in their autobiographies that the lynching of three middle-class black men greatly affected their desire to devote their lives to advocacy.[129] Much of their involvement manifested itself through journalism. Streitmatter stated that "by writing scathing editorials for her Memphis newspaper, Wells-Barnett founded the anti-lynching movement in this country" and still later she played a leading role in America's woman's suffrage movement.[130] According to Streitmatter, Wells investigated reasons for lynching and suggested that "some white women were physically attracted to black men."[131] Lynching was clearly a major theme for some of these journalists.

Wells-Barnett and Terrell were joined by other turn-of-the century women journalists who took up the suffrage banner. In fact, historians who write about nineteenth century black women journalists stress that suffrage was a theme that garnered almost as much of their attention as did lynching.[132] Terborg-Penn pointed out that both Wells-Barnett and Terrell, and other African-American women were suffragists who wrote and spoke frequently on the issue of the black woman's right to vote.[133] The works of such African-American female journalists as Mary McCurdy and Gertrude Mossell appeared in black publications that spread the word about woman suffrage.[134] Giddings maintained that Mary Shadd Cary focused on abolition and women's rights.[135]

Many of the late nineteenth and early twentieth-century African-American women journalists also wrote about education, and topics related to travel and the arts. Most of the women writers were also concerned about morality. Hutton noted that the early newspapers carried messages of "social morality," further reinforced by other messages they delivered "through editorials, anecdotes, and parodies that continually prompted readers about the virtues of frugality, good deportment, temperance, industriousness, and so on."[136]

AUDIENCE

The early black women journalists wrote primarily for the black press and thus a black audience. While the literature indicated that some of the early black journalists wrote for an uneducated populace,[137] it is clear that most of the women wrote for the educated, developing black middle class. The writers reached an even broader audience—that included whites—by writing about art, literature, music, black and white society, education, and other issues. Moreover, some of the journalists wrote articles for the white press and thus also reached white audiences. One of the women, Jacques Garvey, wrote not only for the black masses in the United States, but in African and Caribbean countries.

According to Hutton, the middle class "was not defined by financial standing and family connections comparable to the white upper crust."[138] Rather, the black middle class "aspired almost constantly to respectability through education, temperance, industriousness, upright living patterns, and involvement in a variety of self-evaluation organizations."[139] The audience for the women, therefore, consisted of blacks who had a desire to know about the social changes that were affecting them as citizens. Detweiler elaborated by stating that the black audience consisted of a group of people who wanted to learn about themselves but felt they had no voice in the American newspaper.[140] R. E. Wolseley described the audience of the black press during the period by noting that the black population had access to education, were able to earn a little more income, and were able to give financial support to the press.[141] According to Detweiler, read-

Introduction   17

ers of religious publications were also an audience, as were blacks who were able to vote.[142] Therefore, the audience for these journalistic activists ranged from the black masses to the black middle class, educated and uneducated race members, as well as whites and blacks in the United States and abroad.

REVIEW SUMMARY

The literature clearly has shown that African-American women were actively and successfully working as journalists during the late 1800s and early 1900s. These women worked alongside the editors of the black press, and many of the black females were editors or co-owners of publications. Several other early black women journalists also wrote for the white press. In the introduction to his book, Streitmatter noted that they broke new ground for their race and gender by contributing to the news media.[143] The review of the literature delineated the extent to which historians have not acknowledged the work of the black women and their contributions to journalism. Their names are virtually absent from literature on the history of the white, black, and feminist press. Except for Penn's 1891 book, acknowledgment of the nineteenth-century black women journalists in the history of the black press ranges from a few paragraphs to a few pages in journalism history texts.

During the last thirty years, scholarly examination has uncovered the unnoticed lives and works of turn-of-the-century African-American women, some of whom were journalists. More often than not, however, the women are associated with other professions or in other capacities, such as activism. As a result, these black women journalists are but footnotes in journalism and American history.

IMPLICATIONS OF THE REVIEW OF LITERATURE

The absence of nineteenth-century black women journalists from journalism history is glaring when one looks at the annals of the press. Such a lack of historical acknowledgment created a need for this study. Journalism as practiced in the United States during the late nineteenth and twentieth century sought to inform, persuade, and even entertain.[144] The function of the press, and especially the black press, also included advocacy.[145] The turn-of-the-century African-American women journalists fulfilled all of those roles. Therefore, it is clear that by the standards of journalism and within the context of the period, the women can be called journalists.

Wade-Gayles forcefully argued for the need to study early African-American female journalists, maintaining that such an undertaking "would highlight their contributions while keeping in sharp focus the reality of being Black and Woman in nineteenth century white America."[146] Wade-

Gayles further explained that the study would also inform us of the women's struggle for freedom, their assessment of their contributions to the struggle, and their lifestyles as they "chose to take on the demands of black journalism during the most difficult years of the black press."[147]

Streitmatter stressed that together these women have changed history. The historian explained that "the history of the black press, grounded in a tradition of advocacy, is closely intertwined with the history of America," and as a consequence, "individuals working in the African-American press have been some of the most important leaders of African-American history."[148]

Wolseley argued that "the history and nature of the black press should be put on record, since that press has had a part in our national development."[149] The role and work of the turn-of-the century African-American women journalists also should be investigated, documented, and presented. Hutton wrote that the early black press "has been denied its true place in American journalism and social history."[150] So, too, have the women who worked in that medium been denied.

Works produced during the past quarter century clearly advanced that Ida B. Wells-Barnett was of equal stature with Lincoln Steffens and other giants of the press. And although scholars are generating additional works about Wells-Barnett, the woman still garners little more than a few pages in some works and a few paragraphs in most books on journalism history. Hence, additional research and scholarly attention should elevate Wells-Barnett in the literature.

Likewise, Mary Church Terrell is more acclaimed for her activism on behalf of women and civil rights. However, Terrell wrote hundreds of articles over a six-decade period that have seemingly largely gone unnoticed. Terrell's work and contributions to journalism should receive scholarly attention and inclusion into the historical record, if warranted.

Similarly, although researchers have done much work that provide enlightenment about Alice Dunbar-Nelson as literary figure, much needs to be done regarding her career as a journalist. Because literature has established that Dunbar-Nelson's journalism provided the only means of visibility for her at the turn of the century, it becomes increasingly important to assess her work during that time. Again, such investigation would extend and improve the comprehensiveness of the historical record.

Scholars acknowledged that Amy Jacques Garvey was affiliated with the *Negro World*. It is clear from her private papers and other works that she was a journalist who used her organizational skills to run the newspaper and used her pen to advocate for her race. Because her work as a journalist has not been chronicled, it should be examined and put in the historical record.

Introduction

Many, if not most Americans, do not know about African-American women journalists who wrote during the late nineteenth and early twentieth century. Some of the women continued to write until well into the twentieth century. Therefore, a study of this nature unearths the women, their lives, works, and contributions to journalism and places them in the history of the press.

STUDY PURPOSE AND QUESTIONS

In seeking to determine and describe the women's journalism activities, it is appropriate to look at their lives within the context of the period in which they lived. Thus, this project examines the practices and output of the women by including the themes they addressed and the audience they reached, and it places the women's contributions to journalism in the annals of the press.

In view of the obscurity of most of the women journalists, it was not prudent to include all of the nineteenth-century black women journalists in this study. Such an undertaking would have been unwieldy and unfocused. Thus, this investigation only focused on four late nineteenth- and early twentieth-century black women journalists: Ida B. Wells-Barnett, Mary Church Terrell, Alice Dunbar-Nelson, and Amy Jacques Garvey.

I selected these four women because the literature revealed commonalities in their backgrounds as well as significant philosophical differences among them. Three were born in the South and migrated to the North; the other was born in Jamaica and immigrated to New York. Ida B. Wells was born into slavery, while Mary Church Terrell was born to privilege, and Dunbar-Nelson and Jacques Garvey had middle class parents. During their adult lives, the women lived in urban areas, and they had what Wade-Gayles calls "prestige and influence."[151] Dunbar-Nelson, however, faced a constant struggle for finances, as she and her husband struggled to keep their newspaper and other ventures afloat.[152] All of the women except Jacques Garvey taught school or college and were involved in the club movement and church work. Some of the women did women's work in the home,[153] such as grocery shopping and tending to children, although some of them had the help of domestics who worked for them or an extended network of friends, students, and church members who also helped out.

All of the women succeeded as journalists who wrote for the black press and publications aimed at black audiences. Wells-Barnett, Dunbar-Nelson, and Garvey owned and edited newspapers for a time. For the most part, the white press was not receptive to the women's articles, essays, and columns. Church Terrell noted that the white press routinely rejected her work.[154] Dunbar-Nelson submitted articles that were sometimes published by the white press, while it does not appear that Jacques Garvey ever submitted articles to the mainstream press.

The women addressed many of the same themes, although Jacques Garvey overwhelmingly adhered to the doctrine of black repatriation, self-help, and white exploitation. The four women overwhelmingly agreed that racial and sexual discrimination prevented blacks and women from advancing and kept them in a state of bondage. Hence, they devoted their columns, articles, and pages of their papers to exposing such discrimination and advocating for an end to the practice.

Because more than fifteen books, approximately one-hundred articles, as well as documentaries and references have established Wells-Barnett as a journalist and have highlighted her activities and contributions to the field, this study begins with an overview of her background and works, and uses Wells-Barnett as a benchmark. Of the women the study examines, Wells-Barnett was the only one acknowledged as a journalist by her contemporaries and later, by some historians. Significantly, the review of scholarly works on the women reveals that Wells Barnett, Church-Terrell, Dunbar-Nelson, and Jacques Garvey were engaged in similar activities, and were making the same points in their articles, columns, and other works. Hence, these women together all meet the criteria commonly used to define journalists.

Thus, by looking at the these women, the themes they addressed, the audiences they reached, and their views on issues, I sought insight into the breadth of their contributions to journalism. I have attempted to answer a number of questions. First, what was the background of Ida B. Wells, Mary Church Terrell, Alice Dunbar-Nelson, and Amy Jacques Garvey? I first provide biographical information about the women, including dates and places of birth, parents, education, marriages, and careers to provide historical and social context. My goal is to reveal why the women chose to become writers, editors, columnists–journalists–in a field that white males traditionally dominated.

The nature and types of publications for which the women wrote and the audiences they reached formed the crux of my second question. Such inquiry provided insight about the extent to which the women's voices were heard and by whom.

The third question centered on themes the women addressed. Results indicated that these community organizers and activists were writing about racial and gender issues, as well as social, economic, and political topics; and they also gave attention to religious, literary, historical, and cultural subjects.

My fourth area of inquiry focused on the writing styles of the women. Streitmatter stated that each of the women he chronicled in his book were both racial activists and journalists, "in that order."[155] I examined whether the women focused more on opinion, advocacy, and promotion than on presentation of information. I also gave further attention to the extent to which the women fulfilled the advocacy role of the black press and the manner in which they accomplished their activism through journalism. Ultimately, I not only described the women, their writings, themes, and audiences, but also uncovered the role they played in the histories of journalism, African-Americans, and this country.

METHODOLOGY AND PROCEDURES

To uncover the lives and works of the selected women journalists, this study employed the historical-critical method of qualitative research, using both primary and secondary sources. Because the literature revealed that the women worked for the black press and that they addressed racial and gender issues, this research used the following categories: the early black press, the American press, and the feminist press.

I consulted the women's original works in magazines, newspapers, pamphlets, and other publications. The works included news articles, letters to the editor, editorials, features, and reviews. Major primary sources included the autobiographies of Terrell and Wells-Barnett, as well as the diaries of Wells-Barnett and Dunbar-Nelson. I also attempted to obtain background information through such primary sources as personal papers, letters, memoranda, and other correspondence and notes that the women generated. Terrell's collections of personal papers housed in the Moorland-Springarn Collection at Howard University in Washington, D.C., and Jacques Garvey's papers in the Marcus Mosiah Garvey Memorial Collection at the Fisk University Library Special Collections in Nashville, Tennessee, yielded significant data for this project. Additional primary sources came from other collections related to women, race, and the press. Those sites included the National Archives of Black Women's History at the National Council of Negro Women headquarters in Washington, D.C., and the Marcus Garvey and UNIA Paper Project at the University of California at Los Angeles.

Because Dunbar-Nelson was born in New Orleans and educated at what is now Dillard University, I conducted searches at that school, as well as the libraries at Tulane University and the University of New Orleans. Both Tulane and UNO have special collections, Louisiana collections, and women's collections. Dillard has an extensive Schomburg Collection that yielded microfilm copies of black publications and works by and about African-American writers and speakers. The Amistad Research Center, housed on the Tulane campus, the nation's largest repository of works by and about black people, also contained useful materials.

I believed that oral interviews with relatives who are still alive, acquaintances, and others who have had direct contact with the women would be crucial to the research process. However, attempts to obtain information about the lives, experiences, activities, and works of the women via that avenue were unsuccessful. Moreover, attempts to obtain primary information from courthouses, churches, and government offices also proved unsuccessful.

Secondary sources, including biographies, master's theses and dissertations about the women, as well as references and histories of the black and feminist press provided valuable information. A bibliography titled *A History of Journalism in the Black Community* proved useful because it contained a selected list of one hundred fifteen contemporary black newspapers by state and selected United States libraries with major black history collections. It also listed more than two hundred books, periodicals, articles, dissertations, and theses related to the black press.

EXTERNAL AND INTERNAL ANALYSIS

I employed external and internal criticism to evaluate the historical records. Historians James D. Startt and Wm. David Sloan say "external criticism involves establishing the authenticity of a record" while "internal involves matters of credibility and understanding the content."[156] As suggested by the two authors, this external criticism involved collation or comparing various texts; identification when names and other information were missing; and textual verification to determine if the record was genuine. The internal criticism involved establishing the credibility of the authors, as well as personal records and public documents. Having an understanding of the content was necessary for me to make the best use of it.

Armed with information, I described the careers of the selected black women journalists, attempting to present the information obtained via the historical narrative, "a mixture of explanation based on evidence and intuitive reasoning."[157] Startt and Sloan point out that the narratives, from the historical perspective, "create a perceptive and lasting impression of life."[158]

This book, therefore, tells the story of these women's careers in journalism within the context of the time in which they lived and worked. I have endeavored to present historical facts and to provide insight into the factors that shaped the women's lives and work as journalists, while presenting and evaluating the reasons why the women are not acknowledged in the literature about the history of journalism.

SUMMARY AND IMPLICATIONS

More than a century has passed since Wells-Barnett, Terrell, Jacques Garvey, and Dunbar-Nelson joined other late nineteenth and turn-of-the century black women who worked in media. Yet today the women remain virtually absent from the history of the American press, black press, and

Introduction

feminist press. It may be reasonable to conclude that because of the nature and scope of the women's activism, their work as journalists has been overshadowed. Their accomplishments were so great in many areas; hence their journalism endeavors may have been seen as only a part of the mix and not as a defining part of their work.

During the past quarter century, historians have uncovered, documented, and presented a plethora of works which reveal the extent of nineteenth and early twentieth century women's contributions to American society. However, while scholars, historians, and biographers have singled out the work of some of the women journalists, lesser-known women need to be reclaimed and their lives and contributions illuminated. The role that these women played in the history of journalism should be investigated, and if their contributions warrant it, their history, lives, and works should become a part of the record.

Research such as this project should be conducted to assure that these women journalists will no longer be tokens in feminist history, footnotes in black history, and invisible in journalism and American history. Researchers should continue to delve into the history of these women because their lives were integral components in the history of America and the journalism profession. Such exploration fills a void in scholarship, broadens the intellectual discourse, and makes history more inclusive. Moreover, this research also provides insight relative to the extent to which the issues these women addressed are still predominant in today's society.

CHAPTER TWO

Ida B. Wells-Barnett
Militant Muckraker

> As for myself, I don't care. I'd rather go down in history as one lone Negro who dared to tell the government that it had done a dastardly thing than to save my skin by taking back what I have said. I would consider it an honor to spend whatever years are necessary in prison as the one member of the race who protested, rather than to be with all the 11,999,999 Negroes who didn't have to go to prison because they kept their mouths shut.[1]
>
> Ida B. Wells-Barnett

Armed with that conviction, Ida B. Wells-Barnett[2] set the standard not only as a black woman journalist, but also as a journalist during the late nineteenth and early twentieth century. This daughter of former slaves championed causes that sought to terminate the horrific conditions under which black people lived and the impediments they faced in the years following the Civil War and into the twentieth century. Through journalistic activism, Wells-Barnett called attention to and sought an end to lynching of black men, women, and children. The muckraking journalist used her investigative skills and her pen to fashion stories, letters, and commentaries that took a nation and its white inhabitants to task for lynching and racial and gender discrimination. Wells-Barnett's writings prodded both black leaders and the black masses to seek to elevate themselves and the race.

During the years that she conducted her crusade for an end to lynching, as well as equal justice and rights for blacks, members of the black and white community took note of Wells-Barnett's writings and activities. The white press regularly sought to malign Wells-Barnett, while some of her contemporaries in the black press praised her work and others criticized her personally.³ Wells-Barnett characterized the attacks against her by the *Memphis Daily Commercial* as exceeding all others in its "vigor, vulgarity and vileness."⁴ Members of her race sometimes questioned her motives, accusing her of wanting to be "that Negro woman," or criticized her work as a journalist.⁵ For example, the *Indianapolis Freeman* once ran a cartoon of a barking dog whose head resembled Wells-Barnett's and whose collar was labeled "Iola," Wells-Barnett's pen name.⁶ On the other-hand, fellow journalist T. Thomas Fortune, the owner and editor of the *New York Age*, often praised Wells-Barnett and her talent. He once wrote,

> She has become famous as one of the few of our women who handle a goose quill with diamond point as easily as any man in newspaper work. If Iola were a man, she would be humming independent in politics. She has plenty of nerve and is as sharp as a steel trap.⁷

Of Wells-Barnett, fellow female journalist Lucy Wilmot Smith wrote, "No other writer, the male fraternity not excepted, has been more extensively quoted [sic] none struck harder blows at the wrongs and weaknesses of the race." ⁸ Smith asserted that Wells-Barnett was "an inspiration to the young writers" and that "her success has lent an impetus to their ambitions."⁹ Black editors invited Wells-Barnett to represent their newspapers at their annual press convention in 1889, and they elected her secretary of the National Press Association.¹⁰

Hence, it is has been established that Wells-Barnett was a consummate journalist who stood head and shoulders with the best in her field, black or white. Despite recognition during her time, scholarly neglect of Wells-Barnett during the first quarter of the twentieth century rendered her an asterisk or footnote in journalism histories and textbooks. The last quarter of the century, however, saw a flowering of scholarship about the woman and her contributions to journalism.¹¹

Because of this renaissance, Wells-Barnett's name comes to mind when those who study the press, especially the black press, mouth the words lynching and journalism. Scholars attribute Wells-Barnett's investigative reporting on lynching in the South with exposing the barbaric act and for the passage of laws barring the practice.¹² Journalism historian Roger Streitmatter argued that Wells-Barnett launched "the first full-scale journalistic effort to report and counteract the atrocities," by challenging "the myth behind which the lynch mob had hidden, speaking frankly about the most taboo subject in Victorian America: white women willingly engaging in sexual acts with black men."¹³ Margaret Walker's introduction to Dorothy Sterling's book about Wells-Barnett and two other black women journalists indicated that journalism offered the crusader "scope not only for her writing abilities, but for her dawning commitment to the advancement of her people."[14] According to Walker, "nothing could stop her in her struggle against racism, sexism, and the violent crime of lynching."[15]

Although much has been written about Wells-Barnett during the past thirty years, she is still marginalized in most journalism histories. Therefore, this chapter provides an overview of Wells-Barnett's life and career as a journalist and activist. This study examines Wells-Barnett's activities, works, and contributions, paying particular attention to her writings about lynching and misrepresentation of black males and females. Ultimately, the chapter seeks to establish Wells-Barnett as the benchmark by which other black female journalists of her era should have been or were judged and recognized, and to create a more prominent place for Wells-Barnett in journalism history.

BIOGRAPHICAL INFORMATION

Wells-Barnett was born into slavery July 16, 1862, in Holly Springs, Mississippi, six months prior to the Emancipation Proclamation. She was the first of eight children born to James Wells and Elizabeth "Lizzie" Warrenton. James Wells was the son of his master, and as such, enjoyed relatively more freedom than other slaves.[16] Wells-Barnett pointed out in her autobiography that her father "was never whipped or put on the auction block, and he knew little of the cruelties of slavery."[17] Jim Wells was hired out as an apprentice to a carpenter; therefore, he acquired a trade that would serve him well after emancipation. Lizzie Wells was a cook in the household of the man to whom Jim Wells had been apprenticed. The couple married as slaves and married again after emancipation.

Her father provided the example of activism, assertiveness, and self-reliance that Wells-Barnett exhibited most of her lifetime. Miriam DeCosta-Willis, editor of Wells-Barnett's diary, elaborated on this view when she wrote, "Although Ida learned important lessons on religion, discipline, morality, and housework at home from her mother, she received her political and civic training from her father and other black Holly Springs men.... She chose to emulate her father, not her mother."[18]

An entry in Wells-Barnett's autobiography recounts how her father went into town, bought tools, and set up a carpenter shop and a household after his boss locked him out because he did not vote the way the man wanted. Wells-Barnett stated, "When Mr. Bolling returned he found he had lost a workman and a tenant, for already Wells had moved his family off the Bolling place."[19] Jim Wells was also a trustee of Shaw University and was involved in politics, although he held no office.

Her parents instilled in Wells-Barnett a belief that education was a means for advancement. Although she cannot remember when she started school, Wells-Barnett attended Shaw University in Holly Springs, a school founded by the Freedmen's Aid Society that went from elementary to normal or teacher training. The death of both parents of yellow fever in 1878 ended Wells-Barnett's quest for a formal education. At the time, the sixteen-year-old quit school and took a teaching job in a country school so that she could care for and keep her siblings together.[20] In doing so, Wells-Barnett displayed an independence for which she was forever to be known. The tenacious young woman later described the reaction to her decision by the people who wanted to assist her and her family when she wrote,

> Of course they scoffed at the idea of a butterfly fourteen-year-old schoolgirl who had never had to care for herself trying to do what it had taken the combined effort of father and mother to do.
> But I held firmly to my position and they seemed rather relieved that they no longer had to worry over the problem.[21]

Although Wells-Barnett was unable to graduate from Shaw, later renamed Rust College, at one point, she took summer courses at Fisk University in Nashville, Tennessee. She also sought to educate herself by becoming a voracious reader, attending lectures and symposia, and availing herself of courses offered in communities where she lived and worked.[22] Alfreda Duster, the daughter of Wells-Barnett and the editor of her autobiography, noted that her mother "took advantage of every opportunity to improve her own academic skills with private lessons from older teachers and those skilled in elocution and dramatics," and she "traveled on excursions for teachers to places of interest and value."[23] According to Linda O. McMurry, Wells-Barnett's biographer, Ida's list of works by Dickens, Louisa May Alcott, Sir Walter Scott, Charlotte Bronte, Shakespeare, and others shaped her "ideals and vision of the world."[24] McMurry offered that the reading list was "filled with larger-than-life heroic figures, outcasts, orphans, and underdogs . . . a cast to whom she could easily relate as an orphan who understood the heroic tasks of keeping her family together while enduring scurrilous gossip about herself."[25]

As was the case with other black women journalists of the era, teaching for Wells-Barnett became the means for her to obtain a living. In addition, the position gave her social standing and an opportunity to have influence in her community. After spending a brief time at the country school where she began teaching, Wells-Barnett moved to Memphis, Tennessee, in 1881 when she was nineteen years old and "in search of greater opportunities and a richer cultural life."[26] She taught for two years in Shelby County and, after passing the qualifying examination for teachers, she taught in the Memphis public schools for seven years. Duster noted that her mother "was regarded as a competent and conscientious teacher, devoted to helping young Negroes acquire what she knew was crucially necessary for their future—a good education."[27] During Wells-Barnett's career, she also taught in Marshall County and Tate County schools in Tennessee and for six months in Cleveland County, Arkansas.[28]

Wells-Barnett had already gained a reputation as a crusading journalist and activist when she married the prominent attorney and newspaper editor, Ferdinand Barnett, and moved to Chicago in June1895. Newspapers all over the country wrote about the wedding.[29] Barnett was a widower who had two children and four more were born to his union with Ida.

SEEDS OF ADVOCACY

Wells-Barnett's activism was evident through the following entry she made in her autobiography years later:

> I decided to continue to work as a journalist for this was my first, and might be said, my only love. I had already purchased the *Conservator* from Mr. Barnett and others who owned it, and the following Monday morning, after my marriage, I took charge of the *Conservator* office. My duties, as president of the Ida B. Wells Woman's Club, and as speaker in many white women's clubs in and around Chicago kept me pretty busy. But I was not too busy to find time to give birth to a male child the following 25 March 1896.[30]

Wells-Barnett gave up her newspaper career for a time after her second son was born in 1897 because "she firmly believed in the importance of the presence of a mother in the home during the children's formative years," Duster stated.[31] Although Wells-Barnett did not work outside the home until her youngest child was eight-years-old, she continued to be active in causes on behalf of the race. Of her decision to curtail her public activities, Wells-Barnett wrote,

> I was thoroughly convinced by this time that the duties of wife and mother were a profession in themselves and it was hopeless to expect to carry on public work. I therefore gave up the newspaper and very shortly thereafter resigned from the presidency of the Ida B. Wells Club, after five years of service.[32]

The Barnetts were part of the social elite of Chicago, and they were influential in virtually all civic affairs. Wells-Barnett biographer Mildred Thompson wrote that unlike other members of the black middle class, Wells-Barnett maintained a bond with the black masses and was inclined to be critical of "those whose social position and ambition removed them from the needs of the lower class."[33] Although writing and speaking demanded much of Wells-Barnett, her activism on behalf of social, political, and racial causes continued throughout her life. She established programs and organizations to benefit youth, women, and blacks. Historian Paula Giddings argued that Wells-Barnett "was a catalyst for the creation of a black women's organization."[34] As such, Wells-Barnett formed the Women's Era Club, later renamed the Ida B. Wells Club, the first civic organization for black women. Wells-Barnett was involved in the National Association of Colored Women, an organization of black club women who sought to provide guidance and assistance to blacks. Thompson argued that although "women's club work was a middle-class endeavor, Wells-Barnett's conception of racial solidarity and united effort embraced the lower class, as well." [35] Wells-Barnett's work included encouraging a saloonkeeper in his attempt to establish a respectable theatre for blacks, establishing a kindergarten for young black children who did not have access to the only existing kindergarten for them in Chicago, and being partially responsible for organizing the city's first black orchestra.[36]

At the beginning of the Great Migration of blacks from the South to the North, Wells-Barnett learned that the Chicago YMCA excluded black men, so she organized the Negro Fellowship League settlement house to provide housing, employment counseling, and social activities for them. Wells-Barnett also taught Bible class and served as a probation officer there. She labored virtually alone in this endeavor and others because she had little support from middle- and upper-class blacks who were educated and had ability and influence. Duster wrote that although her mother's "friends and associates in clubs, churches, and social life admired her dedication and hard work, they were not willing to . . . work among the recent migrants who were uneducated, unemployed, and living in such undesirable neighborhoods."[37]

Wells-Barnett was also a founder of the National Association for the Advancement of Colored People in 1910. She played a crucial role in the establishment of its magazine, *Crisis*, because she wanted the organization's members to have the ability to "publish whatever we chose whenever we wished."[38] Wells-Barnett later resigned from the NAACP because she believed the organization was too slow in efforts to uplift the race and had "fallen short of the expectations of its founders."[39]

Her belief in universal suffrage led Wells-Barnett not only to write about the issue but to form the Alpha Suffrage Club in 1913, the first such organization for black women. Wells-Barnett said she showed the women who joined that they could use their "vote for the advantage of ourselves and our race."[40] Under her leadership, the club registered thousands of black women to vote in both local and national elections, and helped elect Oscar DePriest, a black Chicago alderman, to Congress.[41] Although a firm believer in the franchise for women, Wells-Barnett did not place gender progress above that of her race. Historian Rosalyn Terborg-Penn argued that as the woman suffrage campaign gained momentum, "the national leadership emulated the racial attitudes of white women's clubs around the nation."[42] Hence, Wells-Barnett's militancy led her to expose and campaign against racial discrimination in the woman suffrage movement. She reported how the Chicago Woman's Club denied admissions for fourteen months to Fannie Barrier Williams, a black club woman from Chicago.[43] In 1913, when she was told to join black women at the end of the line in the first national suffrage parade for women in Washington, D.C., Wells-Barnett left the parade temporarily then rejoined it alongside white suffragists in the first section. She remained front and center to the end of the parade route—to the consternation of white suffrage leaders who were trying to placate the South.[44]

Later in her life, Wells-Barnett worked to block segregation of schools in Chicago.[45] In 1915, she was part of a delegation that met with President Woodrow Wilson to "call his attention to segregation enforced in the departments of government" and to ask "him to use his influence as president of the United States in abolishing discrimination based on the color line."[46] Wells-Barnett was also active in politics and ran unsuccessfully for an Illinois State Senate seat in 1930.

While writing about lynching, Wells-Barnett understood that international pressure on the United States might be the only means to not only end lynching, but to bring about equal justice for blacks. She, therefore, embarked on an international tour during which she spoke about lynching and the plight of blacks.[47] The British people afforded Wells-Barnett "a platform from which to tell the Negro's side of the gruesome story of lynching, and to appeal to Christian and moral force for help in the demand that every accused person be given a fair trial by law and not by the mob."[48] Largely because of Wells-Barnett's exposes and her activities abroad, the anti-lynching Blair Resolution was introduced in Congress in 1894, and six states passed anti-lynching measures between 1893 and 1897.[49] Although the Blair Resolution failed, North Carolina, Georgia, South Carolina, Ohio, Kentucky, and Texas passed legislation to end lynchings.

BEGINNINGS OF A JOURNALISM CAREER

While teaching provided a source of steady income for Wells-Barnett, she did not enjoy the work. In her autobiography, Wells-Barnett wrote, "I never cared for teaching, but I had always been very conscientious in trying to do my work honestly. There seemed to be nothing else to do for a living except menial work. I could not have made a living at that."[50] Wells-Barnett initially did not imagine a career in journalism, because she knew of no other black women in the field. Moreover, black newspapermen whom she knew earned their living as teachers and ministers.[51] However, journalism not only was the alternative to the monotony and confinement of teaching, but the avenue through which she could help her people and serve as a voice for them.[52]

Seeking to expand her knowledge and skills, Wells-Barnett joined a literary society of fellow public school teachers that met every week. Her involvement in the lyceum would pave the way for Wells-Barnett to embark on her journalism career, for she discovered her talent for both writing and speaking. According to Wells-Barnett, participating in the lyceum "was a breath of life" to her.[53] Lyceum committee members asked Wells-Barnett to edit the publication, *The Evening Star*, when the editor of the group's journal moved to Washington, D.C.[54] Wells-Barnett indicated that the publication was "a spicy journal" that contained "news items, literary notes, criticisms of previous offerings on the program, a 'They Say' column of pleasant personalities—and always some choice poetry."[55]

Through her work with *The Evening Star*, Wells-Barnett came to the attention of the Rev. R. N. Countee, pastor of one of the leading Baptist churches in Memphis and publisher of a weekly called *Living Way*. Countee ran some of the material Wells-Barnett wrote for *The Evening Star*, and he offered her the opportunity to write for the publication. Wells-Barnett shared her first thoughts upon being invited to contribute to *Living Way*, noting that she "had no training except what the work on *The Evening Star* had given me, and no literary gifts and graces." Wells-Barnett wrote that she "had observed and thought much about conditions" as she "had seen them in the country schools and churches." She added,

> I had an instinctive feeling that the people who had little or no school training should have something come into their homes weekly which dealt with their problems in a simple, helpful way. So, in weekly letters to the *Living Way*, I wrote in a plain, common-sense way on the things which concerned our people. Knowing that their education was limited, I never used a word of two syllables where one would serve the purpose.[56]

Early in her career when she was still earning her living as a teacher, Wells-Barnett was concerned about her writing style and had difficulty believing it was good. An entry in her diary on August 26, 1886, reflected her ambivalence:

> I think sometimes I can write a readable article and then again I wonder how I could have been so mistaken in myself. A glance at all my "brilliant?" productions pall on my understanding; they all savor of dreary sameness, however varied the subject, and the style is monotonous. I find a paucity of idea that makes it a labor to write freely and yet—what is it that keeps urging me to write notwithstanding all?[57]

A few weeks later, Wells-Barnett was feeling better about her product. She noted that she "wrote a dynamite article to the G(ate) C(ity) P(ress) almost advising murder!"[58] Her reason for writing the article was her indignation over the lynching of a black woman for allegedly poisoning a white woman. Before long, black newspapers in the country began picking up Wells-Barnett's writings, under the pen name "Iola," and the editors of those publications also asked her to write for them.[59] Her writings primarily in the black press enabled this consummate activist to be a racial and gender advocate.

Scholars agree that Wells-Barnett's early experience shaped her commitment and her activism,[60] which began in 1884 when she was a passenger on a Tennessee train. While traveling to her teaching job six miles away from her home, Wells-Barnett sat in the ladies coach and refused to move to the colored section, as she was directed to do. She struggled and bit the conductor as he tried to forcefully eject her from the car, to the cheers of the white men and women on the train. With torn clothing, Wells-Barnett disembarked at the next station.[61]

Not to be deterred, Wells-Barnett sued the railroad for its discriminatory practices and won a $500 judgment in December 1884. The headline in the white newspaper, the *Memphis Commercial Appeal*, "Darky Damsel Gets Damages," bespoke of the racial climate of the time and the lack of esteem in which whites held blacks.[62] The victory would not stand, however, because the Chesapeake and Ohio Railroad appealed the decision, and in 1887, the Tennessee State Supreme Court overturned the verdict.[63] Notwithstanding the headlines and the possible backlash for her actions, Wells-Barnett displayed the courage of her conviction and continued her work for social justice. Hence, despite many entreaties, Wells-Barnett refused to compromise when the railroad tried to persuade her to settle the suit as it wound its way through the courts.[64]

Wells-Barnett believed her suit was significant and necessary because it was the first case in which a black plaintiff in the South had appealed to a state court since the repeal of the Civil Rights Bill by the United States Supreme Court. She declared that the success of her case "would have set a precedent which others would doubtless have followed."[65]

An April 11, 1887, notation in her diary conveyed the sense of Wells-Barnett's frustration in losing the suit on appeal. She wrote,

> I felt so disappointed because I had hoped such great things from my suit for my people generally. I have firmly believed all along that the law was on our side and would, when we appealed to it, give us justice. I feel shorn of that belief and utterly discouraged, and just now if it were possible would gather my race in my arms and fly far away with them. Oh God is there no redress, no peace, no justice in this land for us? Thou hast always fought the battles of the weak and oppressed.

Come to my aid at this moment and teach me what to do, for I am sorely, bitterly disappointed.[66]

Wells-Barnett also wrote an article about her experience that ran in black publications nationwide. Her contemporary, historian I. Garland Penn, observed that the article for the *Living Way* "introduced" Wells-Barnett "to the newspaper fraternity as a writer of superb ability" and that "demands for her services began to come in."[67]

According to Duster, Wells-Barnett's actions were indicative of her destiny "to defy mobs and become a vigorous crusader against the injustices that beset the Negro people in the post-Reconstruction days in the South."[68]

PUBLICATIONS FOR WHICH WELLS-BARNETT WROTE

While in Memphis, Wells-Barnett saw her articles, letters, and columns published in such papers as the Kansas City *Gate City Press*, the *Little Rock Sun*, the *New York Freeman* which later became the *New York Age*, the *Detroit Plaindealer*, the *AME Church Review*, and the *Washington Bee*. Wells-Barnett also wrote articles that ran in such white papers as the *Memphis Scimitar*.[69] During the later years of her life, the journalist also published "a little paper called the *Fellowship Herald*" in Chicago.[70]

Newspapers in large numbers published and praised Wells-Barnett's articles and letters, and as McMurry indicated, the writer considered herself a "professional journalist" who "desired to be paid for her efforts."[71] Such papers as the *Kansas City Dispatch*, the *Chicago Conservator*, and the *Indianapolis World* asked Wells-Barnett to write articles or serve as a correspondent. Although only in her mid-twenties and earning a meager living as a teacher, Wells-Barnett again exhibited her independence and conviction. In her dealings with the *World*, Wells-Barnett displayed what DeCosta-Willis described as those "leadership skills" that would bring her "fame, if not fortune, in the 1890s as a journalist, club woman, civil rights advocate, and anti-lynching crusader."[72] An indignant Wells-Barnett refused to write for the *World* after its editor offered to pay her with a two-year subscription.[73]

Consequently, Wells-Barnett was becoming a prolific and sought after writer, but was receiving little or no remuneration for her work. That changed when William J. Simmons, the pastor of a leading Baptist church and publisher of the *American Baptist*, a religious newspaper that circulated nationally, offered to pay Wells-Barnett "a lavish sum of one dollar a letter weekly"[74] to be a correspondent for the paper. Years later, Wells-Barnett wrote, "It was the first time anyone had offered to pay me for the work I had enjoyed doing. I had never dreamed of receiving any pay, for I had been too happy over the thought that the papers were giving me space."[75]

Simmons, who was also president of the National Press Association, paid Wells-Barnett's way to the convention of the black press in Louisville, Kentucky, in 1887 in exchange for her writing two articles per month exclusively for the *American Baptist* for six months.[76] Thus, Wells-Barnett became a staff member for a publication, not only receiving regular pay, but also a contract. She credited Simmons with being her mentor and with encouraging her to become a newspaperwoman, writing ". . .whatever fame I achieved in that line I owe in large measure to his influence and encouragement."[77]

Wells-Barnett soon took her journalism career to a new level. When presented with the opportunity in 1889, she purchased one-third interest in the *Free Speech and Headlight*, a small newspaper in Memphis co-owned by the Rev. F. Nightingale, pastor of the largest black church in the city, and J. L. Flemming, who served as the publication's business manager. Wells-Barnett's independent spirit was again evident in this venture. She wrote in her autobiography that she refused to join the paper "except as equal."[78] She shortened the paper's name to the *Free Speech*, and she set out to make the publication profitable. Besides editing and reporting, Wells-Barnett traveled throughout the South to solicit subscriptions and extend the paper's circulation. Displaying her savvy, she appointed correspondents to send news to the paper weekly. No copies of the *Free Speech* exist; however, other newspapers reprinted Wells-Barnett's articles that ran in her publication.

Wells-Barnett's travels were successful, and she discovered she had at last found her real vocation.[79] Decades later she explained, "It was quite a novelty to see a woman agent who was also an editor of the journal for which she canvassed."[80] Wells-Barnett noted that "the *Free Speech* was a welcome visitor, a helpful influence in the lives of our people, and was filling a long-felt want."[81] Moreover, the paper's circulation increased from fifteen hundred to four thousand in less than a year.[82]

The ability to raise money for the paper assured Wells-Barnett that she would have a source of income, especially because her activism and hard-hitting journalism often brought about negative consequences for her. Wells-Barnett lost her teaching job in 1891 when her articles in the *Free Speech* criticized the Memphis board of education for hiring incompetent black teachers and for having poor school facilities for black children.[83] Of her firing, Wells-Barnett wrote: "Of course I had rather feared that might be the result; but I had taken a chance in the interest of the children of our race and had lost out."[84] Explaining that she received little appreciation from the parents, Wells-Barnett added,

> But I thought it was right to strike a blow against a glaring evil and I did not regret it. Up to that time I had felt that any fight made in the

interest of the race would have its support. I learned then that I could not count on that.[85]

That incident early in her career, the manner in which she took a stand, and the reaction of her race members portended a position in which Wells-Barnett would find herself often in her career—that of a lone crusader. She used her words to advocate on behalf of her race, and when she incurred the wrath of her detractors, Wells-Barnett continued along the path she had chosen or sought another avenue through which she could make an impact. That is what she did after her termination from the Memphis school system. In addition to parachuting her into a full-time journalism career, the loss of her job and her resultant travels as a correspondent and representative for her paper gave Wells-Barnett visibility as a journalist.[86]

Fortune offered Wells-Barnett the opportunity to write a twice-weekly column for the *New York Age* after the white mob destroyed the *Free Speech* and friends told her that her life would be in jeopardy if she returned to Memphis. After a short time, Wells-Barnett bought one-fourth interest in the paper in exchange for her subscription list, and she "became a weekly contributor on salary."[87] She accepted the offer because she saw it as "the chance to be of more service to the cause by staying in New York than by returning to Memphis."[88] She explained,

> I accepted their advice, took a position on the *New York Age*, and continued my fight against lynching and lynchers. They had destroyed my paper, in which every dollar I had in the world was invested. They had made me an exile and threatened my life for hinting at the truth. I felt that I owed it to myself and my race to tell the whole truth.[89]

Of the opportunity the *Age* afforded her, Wells-Barnett wrote: "The Negro race should be ever grateful to T. Thomas Fortune and Jerome B. Peterson" because "they helped me give to the world the first inside story of Negro lynchings."[90] The crusading journalist added that she "could never have made such headway in emblazoning the story to the world"[91] if Fortune and Peterson had not displayed courage and vision.

As she grew in stature, and after her move to Chicago, Wells-Barnett saw her articles published in most of the local and national black publications, including the *Chicago Defender*, the *Chicago Conservator*, that her husband owned and she later purchased, the *Cleveland Gazette*, the *Chicago Broad Ax*, and the *Whip*. For those publications, Wells-Barnett produced articles about riots in Elaine, Arkansas; Springfield, Illinois; East St. Louis, and Chicago.[92] Wells-Barnett had traveled to the scene of those riots to obtain first-hand information. The *Chicago Inter-Ocean*, a mainstream publication, carried Wells-Barnett's articles and letters about lynching while she was on her European tours to call attention to the crime.

Wells-Barnett maintained that the *Inter-Ocean* was "the only paper in the United States which had done anything in a systematic way to expose the lynching infamy."[93]

THEMES

Although she had been fired for writing about education, Wells-Barnett continued to write about that topic and to address such other themes as black leadership, misrepresentation of her race, segregated churches, an unjust criminal justice system, and other issues that had an impact on blacks. Scholars agree, however, that despite Wells-Barnett's activism, and her writing and lecturing on a variety of causes and issues, her role in exposing and campaigning against lynching was the most significant of her activities and was the focus of a large body of her journalistic work.[94] Giddings offered that the lynching of three black men in Memphis propelled Wells-Barnett and fellow journalist and activist Mary Church Terrell into the fight for racial equality. The lynching opened "a new chapter in the racial struggle, for they spurred two women to dedicate their lives to the fight against lynching and the malevolent impulses that underlined it," Giddings noted.[95]

Wells-Barnett cited the lynching of Memphis businessman Thomas Moss and his two partners, Calvin McDowell and Henry Stewart, as the catalyst for her activism in the racial struggle. According to accounts of Wells-Barnett, Terrell, and historians, Moss, McDowell, and Stewart opened the People's Grocery Company across the street from a white storeowner in a predominantly black area known as the Curve, just outside the Memphis city limits. The white storekeeper for many years had a monopoly until Moss and his partners opened their establishment.

Because the store was beyond city police protection, Moss, his partners, and several friends armed themselves at their store when they learned that a mob planned to ransack it. In the ensuing conflict, three white people were wounded.[96] Police arrested the three businessmen as well as almost forty other blacks, and the white newspapers called the incident a "black conspiracy."[97] Three days after the incident, a group of whites took the partners from their jail cells, and according to Wells-Barnett, loaded them on a "switch engine of the railroad," and carried them outside the city limits where they were "horribly shot to death."[98] Of the incident, Wells-Barnett wrote in her autobiography,

> While I was thus carrying on the work of my newspaper, happy in the thought that our influence was helpful and that I was doing the work I loved and had proved that I could make a living out of it, there came the lynching in Memphis which changed the whole course of my life.[99]

Moss and his wife, Betty, were Wells-Barnett's best friends in Memphis, and she was godmother to the couple's daughter, Maurine.[100] Wells-Barnett immediately set about to right the grave wrong that she and the Memphis black community believed had been committed. She had been in Natchez, Mississippi, when the lynching took place, and Moss had already been buried when she returned. In a series of editorials, Wells-Barnett embarked on her anti-lynching campaign. She argued that Moss "was murdered with no more consideration than if he had been a dog,"[101] and that economic reprisal was the real reason for the lynching.

Therefore, Wells-Barnett encouraged blacks to take the dying Moss's suggestion and leave Memphis. She pointed out that the city had "demonstrated that neither character nor standing" availed the black man "if he dares to protect himself against the white man or become his rival."[102] Furthermore, there was nothing blacks could do about lynching because they were "out-numbered and without arms," the writer declared. Not content to sit by passively, Wells-Barnett counseled blacks to save their money and leave a town that she said would "neither protect our lives and property, nor give us a fair trial in the courts, but take us out and murder us in cold blood when accused by white persons."[103] In addition, Wells-Barnett urged blacks to boycott the segregated transportation system.

Subsequent articles and editorials responded to other lynchings. A central theme in those articles was Wells-Barnett's charge that white women often initiated relationships with black men. In May 1892, Wells Barnett asserted that the notion of blacks raping white women was a "thread bare lie."[104] The reporter wrote,

> Eight Negroes lynched since last issue of the *Free Speech*. Three were charged with killing white men and five with raping white women. Nobody in this section believes the old thread-bare lie that Negro men assault white women. If Southern white men are not careful they will over-reach themselves and a conclusion will be reached which will be very damaging to the moral reputation of their women.[105]

The *Free Speech* was unrelenting and successful in its crusade, for during a three-month period more than two thousand blacks took Wells-Barnett's advice, left Memphis, and headed for Oklahoma and Kansas City. Wells-Barnett's power as an agent of change through the press was evident because her efforts crippled the Memphis economy.[106] In her autobiography, Wells-Barnett wrote,

> Business was practically at a standstill, for the Negro was famous then, as now, for spending his money for fine clothes, furniture, jewelry, and pianos and other musical instruments, to say nothing of good things to eat. Music houses had more musical instruments, sold on the install-

ment plan, thrown back on their hands than they could find storage for.[107]

As she had done with her suit against the railroad, Wells-Barnett again refused the entreaties of the white citizens. This time she refused to call a halt to the exodus.

The editorials so angered Memphis whites that they reacted. As a result, Wells-Barnett again suffered the consequences for her journalistic activism. While she was travelling to Philadelphia to attend the African Methodist Episcopal Church's general conference, a white mob, at the urging of the *Memphis Commercial Appeal*, destroyed the office of the *Free Speech*. Calling on "chivalrous white men to avenge this insult to the honor of their women," the *Commercial Appeal* wrote, "The black wretch who had written that foul lie should be tied to a stake at the corner of Main and Madison streets, a pair of tailor's shears used on him and he should then be burned at a stake."[108] With her life in jeopardy, Wells-Barnett remained in the North and continued to report about the violence and injustices being perpetrated against blacks. She maintained that she felt she owed it to herself and her race to "tell the whole truth now that I was where I could do so freely."[109]

WRITINGS ABOUT LYNCHING

In June 1892, Wells-Barnett produced a seven-column article on the front page of the New York Age that showed conclusively that her article in the *Free Speech* was based on the "fact of illicit association between black men and white women."[110] Later that year, she produced another article that detailed the number of lynchings, and she refuted the widely accepted premise that lynching occurred because immoral black men raped white women.

Writing in her autobiography, Wells-Barnett explained her tenacious determination to stop lynching. She clarified:

> I found that in order to justify these horrible atrocities to the world, the Negro was being branded as a race of rapists, who were especially mad after white women. I found that white men who had created a race of mulattos by raping and consorting with Negro women were still doing so wherever they could. These same white men lynched, burned, and tortured Negro men for doing the same thing with white women; even when the white women were willing victims.
>
> It seemed horrible to me that death in its most terrible form should be meted out to the Negro who was weak enough to take chances when accepting the invitations of these white women; but that the entire race should be branded as moral monsters and despoilers of

white womanhood and childhood was bound to rob us of all the friends we had and silence any protest that they might make for us.[111]

Beginning with the death of Moss and continuing for decades, Wells-Barnett traveled to investigate lynching, tirelessly poured over articles in white newspapers that reported on lynching, collected data, and wrote pieces aimed at making her readers aware of the crime. By graphically describing what she observed at the scene of lynchings, Wells-Barnett hoped to stir a nation's consciousness and humanity.

A little less than a year after her first articles on lynching, this muckraker produced a twenty-five page pamphlet that described the extent to which lynchings were spreading, castigated the nation for its "indifference" and "apathy," and debunked the myth of lynching as the just punishment for the rape of white women.[112] In what was to become the hallmark of her investigative journalism, Wells-Barnett buttressed her arguments with statistics. Declaring that in the Unites States, "our common country, a government of the people, by the people, and for the people, means a government by mob rule," Wells-Barnett wrote contemptuously that "the land of the free and home of the brave means a land of lawlessness, murder, and outrage; and where liberty of speech means the license of might to destroy the business and drive from home those who excused the privilege contrary to the will of the mob."[113]

The article, clearly aimed at educating the public, revealed that "lynching bees" had "become the favorite pastime of the South."[114] Furthermore, Wells-Barnett maintained that the crime came in various forms, from killing innocent blacks, to destroying their property, to driving people from their homes and livelihood. By way of example, Wells-Barnett detailed the status of blacks in Memphis, noting that many were prospering, well-educated and refined. According to the writer, all of that changed with the lynching of Moss and his partners.[115] Wells-Barnett avowed that she could not describe "the feeling of horror that possessed every member of the race in Memphis when the truth dawned upon us that the protection of the law which we had so long enjoyed was no longer ours." According to Wells-Barnett,

> all this had been destroyed in a night, and the barriers of the law had been thrown down, and the guardians of the public peace and confidence scoffed away into the shadows, and all authority given into the hand of the mob, and innocent men cut down as if they were brutes—the first feeling was one of utter dismay, then intense indignation.[116]

As evidence that lynching involved more than killing blacks, Wells-Barnett explained that Memphis whites sought retaliation by scouring the city for the *Free Speech's* business manager. When the mob was unable to find Flemming, the angry throng "had to be content with Mr. Nightingale who was dragged to the meeting, shamefully abused (although it was known he had sold out his interest in the paper six months before)."[117] Wells-Barnett explained that Flemming "was struck in the face and forced at the pistol's point to sign a letter which was written by them, in which he denied all knowledge of the editorial, denounced and condemned it as slander on white women."[118]

Wells-Barnett maintained that lynching, which began in and gradually disappeared from the western United States, had found its way to the South, where "it has flourished ever since" and where continued the "inhuman butchery of more than ten thousand men, women, and children by shooting, drowning, hanging, and burning them alive."[119] Decrying the lawlessness and "lynching mania"[120] that had now spread to the North and Middle West, Wells-Barnett once described a "ghastly and barbaric lynching" in Texarkana, Texas, of a black man accused of rape. The victim was "strapped" to a tree, his flesh was chipped away, coal oil was poured over his body, and, finally, he was set afire by the woman he was accused of raping. Again, Wells-Barnett charged that "the country looked on and in many cases applauded, because it was published that this man had violated the honor of the white woman, although he protested his innocence to the last."[121]

Wells-Barnett provided statistics that showed that black men—and some black women and children—were lynched between 1882 to 1892 for a variety of offenses, and mostly without benefit of trial. To illustrate that black men were not the only victims, Wells-Barnett related the story of a black woman who was accused of poisoning the woman for whom she worked and lynched when the woman died. Another woman was lynched "after being charged as an accomplice in the murder of her white paramour who had abused her."[122] Commenting that "neither age, sex nor decency are spared," Wells-Barnett criticized "this Christian nation" that was "willingly powerless to send troops to protect the lives of its black citizens," but "free to use state troops to shoot them down like cattle when in desperation the black men attempt to defend themselves."[123]

Wells-Barnett's writings did not merely provide statistics or graphic details of lynchings; instead, the journalist always proposed a remedy. In this piece, she suggested that "a public sentiment strong against lawlessness must be aroused."[124] Continuing, Well-Barnett stated optimistically, "When a sentiment against lynch law as strong, deep and mighty as that roused against slavery prevails, I have no fear of the result."[125] Asserting that every human being deserved a fair trial, and "reformers from the press and pulpit, from industrial and moral association" should demand that,[126] Wells-Barnett used another article to call for the establishment of the Anti-Lynching Bureau of the National Afro-American Council "to investigate every lynching and publish the facts to the world."[127] She further explained that because lynching affected the whole country, the nation should seek to end it, based on "consistency... economy... the honor of white civilization," and "love of country."[128] With regard to consistency, Wells-Barnett protested:

> Brave men do not gather by the thousands to torture and murder a single individual, so gagged and bound he cannot make even feeble resistance or defense. Neither do brave men or women stand by and see such things done without compunction of conscience, nor read of them without protest."[129]

The crusading journalist, intent on holding the nation accountable, further argued that the United States should pay "indemnities for lynching" as the country had done when Italians were lynched in Louisiana.[130] Finally, Wells-Barnett suggested that the white man "should be able to protect the honor of his women" without resorting to "such brutal, inhuman, and degrading exhibitions as characterize lynching bees."[131] With a militancy that defied the era, Wells-Barnett wrote:

> With all the powers of government in control; with all laws made by white men, administered by white judges, jurors, prosecuting attorneys, and sheriff; with every office of the executive department filled by white men—no excuse can be offered for exchanging the orderly administration of justice for barbarous lynching and "unwritten laws."[132]

The article then condemned the silence of "moral and philanthropic forces of the country" that failed "to put a stop to this wholesale slaughter."[133]

Not content to expose lynching in the press, in 1895 Wells-Barnett published *A Red Record*, "the first comprehensive history of lynching."[134] The pamphlet traced the genesis of lynching, from excuses that began with the myth of protecting white womanhood, to the need to stamp out race riots, and finally, to resist black domination via organized terrorism. The latter was the real excuse, Wells-Barnett argued.[135]

Continuing her crusade in the press against lynching, she reasoned in the May 16, 1901, issue of the *Independent* that it was "unspeakably infamous to put thousands of people to death without a trial by jury," adding "it adds to that infamy to charge that these victims were moral monsters, when, in fact, four-fifths of them were not so accused even by the fiends who murdered them."[136]

Wells-Barnett did not back down when her detractors confronted her. She addressed a writer who evidently believed the rationale used to justify lynching when she wrote, "It is this assumption, this absolutely unwarrantable assumption . . . the same baseless assumption which influences ninety-nine out of every one hundred persons who discuss this question."[138] Wells-Barnett pointedly countered that the facts about lynching were easy to obtain via the Associated Press, the press clippings bureau, books, and an annual summary that "influential journals" provide every year. "This record, easily within the reach of every one who wants it, makes inexcusable the assumption that negroes are lynched only because of their assaults upon womanhood," Wells-Barnett asserted.[139]

As with previous articles, Wells-Barnett provided statistics on the number of people lynched and the causes for the lynching from 1896 through 1900. Those statistics, she exclaimed, showed that blacks were lynched overwhelmingly for causes other than rape. Rather, race prejudice again was the lynch mobs' incentive.[140] The year 1900 saw Wells-Barnett supplementing her stories on lynching with a more in-depth piece titled *Mob Rule in New Orleans: Robert Charles and His Fight to the Death*. Noting that she obtained her details from two white newspapers in New Orleans, Wells-Barnett provided "accounts of brutality, injustice and oppression"[141] in the city. The work provided details of the death of Charles, who while being sought for allegedly killing two white police officers, defended himself by killing several other people before being shot, mutilated beyond recognition, and dragged through the streets in a police wagon. Wells-Barnett declared that mob violence "was further shown by the unspeakable cruelty with which it beat, shot and stabbed to death an unoffending colored man, name unknown, who happened to be walking on the street with no thought that he would be set upon and killed because he was a colored man."[142]

Subsequent articles labeled lynching the country's "national crime."[143] In one piece, Wells-Barnett made three "salient" points about the crime. She argued that lynching was "color line murder;" that committing "crimes against white women was the excuse, not the cause;" and that the crime of lynching required a "national remedy."[144] This article again averred that lynching was "wholly political" and its purpose was "to suppress the colored vote by intimidation and murder."[145] Again providing statistics that blacks were lynched for such purported causes as "slapping a child," "colonizing negroes," and disobeying a quarantine," Wells-Barnett said that preventive remedies such as education and agitation had not stopped "the lynching infamy" that "was tantamount to the butchery of men, women and children."[146]

As she had done in previous articles, Wells-Barnett suggested initiatives the country could undertake to stop lynching. She urged "federal protection" for "American citizenship;" action on a bill in Congress that would have provided for "federal prosecution of lynchers;" establishment of a bureau to investigate and publish the details of every lynching; and a conference.[147] Wells-Barnett concluded her article with the assertion that at one time lynching "appeared to be sectional," but the practice was now national and "a blight upon our nation, mocking our laws and disgracing our Christianity."[148]

In 1913, Wells-Barnett was still writing about lynching and criticizing the country's acquiescence. She pointed out that although a "governors' meeting" had formally condemned expressions in support of lynching, "many governors have refused to deal sternly with the leaders of mobs or to enforce the law against lynchers."[149] Noting that political leaders had "accepted the excuse that lynching was just punishment for defiling white womanhood," Wells-Barnett argued that statistics showed blacks were lynched for other reasons. She continued, "In the thirty years in which lynching has been going on in the South, this falsehood has been universally accepted in all sections of our country, and has been offered by thousands as a reason why they don't speak out against these terrible outrages."[150]

Writings about Gender

With the same fervor that she tackled lynching, Wells-Barnett also addressed other issues related to race, especially the misrepresentation of race members and the negative stereotypical portrayal of black women. Through her articles on lynching, Wells-Barnett unmasked the rampant falsifications about her race. Armed with statistics, she proved that black males were not vicious sexual monsters. While challenging the lies about black men, Wells-Barnett, likewise, clearly sought to counter the false and negative image of black women. She emphatically stressed that, contrary to the commonly held view of whites, black women were not immoral, but were the victims of white men's sexual proclivities.[151] In her autobiography, Wells-Barnett expressed her outrage about and the rationale for what had happened to black women. She wrote,

> I found that this rape of helpless Negro girls and women, which began in slavery days, still continued without hindrance, check or reproof from church, state, or press until there had been created this race within a race—and all designated by the inclusive term of 'colored.'"[152]

Clearly, Wells-Barnett was among the black women of the period whom Glenda Gilmore noted "tried to eliminate grist for the white supremacy mill by abolishing the image of the immoral black woman and the barbaric black home."[153] According to Gilmore, black women were portrayed as "immoral scourges" with "low and animalistic urges;" and these stereotypes "applied to all classes, including middle-class leaders."[154] This characterization troubled Wells-Barnett, who was at times painted with the same brush.[155]

Wells-Barnett addressed the cloak of immorality that had been draped around her fellow race women. The writer argued that allowing the misrepresentation of black women as "loose—insatiable, promiscuous, and vulgar,"[156] was a major threat to racial advancement. On January 1, 1887, Wells-Barnett reiterated her disgust about the negative and stereotypical portrayal of black women, declaring that "the taint of immorality"[157] was deeply and keenly held. Moreover, she could not countenance the "jest and sneer with which our women are spoken of, and the utter incapacity or refusal to believe there are among us mothers, wives, and maidens who have attained a true, noble, and refining womanhood."[158]

The view of a woman's role, therefore, was a theme found in Wells-Barnett's articles. Existing scholarship indicate that she was "ambivalent" about her role as a woman in a society where the role of woman was prescribed.[159] Although Wells-Barnett believed in the "ideology of puritanical Victorianism, propagated by her white missionary teachers at Rust University,"[160] she had difficulty accepting the cult of true womanhood.[161] The ideology, according to McMurry, postulated that "the ideal woman" was "submissive". . . "gentle, innocent, pure, and pious," and that "her proper sphere was the home, and her life revolved around her husband."[162] McMurry further indicated that "women were to honor and defer to men and yet provide moral influence."[163] This cult of true womanhood was "used to circumscribe white women and make them dependent" and it "caused black women to prove they were ladies," Gilmore maintained.[164]

Wells-Barnett did not fit into that role. She operated in a field that males dominated. Her autobiography and diary indicate that her interactions were mainly with men who became her mentors. Wells-Barnett had an often-contentious relationship with women and sometimes criticized their weaknesses.[165] Many of the leading women viewed Ida as intractable. Although a founder of the National Association of Colored Women, Wells-Barnett was not invited to appear in the organization's 1899 program when the group met in Chicago. She ran unsuccessfully for the NACW's presidency, and in 1901, delegates openly hissed when Wells-Barnett spoke at the group's national meeting.[166] Wells-Barnett wrote in her autobiography, "Always the personal element. It seems disheartening to think that every single movement for progress and race advancement has to be blocked this way."[167]

Despite her relationship with most black women, Wells-Barnett sought to dispel the negative stereotypes about them. She and other black women journalists, therefore, made the case that the women of their race should adhere to the cult of true womanhood. In one of her first articles, Wells-Barnett told her race sisters that they had not "awakened to a true sense of responsibilities," were not aware of the influence they had, and had not yet "realized the necessity for erecting a standard of earnest, thoughtful, pure, noble womanhood, rather than one of fashion, idleness and uselessness."[168]

In an article, "The Model Woman: A Pen Picture of the Typical Southern Girl," Wells-Barnett expounded on her concept of the "true or ideal woman," especially in the face of derogatory perceptions of women. She noted that "character" was the "typical girl's only wealth," and that "her first consideration was to preserve that character in spotless purity."[169]

Later, Wells-Barnett indicated that black women knew and understood the role they could play in society and in uplifting the race. She related the story of a young teacher who, aware of the sentiments regarding the treatment of blacks, was not content to earn a salary, but also used her teaching as the opportunity to influence students and educate them about how to live upstanding, moral, and productive lives. Wells-Barnett wrote that as the teacher learned of trouble in which former students were involved, "it flashed" in the young woman's mind "that the real want was proper home and moral training combined with mental, that would avert a too frequent repetition of this sad case and that the duty of Negro teachers was to supplement this lack, as none had greater opportunities."[170] According to Wells-Barnett, the teacher's "causal earnest talks made a deep impression," consequently, "the pupils became thoughtful and earnest," viewed school life "as a means to an end," and learned "that there was work out in the world waiting for them to come and take hold."[171]

Wells-Barnett conveyed that even though women adhered to the cult of true womanhood, they were progressive and were making tremendous strides. Writing in the *New York Freeman* in December 1885, Wells-Barnett averred that throughout history women had "won laurels for themselves as philanthropists, statesmen, leaders of armies, rulers of empires." Wells-Barnett wrote that the woman had "gradually ascended the scale of human progress as men have become more enlightened, until in this nineteenth century there are few positions she may not aspire to."[172]

According to Wells-Barnett, the woman had "nobly vindicated her right of equality" in colleges; had "borne herself with credit and honor" in the professions; and had "proven her ability and faithfulness" in "positions of trust."[173] Wells-Barnett added, "Women should be a strong, bright presence, thoroughly imbued with a sense of her mission on earth and a desire to fill it; an earnest, soulful being, laboring to fit herself for life's duties and burdens and bearing them faithfully."[174]

WRITINGS ABOUT RACE

The misrepresentation of her race and gender, Wells-Barnett believed, provided the justification for racial discrimination, another major theme about which she wrote. Early in her career, Wells-Barnett was not afraid to express outrage when she perceived such discrimination. In 1893, she joined her husband, Ferdinand Barnett; fellow journalist I. Garland Penn; and noted abolitionist and activist Frederick Douglass to publish the pamphlet, *The Reason Why the Colored American Is Not in the World's Columbian Exposition*. In addition to writing about the inherent racism of the fair's organizers and administration, Wells-Barnett solicited funds that made possible the publication and distribution of 20,000 copies of the eighty-one page pamphlet. In the preface to the document, Wells-Barnett traced the "large share" of contributions blacks had made to "American prosperity and civilization" since arriving on slave ships in 1619.[175] She then declared that the pamphlet would serve to answer the question of visitors to the exposition who undoubtedly would wonder why black people were not visible or represented in the exposition.[176] The writer professed:

> The labor of one-half of this country has always been, and is still being done by them. The first credit this country had in its commerce with foreign nations was created by productions resulting from their labor. The wealth created by their industry has afforded to the white people of this country the leisure essential to their great progress in education, art, science, industry and invention.[177]

Wells-Barnett was not content to express her views in the pamphlet; therefore, with fervor, she also castigated fair organizers for creating "Colored Folks Day" during the World's Fair. In an article with the headline, "To Tole with Watermelons," Wells-Barnett decried the proposal, calling it a ploy to increase attendance numbers after having ignored blacks and denying them the opportunity of meaningful participation. "The secret of the kindness (?) of the world's fair commissioners is that the attendance at the fair has been very poor all along, and the colored brother has been conspicuous by his absence," Wells-Barnett wrote.[178] And in what was clearly a reference to a common racial stereotype, Wells-Barnett offered sarcastically that "the horticultural department has already pledged itself to put plenty of watermelons around on the grounds with permission to the brother in black to 'appropriate' them."[179] Concerned about misrepresentation of the race, the writer explained: "The sight of the horde that would be attracted there by the dazzling prospect of plenty of free watermelons to eat, will give our enemies all the illustration they wish as excuse for not treating the Afro-American with the equality of other citizens."[180]

By presenting evidence of the success of blacks and women, Wells-Barnett believed that she was destroying negative myths. Wells-Barnett not only criticized the press, she sometimes chastised individuals who believed the commonly accepted views about the race. A statement by Frances

Willard of the Women's Christian Temperance Union led Wells-Barnett to respond that she did not desire to "quarrel with the Women's Christian Temperance Union." Wells-Barnett stated that her "love of the truth" was greater than her "regard for an alleged friend who, through ignorance or design, misrepresents in the most harmful way the cause of a long suffering race, and then unable to maintain the truth of her attack excuse herself as it were by the wave of the hand."[181]

Wells-Barnett biographer McMurry noted that President William McKinley was on the receiving end of Wells-Barnett's venom following a race riot in Wilmington, North Carolina, in November 1898. Wells-Barnett charged, McMurry explained, that the President was "much too interested just now in the national decoration of Confederate graves to pay attention to Negro rights."[182]

Just as she scolded whites, this provocative writer and race woman vented her wrath on members of her own race. Because she believed that black leaders had a special obligation to uplift the race, Wells-Barnett was militant in her criticism of those who did not pick up the mantra, including religious leaders, middle and upper class blacks, and politicians. Early in her career, she took on ministers, whom she believed had abdicated their responsibility to the race. DeCosta-Willis argued that Wells-Barnett "was critical of ill-prepared, corrupt, or insincere clergymen, who did not make 'practical talks' or give people 'guidance in everyday life.'"[183]

A February 1, 1886, entry in her diary indicated what the very religious Wells-Barnett thought about a particular minister whose sermon she had heard during her attendance at two church services that day. Wells-Barnett wrote that the minister's later sermon did not differ from the earlier one and contained "a constant arraignment of the Negro as compared to the whites, a burlesque of Negro worship, a repetition of what he did not believe in, and the telling of jokes together with a reiteration of his text 'ye must be born again'."[184] Wells-Barnett declared that the clergyman lacked "some of the essential elements that compose a preacher," seemed "to be wanting in stability," and lacked reverence.[185]

In an earlier piece, the *Free Speech* exposed a minister who had been caught in an uncompromising situation at the home of one of his female church members. When fellow ministers threatened to boycott the paper because of the article, Wells-Barnett published the names of "every minister who belonged to the alliance."[186] The *Free Speech*, Wells-Barnett wrote, "told the community that these men upheld the immoral conduct of one of their number and asked if they were willing to support preachers who would sneak into their homes when their backs were turned and debauch their wives."[187]

Race spokesman Booker T. Washington was the subject of an April 1904, article. With regard to Washington's urging of industrial education for blacks, Wells-Barnett made the following assertion: "That one of the most noted of their own race should join the enemies to their highest progress in condemning the education they had received, has been to them a bitter pill."[188] As a result of Washington's views, Wells-Barnett protested, "the world which listens to him and which largely supports his educational institutions, has almost unanimously decided that college education is a mistake for the Negro."[189]

Blanche K. Bruce, a black senator from Mississippi, did not live up to Wells-Barnett's expectation of black leadership. She strongly believed that Bruce compromised on racial issues to the detriment of black people, as illustrated when she asked: "What can history say of our Senator Bruce, save that he held the chair of a Senator for six years, drew his salary and left others to champion the Negro's cause in the Senate Chamber?"[190] Bruce incurred Wells-Barnett's indignation for the same reason that other black leaders did—personal aggrandizement at the expense of race progress or perceived weaknesses. In September 1885, Wells-Barnett noted that "wealth served as a shield" against discrimination for black leaders. Two months later, Wells-Barnett stated that she was not aligned with either the Democratic of Republican Party, but she was concerned about whether black leaders were "obeying honest and intelligent convictions." She added, "It is the spirit of intolerance and narrow mindedness among colored men of intelligence that is censured and detested."[191]

Wells-Barnett asserted that the black upper class sought to obtain all they could for themselves and cared little about the black masses. DeCosta-Willis suggested that Ida likely joined others who criticized "secret societies such as the Masons, the Sons of Ham, the Odd Fellows, the Knights of Phythia, and the Knights of Labor."[192]

The sharp-tongued Wells-Barnett criticized political leaders in 1885, with the protest that "some of them do not wish, after getting wealth for themselves, to be longer identified with the people to whom they owe their political preferment."[193] Two years later, Wells-Barnett scolded black barbers, hotelkeepers and black business people for refusing to serve other blacks.[194] An issue of the *Free Speech* in 1889 had Wells-Barnett taking aim at Reconstruction black leaders whom she said had been in power too long and had become more interested in keeping patronage among themselves rather than protecting black rights.[195] On another occasion, Isaiah Montgomery, the black man who had established the town of Mound Bayou in Mississippi, received a severe reprimand for his vote in favor of the "Understanding Clause" in the "infamous" Mississippi Convention of 1890.[196] The clause enabled the state to prevent blacks from voting "without conflicting with the provision of the Fourteenth and Fifteenth Amendments."[197] Wells-Barnett's *Free Speech* editorial argued that "it would have been better" for Montgomery "to have gone down to defeat still voting against this outrageous"[198] measure.

Following the lynching of Moss, an agitated Wells-Barnett asked, "Where are our 'leaders' when the race is being burnt, shot and hanged?" And she answered, "Holding good fat offices and saying not a word—just as they were when the Civil Rights bill was repealed and the Blair Education and Federal Elections bills were defeated."[199]

In 1887, Wells-Barnett criticized black leaders who had asked for separate and unequal schools for black children in Visalia, California. This former teacher assailed such an arrangement, and declared, "consciously and unconsciously we do as much to widen the breach already existing to keep prejudice alive as the other race."[200] Wells-Barnett pointed out that no separate school existed in the state of California until the black people requested it. Admonishing her race, she cautioned,

> To say we wish to be to ourselves is a tacit acknowledgement of the inferiority that they take for granted anyway. The ignorant man who is so shortsighted has some excuse, but the man or men who deliberately yield or barter the birthright of the race for money, position, self aggrandizement in any form, deserve and will receive the contumely of a race made wise by experience.[201]

Even T. Thomas Fortune, the *New York Age* editor who had provided Wells-Barnett with the forum from which she launched her anti-lynching campaign, was not spared. In 1889, when Fortune defended white southerners, Wells-Barnett challenged him, asking: "Do you really and candidly believe that if appealed to in honest the white people of the South 'could not' and would not refuse us justice?" Wells-Barnett answered, "I don't believe it."[202]

Even after she no longer wrote articles on a regular basis for the black press, she expressed her views about black leadership and other issues via letters to the editor. Following a race riot in East St. Louis, Wells-Barnett exclaimed that she was pleased blacks had met, marched, protested, and passed resolutions condemning the killing of blacks. The writer stressed, however, that those actions were only a beginning and certainly not enough, and she suggested that blacks "should have engaged the finest race lawyers to be had on the ground to protect race interest."[203] Absent anyone else doing anything along those lines, Wells-Barnett announced that she was going to the area and she pleaded for "funds to accomplish the task at hand."[204]

Wells-Barnett did not always focus on criticism, protest, and chastisement. Other themes included racial self-help and productivity. When the Blair Education bill aimed at providing federal funding to public schools died in Congress in 1890, Wells-Barnett urged blacks to help themselves. She wrote that it now behooved them to "bestir" themselves "to greater efforts for the education of their children," to save money, and "to make better use of the opportunities." Continuing, Wells-Barnett wrote, "The road to our success lies through the door of moral, intellectual and financial education."[205]

On other occasions she offered praise to blacks as well as whites when she deemed such accolades were warranted. In a scathing article in 1891, Wells-Barnett praised blacks who torched Georgetown, Kentucky, following the lynching of a black man. Her editorial posited that the blacks had shown "some of the true spark of manhood by their resentment." A gratified Wells-Barnett commented that she had begun to think blacks

> hadn't any manhood enough in them to wriggle and crawl out of the way, much less protect and defend themselves. One of the things we may be assured, so long as we permit ourselves to be trampled upon, so long we will have to endure it. Not until the Negro rises in his might and takes a hand resenting such cold-blooded murders, if he has to burn up whole towns, will a halt be called in wholesale lynching.[506]

Wells-Barnett also praised white newspapers when they wrote positively on the race issue. In her diary, she pointed out that *Chicago Inter-Ocean* was the only paper "in season and out" that "had denounced the mob and opened its columns to me for an exposition of lynching methods after my return from England."[207] She singled out the newspapers in Birmingham, England, that covered her speech and "gave columns of reports of our meetings, and splendid editorials."[208]

In singling out other newspapers for acknowledgement, Wells-Barnett reprinted an editorial that used the word "shame" to describe laws in the southern United States that forbade blacks and whites from inter-marrying and imposed fines and imprisonment for blacks and whites who rode in the same carriage.[209] Also garnering praise was a similar piece in a New Castle, England, paper that highlighted Wells-Barnett's declaration that England had "often shown America her duty in the past" and that the anti-lynching crusader had "no doubt" that the country would do so again.[210] Coming in for commendation was yet another newspaper, the *Liverpool Daily Post*, that had chided the *Memphis Commercial Appeal* for its "vitriolic attack" on Wells-Barnett.[211]

Suffrage and Racial Elevation

Wells-Barnett, like other black women who were involved in the suffrage movement, saw it as a means of bringing about reform. These activists viewed enfranchisement as "a cure for many of their ills," including "sexual exploitation," and protection of their right to earn decent wages.[212] Moreover, Wells-Barnett stressed that blacks needed the ballot in order to better their conditions and ultimately to stop lynching. She stated that in many states, the black man "was advised that if he gave up trying to vote, minded his own business, acquired property and educated his children, he could get along in the South without molestation."[213] Continuing, Wells-Barnett wrote, "but the more lands and houses he acquired, the more rapidly discriminating laws have been passed against him by those who control the ballot, and less protection is given by the lawmakers for his life, liberty and property."[214]

Calling the right to vote "sacredness," Wells-Barnett stated that without enfranchisement "there is not sacredness of human life itself. For if the strong can take the weak man's ballot, when it suits his purpose to do so, he will take his life also."[215]

Although Wells-Barnett believed the ballot was essential, she also held that other means of elevation existed. DeCosta-Willis affirmed that Wells-Barnett believed elevation of the race could be accomplished if blacks—especially black men—would relinquish such "vices" as "drinking, gambling, and fornication."[216]

In 1892, she suggested that blacks should return to Africa where they "would be welcomed by their race, and given opportunities to assist in the development of the continent."[217] Wells-Barnett's relationship with black nationalist Marcus Garvey during the 1920s signaled her continuing belief in the efficacy of black repatriation. Giddings noted that the United States Secret Service cited Garvey's "association" with Wells-Barnett as "evidence of his radicalism."[218]

CONCLUSION

The activities and writings of Wells-Barnett during the late nineteenth century and well into the twentieth century clearly show that she was an activist who crusaded on behalf of blacks and women. Moreover, Wells-Barnett deserves the credit she has been given for calling attention to and bringing about laws to curb lynching, for playing an integral role in the establishment of the NAACP and several women's organization, and for being at the forefront of the woman's suffrage movement. She was no stranger to the halls of government, including the White House.

Her contemporaries acknowledged her as a journalist; however, during the latter part of her life and well into the twentieth century, Wells-Barnett's work as a journalist was minimized or ignored, while scholars recognized her work in other areas. Yet, her muckraking journalism was the vehicle through which she waged her campaign against lynching and accomplished her activist agenda. Her articles and pamphlets exposed the crime and proposed national, state, and local remedies. Her speeches, which she often turned into articles or letters for distribution in the press, accomplished the same goal.

The perceptive Wells-Barnett was concerned about how history would treat her when she set out to write her autobiography. She wrote, three years prior to her death in 1930, that she had undertaken the process of writing her autobiography "for the young people who have so little of our race history recorded" and because black youth were "entitled to the facts of race history which only the participants can give."[219] Wells-Barnett asserted, "I am all the more constrained to do this because there is such a lack of authentic race history of Reconstruction times written by the Negro himself."[220]

Scholars during the last thirty years, since publication of the Wells-Barnett autobiography, have elevated Wells-Barnett from the footnotes of American, feminist, and African-American history. Today, in addition to Thompson's dissertation that was published as a book in 1990, at least ten books, several dissertations and master's theses, and more than one hundred articles have been published in magazines, journals and on the Internet about Wells-Barnett's life, activities, and contributions.

Works that deal primarily with Wells-Barnett as a journalist are included in that number.[221] This study found that with the exception of McMurry's comprehensive work, most of the other books give an overview of Wells-Barnett's life and journalism career, but do not examine Wells-Barnett's writings. The books simply reprint articles. In addition, as with most black women journalists who wrote during the late nineteenth century and early twentieth century, even when Wells-Barnett is acknowledged in journalism history and texts, she receives minimal space.

Hence, with works such as this study, the muckraking Ida B. Wells-Barnett, this "brilliant"[222] investigative reporter who has been called militant, angry, a racial agitator, and a social reformer is being elevated from the footnotes of journalism history.

CHAPTER THREE

Mary Church Terrell
Captivating Crusader

> And it seemed to me that the only kind of articles which found favor with the editors was one that emphasized the Colored-American's vices and defects, or held him up to ridicule and scorn. Stories which represented him as being a crapshooter, a murder[er], a bum or a buffoon were considered fine examples of literary art, and appeared in reputable magazines. But those which related his struggles to accomplish something worthwhile against fearful odds were labeled "controversial" and never saw the light of day.[1]
>
> *Mary Church Terrell*

Mary Eliza Church Terrell could have ignored the plight of her race and gender during the late nineteenth century and into the twentieth century. Terrell was born to a life of privilege, for her father was the south's first black millionaire.[2] Terrell wrote in her autobiography, *A Colored Woman in a White World*, that her father bought property in Memphis during the Yellow Fever epidemic of 1879, and "he invested every penny he had saved in real estate which was being offered at a bargain."[3] He and his ex-wife gave their daughter virtually everything she could desire—love, an education at one of the country's renowned private colleges and travel abroad. Therefore, it would have been easy for Terrell to remain aloof and unconcerned, sheltered from the difficulties blacks encountered during the post-Civil War era. Instead, this daughter of a former slave chose to become an advocate for blacks and women through her work as a journalist and activist. Terrell has been called one of the leading twentieth-century black women activists. References and other works dub her a poet, lecturer, writer, suffragist, and educator.[4] However, scholars rarely acknowledge Terrell as a journalist when documenting the history of the press.

In her 1990 book about Terrell, Beverly Washington Jones summed up the existing scholarly designation of Terrell's life and work. The author noted that "Terrell saw her role as elevating her race though interracial understanding," and "to achieve this goal, she was active in racial organizations, wrote prolifically, and traveled widely delivering lectures."[5] Rosalie Massery Sanderson, author of a master's thesis on Terrell, pointed out that the woman was always conscious of her "personal double handicap of sex and race," and "she attempted throughout her life to ameliorate the plight of women and Negroes, and particularly that of Negro women."[6] Sanderson added that Terrell's "efforts took diverse forms as she spoke on countless platforms throughout the country, wrote for various Negro and white periodicals, participated in a variety of clubs and organizations, and represented her sex and race at several international congresses."[7]

Like other late nineteenth-century and early twentieth-century black women journalists, Terrell skillfully used the press as a primary vehicle through which she commented on society's ills, urged blacks to live moral and productive lives, and sought equal rights and protection for women. Terrell lectured extensively and wrote hundreds of articles for magazines, newspapers, and other publications. She used the press to inform, entertain, and persuade. Through her writings, Terrell argued passionately for civil rights and social justice. Hence, it is clear that by the standards of journalism as practiced during the period, Terrell was a journalist. Terrell was able successfully to exercise her leadership role as a journalist to advance her activist agenda and argue for basic rights and privileges for women and blacks for more than six decades.

BIOGRAPHICAL INFORMATION

Mary Eliza Church was born on September 23, 1863, in Memphis, Tennessee, during the closing years of the Civil War to Robert Reed Church and Louisa Ayers Church. Mary and her brother, Thomas Ayers Church, lived during a period that spanned the emancipation of blacks through the advent of the Civil Rights Movement in this country. In her autobiography, published in 1940, Terrell explained, "I was born at a time when I did not have to go through life as a slave. My parents were not so fortunate, for both were born as slaves. I am thankful that I was saved from a similar fate."[8]

Terrell's parents were determined to shield their young daughter from the racism of Memphis and to give her an excellent education. Therefore, when she was six years old, her mother, who was divorced from her father at the time, sent Mollie, as they called her then, to school in the North. The parents believed the public schools for blacks in Memphis were inadequately funded and substandard. Terrell first attended the Antioch College Model School in Yellow Springs, Ohio, which she believed was the "forerunner of the kindergarten in the United States."[9] Her mother also believed that children should learn at least two foreign languages, so Mrs. Church engaged a young woman to teach German to Mary.

After two years at the Model School, Terrell attended public school, where she excelled as she enjoyed her work. She noted in her autobiography, "I cannot recall that I ever had to be forced to study. I was ambitious to stand at the head of my class and I was willing to pay the price. I was always curious to know what my books were going to say next."[10] That curiosity and desire to learn led Terrell to decide, while she was still in high school, to take classical courses in college, although her friends cautioned her not to do so. As her friends explained, traditionally, only men who wanted to earn a bachelor of arts pursued the gentlemen's course, as it was called. Terrell received almost every literary honor in high school, and she repeated the same feat in college.[11]

Terrell wrote poetry as a student at the Model School in Yellow Springs, but she began what was perhaps her first journalistic endeavor when she served as one of the editors of the Oberlin *Review*.[12] Terrell first saw her name in print when it appeared in the *Review*, where she was listed as one of the editors representing her literary society, Aelioian. Although Terrell wrote with "fear and trembling,"[13] she, nonetheless, contributed several editorials to the journal.[14] Of her early writing, she stated,

> I always placed a very low estimate upon anything wrote. I was never satisfied with my essays. I usually felt like tearing them up and was ashamed when I handed them to my teachers. I certainly had a bad sense of inferiority when I appraised anything I wrote.[15]

Terrell successfully completed the rigorous program at Oberlin College, becoming one of three black women to earn the A.B. degree in 1884. This accomplishment was clearly significant to Terrell, for she noted in her autobiography that before 1884 "only two colored women had received that degree from any college in the United States or anywhere else in the world . . . so far as available records show."[16] After graduation and at the behest of her father, Terrell moved back to Memphis to live what her father called the life of a southern "lady."[17] Robert Church wanted his daughter to occupy herself with social amenities, and he did not want her to "degrade" herself by working.[18]

In 1885, Terrell moved to Wilberforce, Ohio, to accept her first job at Wilberforce University, one of the nation's oldest historically black colleges and preparatory schools. For a sum of forty dollars a month, Terrell taught five classes, played the organ, and was secretary to the faculty for two years. Although Church did not want his daughter to pursue a teaching career, Terrell believed she acted correctly by choosing to use her training to advance her race.[19]

After two years, Terrell accepted a teaching job at M Street High School, the black school in Washington, D.C. There she met fellow teacher Robert Herberton Terrell, whom she would later marry. Terrell spent one year teaching at the high school, and then embarked on a European tour with her father to England, Belgium, Switzerland, and France. Because she wanted to further her education, Terrell remained in Europe after her father returned to the states. For the next two years, the young woman spent time studying languages and history in Switzerland and Germany and immersing herself in European culture.[20]

When Terrell returned to the United States, Oberlin offered her a job as registrar, then the highest position ever proffered a black woman by a leading college. She declined and resumed her post with the public school system in the nation's capital, where she taught Latin and German for one year. In October 1891, in what the *Washington Bee* called "the most notable event that has ever taken place in the South,"[21] Mary Church married Robert Terrell. He was the first black male to graduate from "Washington's colored high school, then the foremost public school in the country for black youth."[22] Robert Terrell next earned a law degree from Harvard University and then became a teacher, principal, and lawyer.[23] President Theodore Roosevelt first appointed Robert Terrell judge in the municipal court of the District of Columbia in 1902. Presidents William Howard Taft, Woodrow Wilson, and Warren G. Harding all reappointed Judge Terrell.[24]

The marriage proved a partnership, for Robert Terrell not only supported his wife, he also encouraged her to use her education and talent to speak throughout the country on behalf of woman suffrage and her race.[25] In addition to writing and organizing women's club activities, Terrell traveled thousands of miles each year to lecture.[26]

RACIAL IDENTITY

Although Terrell had grown up with the privileges of wealth and education, her knowledge of her parents' status under slavery and the conditions that blacks continued to face may have planted the seeds of advocacy that Terrell dedicated her life to cultivating. A number of incidents shaped her racial identity and contributed to her advocacy on behalf of blacks. Terrell vividly described in her autobiography a night shortly after the end of the Civil War when someone shot her father in the head and left him for dead at his place of business during what was called the "Irish Riots" in Memphis.[27] Terrell explained, "He had been warned by friends that he was one of the colored men to be shot."[28] Terrell's autobiography also detailed her first encounter with what she called the "Race Problem." The experience occurred when Terrell was a four-year-old child who was accompanying her father on a train trip. The fair-skinned Robert Church, who was already a prospering businessman, left his daughter in the first-class car he always occupied with whites when he traveled, and he retired to a smoker car. A conductor tried to remove the young girl to a car designated for blacks and only relented when Church returned to the car with a pistol in hand.[29] On another occasion, Terrell recalled an incident that taught her a lesson she said she never forgot. It occurred when white classmates were "joking and chatting about their 'sparkling eyes,' and 'rosebud' mouths," and Terrell asked "haven't I got a pretty face too?"[30] Decades later, Terrell recalled her reaction when the girls responded that she had a "pretty black face." She explained in an entry in her autobiography,

> The shouts of laughter that went up from that group of young women rings in my ears to this day. For the first time in my life, I realized that I was the object of ridicule on account of the color of my skin. I was shocked, embarrassed and hurt. I was glued to the spot and could not budge an inch. I seemed to lose the power to think as well as to move.[31]

Terrell's racial identity was further solidified when she was asked to play the part of a "Negro servant who made a monkey of himself and murdered the king's English" in a school production. Of the incident, Terrell wrote, "I decided not to take the part. I knew this role had been assigned to me solely because I was a colored girl, and I was embarrassed and hurt."[32]

As an adult, Terrell's tenacity in addressing racial discrimination was evident when she embarked on a quest to purchase a home. Real estate agents in Washington, D.C., were not showing Terrell the kind of homes she was interested in purchasing because she was a "colored woman."[33] She explained in her autobiography,

> I felt then, as I feel now, that people who are discriminated against solely on account of race, color, or creed are justified in resorting to any subterfuge, using any disguise, or playing any trick, provided they do not actually break the law, if it will enable them to secure the advantages and obtain the rights to which they are entitled by outwitting their prejudice-ridden foes.[34]

Seeds of Advocacy

Terrell's recognition of the obstacles that her race faced, the attitudes of white Americans toward blacks, and the lack of acknowledgment of her people's contributions provided the impetus for her to advocate on their behalf through journalism. Terrell made a commitment to dedicate herself to showing racial pride and uplifting her race through her writing, speaking, and other works.

While attending a private school in Lausanne, Switzerland, and studying German in Berlin on her European study trip, Terrell wrote that she realized "those radiant dreams . . . had filled my head and heart for years."[35] However, such visions did not prevent Terrell from losing sight of her racial identity and exhibiting racial pride. She maintained that while traveling, she always told people with whom she was associated how the United States classified her and other members of her race. Terrell also sought to interest people "in the marvelous progress which we have made as a race."[36] She continuously revealed her racial identity to her foreign teachers, who plied her with questions and expressed "genuine interest" in black people. "I felt that I could not be loyal to my race if I did not pursue such a course,"[37] Terrell wrote.

Her advocacy for blacks reached beyond her travel experiences or her role in the classroom where she taught. She accepted an appointment to the Washington Board of Education, thus becoming the first black woman to serve on a board of education in the United States. Terrell wrote, "I realized what a tremendous responsibility was resting upon me and what it would mean to my race if I made a serious mistake."[38] As a board member, Terrell was responsible for the appointment of the first black director of music for the black schools and for securing funding for salaries for black teachers. She also conceived and promoted the idea of celebrating a day in honor of Frederick Douglass because she believed that the recognition would help teach black children "self-respect and pride in their own group."[39] Terrell also made trips to Congress to obtain funds for the public schools and equal funding for the black schools.[40] After serving six years, Terrell resigned the post when her husband became principal of a high school in the city. When the board was later abolished and replaced, Terrell was the only member of the previous board to be reappointed.

Even while serving on the board of education, Terrell was forging an activist agenda in other capacities, including suffrage. Perhaps, more significantly, her association with the woman's suffrage movement sparked her interest in club work among black women. Sanderson stated that through Terrell's involvement with the movement, she realized that the work of "dedicated individuals" could be more effective through organization.[41] Hence, Terrell became a founder and the first president of the

National Association of Colored Women (NACW), a group formed by the merger of the Colored Women's League of Washington and the National Federation of Afro-American Women. The black club women movement had its genesis from a testimonial banquet that fellow black woman journalist Victoria Earle Matthews coordinated in support of Ida B. Wells in October 1892, following her exile to New York and as she embarked on her anti-lynching crusade. The event brought together black women from Boston, New York, and Philadelphia.[42]

As the guiding force behind the NACW, Terrell sought to carry out the group's mission "to foster unity of purpose, to consider and determine methods which will promote the interest of colored people in any direction that suggests itself."[43] Terrell believed it was the duty of every black woman to do everything in her "power to save the children during the early, impressionable period of their lives."[44]

Advocacy on behalf of children, women, and blacks became the cornerstone of Terrell's journalism career. However, the lynching on March 9, 1892, of Memphis businessman Thomas Moss, a friend of Terrell since childhood, cemented her resolve to forgo a life of comfort and security to use her writing and activism to expose injustices and chronicle the accomplishments of blacks and women.[45] It is significant to note that Wells-Barnett cited the same incident as the catalyst for her crusade to end lynching.

The Moss lynching occurred after he and two other black men opened a store that competed with a white storekeeper in a black section of Memphis. According to Terrell, blacks stopped patronizing the white establishment and began to shop in Moss's store "because the supplies he sold were more reasonable and were exactly what they were represented to be, while the patrons themselves were treated right."[46] Of this pivotal event and its impact, Terrell wrote,

> So angry did the white storekeeper and some of his friends in the neighborhood become that they decided to break up Tom Moss's store, and deliberately started a row to do so. They called in the police who placed the owners of the colored store in jail, and the next night all three were taken out by a mob and shot to death. Thus, Tom Moss, who left a wife and several children, and the two others were murdered, because they were succeeding too well. They were guilty of no crime but that.[47]

Because of this incident, Terrell became convinced that she could not live a life of leisure in the face of such injustice against her race. Journalism became one of the avenues through which she sought to expose, ameliorate, challenge, and comment on the practices of the white power structure.

PUBLICATIONS FOR WHICH TERRELL WROTE

Many of the leading newspapers and magazines that were "published either by or in the interest of colored people" carried Terrell's byline.[48] As was the case with many black women journalists of the period, Terrell wrote articles for the *Woman's Era,* a magazine published in Boston by fellow activist Gertrude Mossell. This publication sought to chronicle the work and accomplishments of the black club women movement. The *Woman's Era* and, later, *The National Association Notes* were the official organs of the NACW. Terrell was also a contributor to the African Methodist Episcopal's *AME Church Review.* Scholars maintain that religious publications provided the opportunity for black females to become "journalists of consequence."[49]

Terrell also wrote a column titled "Women's World" for the *Colored American*, a Washington, D.C., newspaper. Her work was fast becoming recognized, and T. Thomas Fortune next asked Terrell to write short articles that appeared under her byline on the editorial pages of the *New York Age* at a rate of four dollars a week.

Magazines for which Terrell wrote included the *Southern Workman,* the NAACP's *Crisis,* the National Urban League's *Opportunity,* the *Indianapolis Freeman,* the *Baltimore Afro-American,* the *Washington Tribune,* and the *Howard Magazine* that her brother published.[50] Terrell commented upon current events in a regular column that ran in the *Norfolk* (Virginia) *Journal and Guide* during the 1920's. Although the pay was small, Terrell also enjoyed writing about a variety of issues as a regular contributor to *The Voice of the Negro,* which billed itself as "the most closely read periodical that the race has."[51]

Although a prolific writer for and contributor to the black press, Terrell often faced refusals when submitting articles to the white press. She maintained that the white press rejected her stories because they contained references to racial issues. Terrell explained in her autobiography that she "soon discovered that there are few things more difficult than inducing an editor of an average magazine to publish an article on the Race Problem, unless it sets forth the point of view which is popularly and generally accepted."[52] She continued by pointing out that editors did not want "to know a colored woman's opinion about her own status or that of her group," and "when she dares express it, no matter how mild or tactful it might be, it is called 'propaganda,' or is labeled 'controversial.'"[53]

To illustrate her point, Terrell recalled a time when the *North American Review* magazine ran her first rebuttal to an article that attacked a black man. However, the editor refused to run a subsequent article. Instead, the editor advised Terrell to delete some references to race relations and to submit the piece to an English magazine noted for its high literary quality.

Terrell said it soon dawned upon her that the powers that be at the *North American Review* rejected her article "not because of its mediocrity or inferiority, but because of the indisputable facts presented by."[54] The English magazine, *Nineteenth Century and After*, ran the article.[55]

Even while magazines spurned Terrell's articles, the editors praised the pieces and suggested that she submit articles on any subject but the race problem.[56] On one occasion, an editor told Terrell that "he would not think of publishing an article showing the progress of colored women because colored people on general principles were 'too cocky' as it was."[57] A "first-class publishing house" also submitted the article to several leading magazines and was promptly rejected, Terrell stated.[58] Such experiences discouraged Terrell, and as a result, she did not submit an article on the "race problem" to editors in the United States for many years.[59]

Although the white press routinely refused Terrell's articles, she continued journalistic activities and found other ways to get her views into print. She submitted articles and quite a number of letters to the editor that such papers as the *Washington Post,* the *Sunday Boston Globe,* the *Boston Herald,* and the *Washington Evening Star* published.[60]

Through those mainstream organs, Terrell reached a broad audience by writing about art, literature, music, black and white society, education, and other issues about which a diverse audience may have been interested. However, Terrell wrote primarily for the black press and thus a black audience composed of a developing middle class. Members of that group had access to education, were able to read, had a desire to know about the social changes that were affecting them as citizens, and sought respectability. In addition, blacks that constituted Terrell's audience wanted to learn about themselves but felt they had no voice in American newspapers and magazines.[61]

Terrell stated in her autobiography that letters to the editor were the avenues she used to get her views published in the white press. A series of letters to the editor of the *Washington Post* in the 1930s and 1940s attests to this. The letters overwhelmingly addressed misrepresentation of the race. In one letter, Terrell called upon "the American press to deal justly by the colored soldiers in reporting the part they played in the hostility with Mexico." [62] Press accounts had called black troops "completely disorganized."[63] Stressing that the press "was not giving soldiers of any race a square deal" by sending out reports which caused the public to hold black soldiers up to ridicule or look down upon them with contempt, Terrell wrote,

> In spite of nearly three hundred years of oppression in the past, in spite of the hardships and humiliation to which the best and worthiest Colored people are subject in the country everyday, the pure and

> unadulterated loyalty of the Colored American cannot be questioned. . . . Justice, therefore, demands that the American press should refuse to publish reports which injure the reputation of Colored soldiers by representing them as lacking in discipline and valor and which encourage the public to discredit what they say or do.[64]

Terrell maintained that General George Pershing's account rendered the press's characterization inaccurate. Pershing had stated that black soldiers "showed the greatest courage and exhibited the most sterling fighting qualities."[65]

Yet another letter to the editor praised a Mr. Alan Barth for remarks he had made at a League of Women Voters luncheon. Terrell noted that Barth's statements "showed the deplorable conditions under which colored people lived" and that "the words may well be instrumental in correcting some of them."[66] The writer added, "People may know on general principles that certain injustices exist, but they are often indifferent and not moved to do anything about them unless somebody definitely calls their attention to them as Mr. Barth did."

The *Washington Post* Letters to the Editor section was the destination of another piece that Terrell wrote. This one commended the *Post* for an editorial that condemned the release of three white men in Honolulu who lynched someone. Terrell noted the hypocrisy of most of the press and members of the U.S. Congress which had urged that the convicted men not only be released, but pardoned, while at the same time the press and members of Congress decried the kidnapping and murder of the Lindbergh baby. Terrell wrote,

> One day they condone crimes committed by those who have the advantage of education, environment, wealth and position in order to wreak vengeance upon a man who was accused but not convicted of wronging them and the next day they call loudly for suppression of crime when the country is shocked by the underworld's brutal murder of a baby.... But so long as the representatives of this government and a large portion of the citizens plus the daily press put their seal of approval upon lynching and lawlessness by demanding the freeing from punishment of self-confessed murderers and their accomplices who have taken the law into their own hands for any reason whatsoever, it will be impossible to uphold the majesty of the law in the United States and its shameful criminal record will continue to grow.[67]

THEMES

Through a variety of publications, Terrell reached a diverse audience by writing about a broad range of issues and topics. Eighty-seven of Terrell's columns, essays, articles, and letters to the editor reviewed for this chapter revealed the multidimensional nature of the issues and topics she addressed. She wrote about race, gender, suffrage, temperance, discrimination, employment, racial productivity, education, and virtually any issue on the national and international agenda for almost three quarters of a century. Terrell also wrote freelance travel stories and articles on art, literature, music, black and white society, and other issues of interest to a diverse audience.[68]

As did other early black women journalists, Terrell wrote mostly for black publications and thus a black audience composed of a developing middle class. Therefore topics that sought to present the truth about the race and to inform blacks about issues that affected them were mainstays of Terrell's output. Her writings dealt with such familiar themes of the black press as the legal, social, economic, and political conditions of African Americans and women.[69] Specific favorite themes included race wrongs and race progress, as well as individual achievement, Jim Crow laws, and the right for men and women to vote.[70] Terrell sought to offset misrepresentation of blacks in publications, to portray them as useful members of society, and to provide them with their own forum. These were the same goals set forth in 1827 on the pages of *Freedom's Journal*, the first publication owned, operated, and published by blacks.[71] In keeping with the mission of black publications, Terrell also sought to stress character development among blacks and to encourage them to seek and obtain their civil rights.

WRITINGS ABOUT RACE

Race was an early and constant theme of Terrell's journalism career; therefore, she devoted considerable attention to the white press's propensity to misrepresent her race in the United States and abroad. In an 1893 article written for *Ringwood's Afro-American Journal of Fashion*, Terrell likened those who seized upon portraying blacks as mentally, morally, and physically deficient to geese, birds that Terrell stated served as "synonyms for silliness and stupidity."[72] Terrell wrote, "Like geese, they mean well, and their hissings do no harm among thoughtful people who readily see the flaws in their arguments."[73] She countered, however, that because many people did not have the time to devote to analysis, the "specious syllogisms, invented to prove false propositions, may be accepted as genuine philosophy."[74] Thus, negative stereotypes prevailed.

In one instance Terrell responded to a Dr. Binton, who was on a quest to prove that black youths were mentally inferior.[75] After taking verbal jabs at Dr. Binton, Terrell explained that the lack of progress of young blacks in school was not because of their mental capacity, but because of their inability to pursue an education beyond the age of fourteen or fifteen. "The girls are needed home to help do the house work, when not obliged to earn their livelihood, and the boys must then begin their trades, or at least support themselves," Terrell wrote.[76] The coverage of Dr. Binton's and other similar articles and columns displayed a pattern in the white press, Terrell believed, and thus, it remained a major theme of her journalistic activism. As the quotation at the beginning of the chapter indicated, Terrell was convinced that the mainstream press was unfair, biased, and mean-spirited in its coverage of blacks. She maintained that the press had no interest in conveying realistic portrayals of blacks, but highlighted stories that emphasized the black person's vices and defects, or held him up to ridicule and scorn.[77]

In November 1927, Terrell addressed the issue of misrepresentation by focusing attention on the absence of blacks and Native Americans from the historical literature. She praised Native Americans who were protesting historians' treatment of them. Terrell suggested that "the attitudes of black and white children toward the Negro race would be different if those who write the histories which are taught in our public schools could be persuaded to devote even a little space to the contributions which colored people have made to the growth and prosperity of this country."[78] Terrell was aghast that because of misrepresentation and lack of acknowledgement of the race, black children heard "little that is commendable and good which is accomplished by representatives of their race." Of the effects on black children, Terrell wrote,

> If they do not read the newspapers themselves, they hear their elders or the white people with whom they come in contact talking about the awful crimes which colored people commit. After a while colored children reared in such an atmosphere learn to believe that members of their group are noted chiefly for their vices and defects and from the very nature of the case, they can have little respect for their group."[79]

Five years after making that observation, Terrell used her column to place on the record the contributions of black soldiers to the birth of this country. Terrell maintained that although black soldiers fought alongside white soldiers in the Revolutionary War, very little was known about "the valuable service they rendered."[80] Terrell also pointed out that the soldiers had been promised freedom, but "many who had battled hard for American's independence were re-enslaved."[81]

Near the end of her career and life, Terrell was still tackling misrepresentation. In a 1949 letter to the editor, Terrell called upon the *Washington Post* to stop using the word Negro. She argued that the word was "a misnomer from every point of view" that did not "represent a country or anything else except one single, solitary color."[82] As further argument, she stated that a female Negro would have to be a negress, an "ugly, repulsive word—virtually a term of degradation and reproach."[83]

Such views were found throughout Terrell's writings and illustrate her unyielding quest to set the record straight regarding the contributions of blacks and the lack of acknowledgement by whites.

Race relations were yet another theme found frequently in Terrell's writings. In a 1904 article for *The Voice of the Negro,* Terrell shared her views about race relations with readers "across the sea."[84] Pointing out that there was "absolutely no prejudice against a man on account of the color of his skin in France," Terrell observed that it was "impossible for the average foreigner to comprehend the race problem, as it presents itself in the United States."[85] England, according to Terrell, had a "slight antipathy toward all dark races," but nevertheless placed no "obstacles in the path of representatives of the dark races who possess extraordinary gifts."[86]

It was unfortunate, Terrell believed, that the Unites States did not share the view of Europeans toward blacks. Following World War I, Terrell wrote that blacks were "more disillusioned than at any time since slavery," adding that "they staked all their hopes on bettering their conditions upon the outcome of the war and they felt that they have been left out."[87] Blacks believed the country's declaration that it was going to war to fight for democracy would also apply to improved race relations and democracy in the United States. Such was not the case, as Terrell explained in the following passage:

> Since the War, one hears practically nothing about Democracy. Not only has no real, concerted effort been made to establish it in the Unites States, leaving the "World" entirely out of consideration, but it is almost never referred to and is rarely, if ever discussed. Therefore, colored people have lost faith in the white man. The majority now believes that race prejudice is so innate in the white United Statesian, that even though he promised to eradicate it, he is mentally, morally and spiritually incapacitated to do it. The spirit may indeed be willing. It is only fair to give the white man here the benefit of the doubt, but the flesh is too weak. Colored people have about reached the conclusions that the white United Statesian is so irrevocably, hopelessly steeped in race prejudice that nothing but a miracle can change his attitude toward his countrymen whose skins are dark.[88]

Terrell's articles reflected the outrage she felt about wrongs blacks suffered at the hands of whites, especially white southerners. She once wrote: "The South has for years been spreading propaganda against the colored man, not only all over the United States, but all over the civilized world."[89] As did her contemporary, Ida B. Wells-Barnett, Terrell blasted the South for its practice of lynching blacks for allegedly raping white women. The true case of lynching, Terrell wrote, was due to the "virulent race hatred and the lawlessness of the South."[90]

Two decades earlier, Terrell had written an article on peonage, arguing that the convict lease system in the South—hiring out of short-term convicts to companies or individuals that needed workers—was a "modern regime of slavery" that "in some ways" was "more cruel than that from which their parents were emancipated forty years ago."[91] Terrell held that the system was based on convicting blacks on "trumped-up charges" and "throwing them into dark, damp, disease-breeding cells, when they were not working."[92]

In yet another jab at the South, Terrell stressed that even among "Southerners who are supposed to be intelligent, just and broadminded, the colored man's vices are exaggerated beyond a semblance of truth, in spite of the facts that his accusers are responsible for many of them themselves."[93] Terrell lamented that the black man's "defects are emphasized in every possible way, his moral nature fluted, and his mental ability underestimated and scoffed at."[94]

Terrell further acknowledged a white Southerner's view that there was "great need of missionary work among colored people," in the South, but concluded that "the need of earnest, consecrated, Christian missionaries among the masses as well as the upper class of the white South is just as urgent, more urgent perhaps, than the work among colored people in that section."[95] In the same article, Terrell asserted that to "study the race problem from whatever view one may, he cannot help reaching the conclusion that the dominant race in the South must be regenerated and lifted to a higher spiritual plane, before this problem can be solved."[96]

This line of writing coincided with morality of the race, another of Terrell's favorite topics. In a response to "well-meaning whites" who told Terrell of the "great deal of immorality among colored people," the columnist observed that she wished the critics had attended a conference at which she had just spoken. "They would have learned many things which would have made them uncomfortable indeed," including the fact "that white people need to improve their morals" because "social diseases had greatly increased" among them. Terrell had informed the conference attendees that it was "impossible to talk intelligently about the morals of colored Americans today without referring to the debasing effects of slavery upon the race . . . breeding slaves for gain," and "little protection for colored women from the men who debased them."[97]

These examples further illustrate Terrell's views on discrimination. In 1923, while chastising the president of Harvard University for his refusal to admit black students to dormitories, Terrell ultimately blamed the South. She wrote: "It is so subversive of the principles for which Harvard has always stood, it so wounds the sensibilities and blasts the hopes of colored people."[98] She concluded that the president's "counselors in the South" had persuaded the president to "bar colored students from the privileges and the opportunities offered of the Freshmen" at Harvard.[99]

In another case, a subhead in Terrell's "Up-To-Date" column in 1928 again reflected her view. The subhead read: "South Not Only Place Where Law Fails to Protect Colored." The blurb pointed out that a judge in Chicago had "severely rebuked" a jury for recommending only a one-year sentence in prison for a man accused of raping a sixteen-year-old black girl. Terrell said the assistant attorney general had called the jury's action a "disgrace." Terrell asserted that the judge deserved thanks for calling the jury's action "a travesty on justice" and for chastising the defendant's lawyer who had said that blacks who lived in certain sections of Chicago were immoral. Terrell concluded that portion of her column with the recognition that it was rare that "slanders hurled against colored people in or out of the Court are resented by white people who have the power to protect the maligned group."[100]

Through letters to the editor and articles, Terrell also commented on discrimination in the nation's capital. She pointed out in another article that a "black woman could walk the streets of Washington, D.C., with money in her pocket" but still be unable to buy food because the restaurants were segregated.[101] Further, a letter to the *Washington Post* praised the American Psychological Association for voting never to meet in Washington, D.C., "until such time as additional progress has been made toward treatment of minority groups."[102] Terrell stressed that the association was helping the cause of blacks "by forcibly calling attention to the prejudice and discrimination" that victimized black people in the capital.[103]

Terrell, likewise, objected to what she called Congress' mistreatment of Washington, D.C. Noting the racial makeup of the city and commenting that many believed Congress was reluctant to enfranchise blacks "because colored people will practically hold the balance of power," Terrell wrote that the citizens of D.C. paid more taxes than they thought they should, shouldered more financial burden than they should bear, and had an increase in the number of school children, but not enough teachers because they did not have the vote. Continuing, she explained: "They are today disfranchised as they have been for many years. They have to beg Congress to give them what they need.[104]

Lack of employment opportunities for blacks was yet another theme that ran through Terrell's articles and columns over the years. In 1905, she wrote that the effect of Jim Crow laws in the South was forcing many black men to seek new homes in the North and assume a white identity. The *Boston Herald* headline and explanation that accompanied Terrell's extensive article offered that the writer would tell "how members of her race abjure friends and family to join 'the other side.'"[105] Terrell's article delineated experiences of black men and women who secured work in such occupations as department store clerks and tailors because employers believed they were white. Blacks engaged in this practice, the writer argued, because it may have been the only avenue through which they could secure work or obtain decent pay. As proof of her premise, Terrell highlighted the case of a young black woman in Washington "who did not show a trace of her African ancestry," and was, therefore, employed as a forewoman in an upscale dress shop for women. The young woman was discharged when her employer "learned that the fatal drop was coursing through her veins somewhere."[106]

Again and again, Terrell provided examples of blacks who had been denied employment on the basis of race or had been discharged when employers learned their racial identity. Terrell traced the plight of young men who had been educated in some of the finest schools, or had become skilled craftsmen and hotel waiters—only to be refused employment. Terrell concluded that although some blacks who foreswore their race had better access to opportunity, the "vast majority do not yield to the temptation of passing for white."[107]

Twenty-five years after the initial article, Terrell again addressed employment when she took the Pullman Company to task during the Brotherhood of Sleeping Car Porters' strike for better wages, and she praised the white press that supported the porters. Terrell pointed out that "editorials in some of the biggest and best newspapers in the country have shamed the Pullman Company for the measly, stingy way in which it is treating its efficient employees."[108] Believing that the strike was justified, Terrell offered,

> Nobody in the United States who has to buy food and clothing and pay rent believes that a man can support himself and his family on $72 a month…And yet that is what men who render such important and efficient services are required to do. If these victims of such flagrant injustice were willing to accept such degrading conditions without a protest they would be less than men.[109]

Explaining the viewpoint of the dominant economic power structure in this conflict, Terrell wrote, "the officials of some labor organizations are not spending sleepless nights devising ways and means of adding Negro workmen to their ranks."[110] Terrell added that few trades were open to blacks, and that members of her race were overworked and paid little.[111]

Economic deprivation caused by lack of employment continued to trouble Terrell throughout her life and was reflected in her writings. In a piece titled "Some Aspect of the Employment Problem, As It Concerns Colored

People," Terrell stated: "There is no phase of the race problem more important and more vital than a colored man's status as a wage earner in the U.S." because his "very life" depended upon his "ability to earn a living and pursue his happiness."[112] So rampant and insidious was racial prejudice that the trade unions passed resolutions barring black workers, Terrell noted. After having been chastised by a young man who objected to her assertions of discrimination in the unions during a speech, Terrell said she felt vindicated when she saw a headline the following December that read, "The American Federation of Labor Draws the Color Line." The subhead was as follows: "The Trade Unions Bar the Negro."[113]

Terrell had begun her article on employment with the declaration that it was "impossible to imagine a condition more harrowing and maddening than one's inability to secure employment solely because of the color of his skin."[114] Nevertheless, this was the condition that confronted "thousands of well-educated, capable, skillful men and women in the United States."[115] Continuing, she noted,

> In order to clothe, feed and shelter their children [sic] many a colored father, well fitted to do clerical work, let us say, or fill some other better position for which his superior education has admirably fitted him is obliged to eke out a miserable existence in some menial pursuit for which he receives a starvation wage. It is growing more and more difficult for colored people to secure employment even in the so-call menial pursuits.[116]

Terrell called such denial of opportunity a "boycott against us," and she urged blacks to "stem the tide of popular disfavor" against them by building "up a reputation for reliability and thorough proficiency."[117]

While focusing attention on the actions that negatively affected blacks, Terrell also urged her fellow race members to be productive. Nowhere was this summons more apparent than in the stated mission of the NACW. As a founder and the first president of the organization, Terrell called upon it and "all organizations of colored women and colored men formed for the elevation or improvement of the race along any line of human endeavor...to do everything in their power" to help the race.[118]

Gender Advocacy through Journalism

While Terrell was unabashed in her advocacy on behalf of her race, she was equally aggressive in using journalism to advocate for her gender, focusing special attention on black women. Terrell believed black women had a unique role to play at that point in the history of the race and country. The work that black women were doing with children was a source of pride for Terrell because she believed that the answer to the race problem rested with the youth. She asserted strongly in the January 1900 *AME Church Review* that the "real solution to the race problem, both so far as we, who are oppressed and those who oppress us are concerned, lies in the children."[119] Terrell urged NACW members to devote themselves "enthusiastically, conscientiously, to the children with their warm little hearts, their susceptible little minds, their malleable, pliable character." She continued with the pronouncement that "through the children of today, we must build a foundation of the next generation upon such a rock of integrity, morality, and strength, both of body and minds, that floods of proscription, prejudice, and persecution may descend upon it in torrents and yet it will not be moved."[120]

Terrell detailed the accomplishments of the NACW, which had only been in existence three years. She indicated that clubs were spearheading initiatives to help delinquent girls and to repeal Jim Crow laws. Terrell said the clubs had "fulfilled a duty to children" by establishing kindergartens that were "the saving grace for the little ones," and day care centers to assist working mothers.[121]

Terrell clearly felt that she and other women of similar status were in a unique position to influence change. She suggested that the "more intelligent and influential" among them do as much as they could "to uplift those beneath them." Further, Terrell asserted,

> policy and self-preservation would demand that we get down among the lowly, the illiterate, and even the vicious to whom we are bound by the ties of race and sex, and put forth every possible effort to uplift and reclaim them. It is useless to talk about elevating the race if we do not come into close touch with the masses of our women so we may correct many of the evils which militate so seriously against us, and inaugurate the reform without which, as a race, we cannot hope to succeed.[122]

Black women were making tremendous contributions, and Terrell believed their accomplishments, especially through club work, were proof that they deserved suffrage and social and economic equality. In the *Indianapolis Freeman* on December 24, 1898, Terrell explained that "for years either banding themselves into small companies or struggling alone, colored women have worked with might and main to improve the condition of their people."[123] Terrell added that black women united their forces because they saw "the necessity of systematizing their efforts and working on a larger scale."[124] As if to illustrate that her peers were as capable as white women of undertaking such a task, Terrell asked rhetorically,

> If the women of the dominant race with all the centuries of education, culture and refinement back of them, with all their wealth of opportu-

nity ever present with them, if these women feel the need of a mothers' congress that they may be enlightened as to the best methods of rearing children and conducting their homes, how much more do our women, from whom shackles have but yesterday fallen, need information on the same subjects![125]

Pointing out that the efforts of its member clubs "have been crowned with success,"[126] Terrell conveyed the activities in which club women engaged on behalf of the race. She noted that club work ranged from "bringing the light of knowledge and the gospel of cleanliness to their benefited sisters on the plantations," to "discussion and instruction as to the best way to sweep, dust, cook, wash, and iron," to rescuing "fallen women and tempted girls."[127]

In a speech later reproduced as an article, "Progress and Problems of Colored Women," Terrell offered that if anyone would seek her opinion about what gave her hope for black people's development in America, her answer would be the "splendid work with which the women are doing to elevate and regenerate the race."[128] In glowing terms, Terrell stated that as soon as black women "had filled their heads with knowledge," their "hearts yearned to dispense blessing to the less fortunate of the race."[129] She asserted that black women worked in every conceivable way "with tireless energy and zeal ... to elevate their race."[130] Writing in *The Voice of the Negro* in July 1904, Terrell pointed out that "during the past forty years, there is no doubt that colored women in their poverty have contributed large sums of money to charitable and educational institutions as well as to the foreign and home missionary work."[131] In a front page article in the *New York Age,* Terrell maintained that black women had "often struggled single-handed and alone against the most desperate and discouraging odds, in order to secure for themselves and their loved ones that culture of the head and heart for which they hungered and thirsted so long in vain."[132]

Not only did Terrell inform her readers of the work of black women, she also held that her sisters were the moral compasses of her race. In a piece that ran in the *Memphis Weekly Sentinel,* Terrell explained that "if the moral standard is to be raised at all, it must be by her who sows the first seeds of virtue in the plastic mind of the child, where there are no weeds and thistles to choke and strangle them, ere they can spring forth and bear fruit."[133] Terrell praised "mothers, teachers, and friends," and she urged them to provide guidance and instruction, speaking kindly to them, and whetting "their appetites for knowledge by helping with homework."[134]

Terrell also commented on the progress black women had made as they navigated the political and social landscape, noting the challenges and obstacles heaped upon them as they endured the double burden of racial and gender discrimination. One of her first articles for *The Voice of the Negro* highlighted the challenges. Terrell wrote that her race sisters had been "handicapped on account of their sex, but they are almost everywhere baffled and mocked because of their race. The writer elaborated:

> Not only because they are women, but also because they are colored women are discouragement and disappointment staring them in the face . . . But in spite of the obstacles encountered, the progress made by colored women along lines appears like a veritable miracle of modern times.[135]

Being twice burdened, in Terrell's opinion, did not deter black women. The writer explained that the women were making progress that compared favorably with "that of their more fortunate sisters, from whom the opportunity of acquiring knowledge and the means of self culture have never been entirely withheld."[136]

Terrell devoted columns in the *Norfolk Journal and Guide* to the desperate and discouraging odds codified in laws that discriminated against women. Terrell, an ardent suffragist, related an incident in which a man who had deserted his wife and young son was allowed under the law to obtain property the son had acquired as an adult even though the father had contributed nothing to the livelihood of the mother or son.[137] Terrell also cited a Maryland law that allowed a divorced father to name someone other than his children's mother as their guardian and a Rhode Island law that made fathers the sole guardians of their children.[138] It was Terrell's view that women were in those positions of powerlessness because they did not have the franchise.

These types of laws and occurrences motivated Terrell to argue forcefully and publicly for woman's suffrage through journalism. For Terrell, the vote was a means of racial uplift and the avenue through which black women could elevate themselves, making further progress. Terrell had written about suffrage while she was a freshman at Oberlin with an essay titled, "Resolved, There Should Be a Sixteenth Amendment to the Constitution Granting Suffrage to Women."[139] Decades later, in 1898, Terrell stood at a meeting of the National American Woman Suffrage Association (NAWSA) to acknowledge her belief that women should have the franchise. Of the occasion, Terrell wrote in a later article,

> Although the theatre was well filled at the time, comparatively few rose. I was among the number who did. I forced myself to do so. In the early 1890s it required a great deal of courage for a woman publicly to acknowledge before an audience that she believed in suffrage for her sex when she knew the majority did not.[140]

The association invited Terrell to speak "as a colored woman" during its biennial session. The activist's rise in stature in the suffrage movement was evident when, a few years later, she addressed the gathering "as a woman without regard to race."[141] For the first appearance, Terrell delivered an address titled "The Progress and Problem of Colored Women," that was well received. She subsequently delivered a talk that was more encompassing of gender issues and was titled "The Justice of Woman Suffrage." According to Terrell's notes, the *Boston Transcript* praised her speech in an article and editorial.[142]

Participating in the suffrage movement was not without its obstacles for Terrell and other black women, because of white women's prejudice and discrimination against black females in women's groups.[143] Moreover, white suffragists were largely indignant that black men were enfranchised ahead of them.[144] For reasons such as these, despite being well-received by some suffragists, two years after addressing the NAWSA, the General Federation of Women's Clubs denied Terrell the opportunity to deliver greetings on behalf of the NACW at a convention because of protests from southern clubs in 1900. Terrell did speak before other white groups that year, and while talking about the needs of black women, Terrell indicted white women for their "prejudice and lack of sympathy" toward blacks, and their failure to assist African Americans who shared their same goals.[145]

Suffrage was the focus of her article in the February 10, 1900, *Washington Post*. Terrell explained that the woman suffragist of the day was unlike the "agitator of a quarter of a century ago." By way of comparison, Terrell pointed out: "The mannishly-attired, short-skirted, short-haired woman who for so many years was the butt of the satirist and the cartoonist, has been shoved off the board, and in her place stands the cultured, womanly woman of the twentieth century."[146] The *Post* article included a portion of the text of "Justice of Colored Women," a speech Terrell had delivered at the thirty-second annual convention of the NAWSA. The speech and subsequent article illustrated the degree to which Terrell chastised those who denied the vote to blacks and women. Terrell wrote that the United States was founded on the principles of "government of the people, for the people, and by the people" but "the elective franchise is withheld from one-half of the citizens, many of whom are intelligent, cultured, and virtuous."[147] Terrell argued that it was implausible for the government to bestow the vote to half of the citizenry, "some of whom are illiterate, debauched, and vicious," because they "were shrewd and wise enough to have themselves born boys instead of girls, or who took the trouble to be born white instead of black."[148] Elaborating on her view that women wanted and deserved suffrage, Terrell argued,

Even if it were true that the majority of women are so ignorant of the full significance of their political disfranchisement that they are willing to remain in subjugation, such ignorance and apathy could not justly be used as an argument in favor of perpetuating a system of injustice. Neither could it by any feat of logic or legerdemain of reason be construed as an argument against granting full suffrage to the women who have sufficient intelligence to desire it.[149]

A little more than a decade after her article in the *Post,* Terrell wrote an article for the September 12, issue of the NAACP's *Crisis* magazine. In the piece, Terrell criticized both black men and black women who opposed suffrage. Noting that "the intelligent colored man" who opposed suffrage was rare, Terrell wrote,

It is queer and curious enough to hear an intelligent colored woman argue against granting suffrage to her sex, but for an intelligent colored man to oppose woman suffrage is the most preposterous and ridiculous thing in the world. What could be more absurd than to see one group of human beings who are denied rights which they are trying to secure for themselves working to prevent another group from obtaining the same rights?[150]

Three years after the article in *Crisis,* Terrell used the magazine again to make virtually the same argument she had made previously regarding woman suffrage. Terrell began with the assertion that even if she believed women should be denied the right of suffrage, "wild horses could not drag such an admission from my pen or my lips."[151] Again, she noted that the very arguments that were used against granting the right of suffrage to women were offered by those who had disfranchised black men. Terrell added that "nothing could be more inconsistent than that colored people should use their influence against granting the ballot to women, if they believed that colored men should enjoy this right to which citizenship confers." [152]

Terrell was still championing the cause of black women suffrage in 1928, long after passage of the nineteenth amendment. In a December 1, *Chicago Defender* article, Terrell commented that the Republican Party "had a right to feel that it has acted quite handsomely toward white women," but the party had not given recognition to women who were not white.[153] Pointing to newspaper articles that detailed tactics used in Virginia to prevent black women from voting, Terrell offered,

The treatment to which these women were subjected when they tried to exercise their right of citizenship was outrageous. The registration officers asked them all sorts of ridiculous questions when they sought to qualify as voters and did everything in their power to prevent and discourage them from voting.[154]

Terrell stated that the "women who belong to the disfranchised group in a large section of this country would welcome the opportunity of changing and improving their condition if they could get it."[155] Somewhat sarcastically, Terrell wondered "if the president and vice president nominees of the Republican Party really know the conditions under which many women who have always been loyal to it and to this government are living?" Terrell answered her own question by suggesting that if the nominees did not know, "somebody should tell them."[156]

Just as the difficulty of obtaining the franchise concerned Terrell, so did the obstacles the women faced in obtaining employment. Terrell observed that "with the exception of teaching, nursing and sewing, there is practically nothing that a colored woman can get to do in the United States, no matter how well educated, skillful or prepossessing she may be, nor how great may be her need."[157]

OTHER THEMES

Terrell persisted in waging a campaign through her writing to impress upon members of her race that they could improve their lot, despite economic hardships that blacks and women faced. A November 3, 1928, column in The *Chicago Defender* referred to a study that indicated that older people had the same capacity to learn new things, as did younger people. Terrell advised, "We don't want to hear adults excusing themselves for their disagreeable habits on the ground that since they learned them in childhood, they are too old to break away from them in old age."[158]

In what could serve as proof of what blacks could achieve, Terrell wrote in a November 1927, "Up-to-Date" column that black voters were instrumental in electing the mayor of Memphis because they believed the mayor when he said he would "give them a square deal." Blacks realized their power, and as a result, "colored people all over the South are rubbing their eyes and waking up politically," according to Terrell. She added that better days would come "when colored people all over the country used their ballots to promote the welfare of their race."[159]

Terrell offered additional proof of her race's potential the success of individuals, organizations, and institutions in the black community. This theme was consistent in articles that appeared in the black and white press from the early days of Terrell's professional and activist career until the waning days of her life. In an "Up-To-Date" column, Terrell wrote, "if those who write the histories which are taught in our public schools could be persuaded to devote even a little space to the contributions which colored people have made to the growth and prosperity of this country, the attitude of both black and white children toward the race would be entirely different from what it is today."[160]

Terrell shared the philosophy of black intellectual W.E.B. DuBois and other contemporaries who believed that they could elevate the race in the eyes of the dominant group by calling attention to the talent, brains, and accomplishments of individual race members.[161] In a *Washington Post* article, Terrell outlined the accomplishments of Ernest Everett Just, a Howard University student who was "engaged in important research and laboratory work in Naples, Italy."[162] In a later article, Terrell referred to Just as a "well-known scientist" and stated that "by those competent to judge, he is acknowledged to be the world's leading authority in his field." Terrell gave biographical information about Just, then a glimpse of his education, the challenges he faced, and how he overcame them. She pointed out that Just was a zoologist and physiologist who had been the only magna cum laude in Dartmouth's 1907 class, had received his Ph.D. in 1916 from the University of Chicago with the same distinction, and had gone on to do research that "may throw light on a cure for cancer."[163]

Terrell also praised and acknowledged Samuel Coleridge Taylor, whom she called "a great Anglo-African composer,"[164] and fellow virtuoso, Levi Dawson,[165] whom Terrell said "had written the first Negro symphony ever composed."[166] Of Coleridge-Taylor's "*Hiawatha's Wedding Feast,*" Terrell stated that his concert proved "there is no musical Parnassus too lofty or too steep for colored people to scale."[167] Terrell called the poet, Phyllis Wheatley, an "African genius."[168] In 1923, Terrell shared her positive recollections of Frederick Douglass in a lengthy article that ran in *National Notes*.[169] Thirty years later, she penned an article for *Ebony* magazine titled "I Remember Frederick Douglass."[170] The black actress Lula Bell was the subject of Terrell's praise in 1927. According to Terrell, the play that Bell had been starring in for two years was "proof of the fact that we have made progress along theatrical lines."[171]

During her career, Terrell wrote about other notable blacks, including Booker T. Washington and George Washington Carver. Moreover, Terrell highlighted progress and success of black institutions, including churches, schools, and colleges. In an untitled article about George Washington Carver, Terrell wrote that "professor Carver has made almost everything from the peanut but dynamite."[172]

While race accomplishments, discrimination, unequal representation, race pride and elevation were the focus of many of Terrell's articles and columns, she also wrote about other topics aimed at simply educating, informing, and entertaining readers. Terrell penned articles about her experiences in politics, black society, and social functions in Washington, D.C.,[173] and Christmas at the White House.[174] While serving as director of the Eastern District Work Among Colored Women for the Republican

Party, Terrell shared her feelings about being at the National Republican Headquarters to work in a campaign. Terrell proffered:

> It seemed too impossible to be true. In the wildest flight of a lurid imagination who would have dreamed only a few years ago that a colored woman would be appointed to take charge of the women of her race either in the East or the West in a campaign to elect a President of the United States?[175]

In the publication that her brother edited, Terrell explained that her task was "to get as many colored women to vote for Harding and Coolidge as I could."[176]

In *The Voice of the Negro* in April 1904, Terrell went to great pains to illustrate that members of black society were as educated and refined, perhaps more so, than members of white society. To contrast white society with Washington's black social class, Terrell wrote that no member of the black group had given a dinner for his dog and invited his friends, as a white socialite had done. The columnist further added that no young black woman "clad in rich evening robes" had ever "walked into a public fountain after a theatre party and come forth wet to the skin, as did a certain young belle in the exclusive circles of Baltimore a few years ago."[177] Anyone attending a function given by "the society of colored people" would "see women as tastefully arrayed, as refined, as correct in their use of the English language, as graceful in carriage as ever rivaled Terpsichore in the maizy dance," Terrell maintained.[178] Continuing, Terrell wrote that it would be "impossible to circulate very freely at such a function without meeting graduates who hold diplomas from Harvard, Yale, Cornell, Oberlin, and other renowned institutions of learning."[179]

Delineating differences among blacks was also a theme Terrell addressed in this same article. Terrell stated that "the various sets and cliques in the social whirl are in number like unto the sands of the sea." Further illustrating her point, Terrell added, "If all colored people look alike to some folks, they all do not look alike to one another, when it comes to drawing the social line."[180]

Exactly one year after her article on black society ran in *The Voice of the Negro*, Terrell provided insight into what blacks did during inauguration week. She stated,

> Never before in the history of the United States were so many distinguished colored people gathered together in one city at the same time as there were in Washington during inauguration week. From all parts of the country they came in, crows, eager to see and pay homage to the great American who stands for a square deal to every man without

regard to race, color, condition or creed, so long as he be decent and honest.[181]

Terrell indicated that more than 1,000 blacks attended balls, receptions, and other functions, and their ranks included "doctors, lawyers, merchants, and writers galore," as well as elected and military officials, and judges.[182]

Terrell interviewed the President's secretary for an article on Christmas at the White House that was replete with photographs of first lady Alice Roosevelt and the Roosevelt children. Relating bits of information about how the family had celebrated past Christmases, Terrell also provided insight into the activities and behavior of the Roosevelt children. Terrell concluded that her observation of the children both during her visit to the White House and on other occasions assured her that they were "absolutely free from prejudice on account of color."[183] The writer cited as an example an occasion when young Quentin Roosevelt lifted the black steward's son so that the child could see a table that had been decorated for a state dinner.[184]

A story about the first convent for black girls in the United States further illustrated the multidimensional themes Terrell addressed. Terrell praised the work of the Order of Oblate Sisters of Providence that she said had its genesis in the French Revolution when thousands of French and Catholic refugees fled riots in Santo Domingo and arrived in Baltimore.[185]

Those who fostered interracial cooperation, another of Terrell's favorite themes, garnered her praise. She called suffragist Susan B. Anthony a friend.[186] Philanthropist Julius Rosenwald was also a subject of Terrell's praise because he established a fund to educate black children in the South.[187] Likewise, the *Public Ledger* newspaper received accolades from Terrell for expressing sentiments on behalf of what she termed "justice and right." Terrell wrote, "I am particularly grateful to the editor for stating that if intolerance and injustice and prejudice are to be eliminated, if white and colored races are to live side by side in peace and harmony, a beginning will have to be made with the children."[188] Similarly, Terrell had accolades for organizations that were celebrating the centennial of Harriet Beecher Stowe. Terrell wrote:

> Few authors have rendered the cause of liberty such striking and signal service with the pen as did Harriet Beecher Stowe. By colored people in the United States her name will ever be spoken with grateful, affectionate reverence, her memory will always be cherished, and her praise forever sung.[189]

Interracial harmony was also the point of a letter to the editor of the *Washington Star* in which Terrell noted that although the schools of

Washington, D.C., were still segregated, blacks and whites who served on the Board of Education worked together in peace. "It is incumbent upon all good citizens who really believe in democracy to work with might and main to have this pattern spread all over a wider field," Terrell urged.[190] Even Washington, D.C. won recognition. Writing in the *Evening Star*, Terrell indicated that the District of Columbia had established a school for blacks before emancipation.[191] According to Terrell, the first schools were held in churches, sometimes in the auditorium, but usually in the basement which generally rented for $10 or $15 per month.[192]

CONCLUSION

Terrell wrote about issues that affected her race and sex throughout the late nineteenth century and well into the twentieth century. She wrote about the plight of black women and children, and the denial of rights for all women. She covered many topics of general interest. Terrell's writing, which reflected a vast breadth of knowledge and experiences, was one of the means by which she educated blacks and whites in the United States and abroad. Terrell used the columns of newspapers and magazines to chastise those whom she felt mistreated women and blacks or to praise those who had done something or said something on behalf of her race and sex.[193] Still, historians do not acknowledge Terrell as a journalist; nor do scholars recognize the body of her journalistic work.

Terrell received tremendous acclaim for her endeavors that paralleled what many black men did during her lifetime. The pages of books, biographies, and even Internet articles refer to Terrell as a suffragist, activist, race spokeswoman and leader, lecturer, and founder of national organizations. Terrell is recognized as a pioneer, for she was one of the first black women to obtain a bachelor's degree from a prestigious college, to be offered a high-ranking position at a college, and to serve on a board of education anywhere in the United States, among other accolades.

It may be reasonable, therefore, to conclude that because of the nature and scope of Terrell's accomplishments, her work as a journalist has been overshadowed. The secondary sources examined for this chapter contained few, if any, references to Terrell as a journalist. As noted, Terrell wrote in her autobiography about her "attempts to succeed as a writer" but she never once used the term "journalist."

Perhaps it is just a matter of semantics and that the word "writer" may be interpreted as "journalist." However, a writer can also be a novelist, poet, author, or playwright. A journalist writes to inform, persuade, entertain—and as in the case of the black press and the early white media—to advocate. Terrell did just that as she contributed hundreds of articles to newspapers, magazines, and other publications during a career that spanned sixty-seven years. Journalists and activists today are still addressing many of the issues to which Terrell called attention and the causes she espoused. Thus, Terrell should not only be acknowledged as a journalist, but the body of her journalism work should be recognized as the avenue through which she promulgated and advanced her activism.

CHAPTER FOUR
Alice Dunbar-Nelson
Writing During the Jim Crow Era

> So the man of color. He was told some generations ago, 'Thus far shalt thou go,' and he still believes it. He has only to lift his huge racial might and brush aside the frail barriers separating him from the outside of things where he has been relegated, and step into a promised land–but he does not know that the barrier that seems so huge and real is after all–nothing but a few frail lies laid on end, and he looms above them and can step over them.[1]
>
> *Alice Dunbar-Nelson*

Alice Ruth Moore Dunbar-Nelson lived most of her adult life known as the widow of one of the country's premier black poets and writers, Paul Laurence Dunbar. In recent decades, Dunbar-Nelson gained notoriety in her own right as an author, playwright, and poet. However, Dunbar-Nelson was more than those characterizations. She was a journalist who wrote for newspapers and other publications during the Jim Crow era in this country.

Although she has received acclaim within the last quarter century for her literary works, Dunbar-Nelson remains largely unrecognized and "invisible" as a journalist.[2] Many sources associate Dunbar-Nelson with other professions and activities. For example, biographical references that include entries about Dunbar-Nelson also do not identify her as a journalist. Gayle Hardy's *American Civil Rights Activists* referred to Dunbar-Nelson as an "author, teacher, social worker, public speaker," and as an advocate for African-American rights and women's rights and suffrage." Hardy did not call her a journalist.[3] Gloria Hull, the editor of Dunbar-Nelson's diary, stated that she was active in "many civic, racial and women's causes," but made little mention of Dunbar-Nelson as a journalist.[4]

Hence, Dunbar-Nelson joins other late nineteenth-century and early twentieth-century black women journalists known more by their racial and gender activism.[5] Like the other women, Dunbar-Nelson specialized in articles on or for children and women, often wrote for and edited publications of religious organizations, and contributed freelance stories to many black and white publications.[6]

Notwithstanding those contributions, dozens of works on the history of journalism and the history of the black press reviewed for this chapter had no mention of Dunbar-Nelson as a journalist. A 1982 article by scholar and educator Gloria Wade-Gayles included Dunbar-Nelson in a group of Southern black women journalists, and thereby provided the impetus for this chapter.[7] Subsequent reviews of other sources also revealed that Dunbar-Nelson not only wrote for and edited publications, but was also a co-owner of *The Wilmington Advocate*, a Delaware newspaper.[8]

The author of a dissertation that focused on Dunbar-Nelson as a literary figure asserted that the woman's journalism provided the only means of visibility for her at the turn of the century.[9] Ruby O. Williams maintained that although poetry and short fiction seemed among Dunbar-Nelson's "first literary loves, the only fairly-accessible outlet for her writing was journalism."[10] "When most other avenues closed, she did manage to get articles and essays published in black newspapers and journals."[11] Another writer who explored Dunbar-Nelson's literary contributions stated that her status as a literary figure "is lowered since the more belletristic genres of poetry and fiction are more valuable than the noncanonical forms–notably the diary and journalistic essay–that claimed so much of her attention."[12] Thus, some literature acknowledge Dunbar-Nelson's journalistic career, but still devote scant attention to her contributions, if any, to the field.

Dunbar-Nelson's journalistic activism was a bold endeavor when one considers the Jim Crow era in which she lived. It was a time when blacks were disfranchised, encountered economic exploitation, and were subjected to other forms of degradation and humiliation.[13] It was within that context that Dunbar-Nelson defied the norms of the day by embarking on a career as a journalist.

Although scholars have produced much work about Dunbar-Nelson as a literary figure, additional exploration of her journalistic activities is needed. This chapter, therefore, examines Dunbar-Nelson's career as a journalist and pays special attention to the themes she addressed, the publications for which she wrote, and her writing style. The chapter does not address Dunbar-Nelson's literary works that include poems, short stories, plays, and novels. Rather, the chapter focuses on some thirty selected columns, editorials, and reviews in an effort to ascertain Dunbar-Nelson's place in the history of journalism. As with other early black women journalists, much of what they wrote has not been preserved or is inaccessible. For example, copies of the *Wilmington Advocate*, the paper that Dunbar-Nelson co-owned and co-edited, no longer exist. Likewise, columns for various publications often did not carry the women's by-lines.

BIOGRAPHICAL INFORMATION

Alice Moore Dunbar-Nelson was born in New Orleans, Louisiana, on July 19, 1875. She was the second of two daughters of Creole parents, Joseph and Patricia Wright Moore.[14] Dunbar-Nelson attended the public schools in New Orleans. In 1892 and at the age of 15, she graduated from Straight College, now known as Dillard University, where she received a broad and challenging liberal arts education.[15] Hardy maintained that although Dunbar-Nelson graduated from Straight's two-year teaching program, while in college, she also took courses in nursing, stenography and law, as well as literature classes. She played the violin, cello, and mandolin in classical and popular groups.[16] Hull stated that a "beautiful" and "talented" Dunbar-Nelson had a "prominent place in Black and Creole society, especially musical and literary circles"[17] in New Orleans. Violet Bryan, the author of a book about Dunbar-Nelson's literature, stated that she "was among an impressive group of Negro elite" and that she "was an active member of the New Orleans social community at a very young age, as elementary school teacher, journalist, and participant in the city's social and literary circles."[18]

Research about Dunbar-Nelson reveals she was a "lifelong student"[19] who earned a master's degree from Cornell University and studied at Columbia University, the Pennsylvania School of Industrial Art, and the University of Pennsylvania.[20] According to Hull, while at Cornell, Dunbar-Nelson "produced a thesis on the influences of Milton on Wordsworth that was so insightful that scholars such as Professor Lane Cooper wrote to her for information and an article based upon it was published in *Modern Language Notes* in 1909."[21]

Williams explained, "The diligence which characterized Alice's pursuits of a formal education also characterized her informal, self-directed studies" and led her to "read an assortment of newspapers, magazines, and books," and attend lectures and "every worthwhile musical, play, and movie that came to Wilmington, Washington, D.C., Philadelphia, or New York."[22]

Dunbar-Nelson began her first job as a teacher in New Orleans, and held the position from 1892 through 1896. She also taught in elementary and high schools, colleges, public schools, and correctional institutions over a period of thirty-seven years. One year after moving with her family from New Orleans to West Medford, Massachusetts, in 1896, Dunbar-Nelson secured a teaching post in Brooklyn, New York, and held it until 1898. From 1902 to 1920, she taught, headed the English department, and served as an administrator at Howard High School, the only school for blacks in Delaware.

Dunbar-Nelson continued to teach after the regular school year adjourned for the summers. During those months, she directed sessions for in-service teachers at State College for Colored Students (now Delaware State College) in Dover, and she worked at Hampton Institute in Virginia.[23] Williams indicated that because of Dunbar-Nelson's "modest income, her social demands, and family needs, . . . her education had to be arranged around her limited funds and her rigorous teaching schedule."[24]

Teaching for Dunbar-Nelson and other female black journalists provided a steady income. According to Williams, the vocation meant that Dunbar-Nelson, "a Black woman with limited professional and economic opportunities, would have a definite, although small, income."[25] While Dunbar-Nelson "loved teaching . . . undoubtedly she must have known that her talents exceeded those required for a teacher."[26] Therefore, this immensely talented woman continued in the profession even while trying to succeed as a literary figure and journalist.

She displayed a concern for her students by making a commitment to young people beyond the school environment.[27] While teaching in New York, Dunbar-Nelson joined fellow journalist Victoria Earle Matthews in establishing the White Rose Mission, a home for girls in Harlem. Between 1920 and 1928, Dunbar-Nelson taught English and typing at the Kruse Home for Girls, an institution she helped found.[28]

In 1898, Alice Moore married the renowned black poet and author, Paul Laurence Dunbar, and gave up her teaching post to move to Washington, D.C. Written accounts indicate that the couple respected each other professionally, but the marriage did not last. "This second period of Dunbar-Nelson's life," Hull stated, was "most notable for the event that assured her claim to fame," her marriage to Paul Laurence Dunbar, the poet from Ohio whose dialect verse catapulted him into prominence as America's first black litterateur.[29] The couple separated in 1902, and Dunbar died in 1906. According to Hull, although the "union was brief, its influence on her was permanent. Forever after, she played the role of a great man's widow, a role that was her insurance against obscurity and was a concrete means of livelihood."[30]

Alice moved to Wilmington, Delaware, after she and her husband separated; she made the state her home for thirty years. Dunbar-Nelson wrote in her diary that she married fellow teacher Henry Arthur Callis in 1910, but they were divorced later at an unknown time.[31] In 1916, Alice married

Robert J. Nelson, a journalist, widower, and father of two children. Together the couple had four children.

She moved to Philadelphia in January 1932 when her husband was appointed to the Pennsylvania Athletic Commission. She continued her civic, literary, and social activism until she died of heart failure on September 18, 1935.

SEEDS OF ADVOCACY

Even while married, Dunbar-Nelson devoted a great deal of her time to political and social activism. Bryan pointed out that Dunbar-Nelson's activism began while she was a student at Straight College. There she became a member of the Comite` des Citoyens, an organization that "struggled for the rights of blacks to ride any streetcar in the Plessey versus Ferguson court case."[32] Early on, Dunbar-Nelson was active in the black women's club movement. According to Hull, Dunbar-Nelson wrote about "good work being done by Afro-American women in Boston, Colorado, New Orleans, Philadelphia, Tuskegee and other places through mothers' meetings, journalism, hospitals, aid for soldiers, and the like."[33]

Hardy highlighted Dunbar-Nelson's activism, noting that during succeeding years she served as a field organizer in the Middle Atlantic States women's suffrage movement in 1915. Dunbar-Nelson founded the local chapter of Circle of Negro War Relief, an organization that provided assistance to black soldiers and their families during World War I. This consummate activist toured the South in 1918 as the only known black field representative of the Woman's Committee of the United States Council of National Defense. Her task was to gather information and assist nine states in organizing black women for the war relief effort in 1918.

Two years later, Dunbar-Nelson and other members of the State Federation of Colored Women founded the Industrial School for Colored Girls in Marshalltown for delinquent and homeless young females.[34] Dunbar-Nelson was the first black woman to serve on the State Republican Committee of Delaware, and she was the chair of the League of Colored Republican Women in 1921. In that position, she directed the political activities of the black women members.[35] A year later, she headed the Delaware Anti-Lynching Campaign, a group that lobbied for Congress to pass the 1922 Dyer Anti-lynching Bill.[36]

As executive secretary of the American Interracial Peace Committee, Dunbar-Nelson enlisted "black involvement in interracial and world peace."[37] In doing so, according to Williams, Dunbar-Nelson "directed the consciousness of America toward interracial peace"[38] by sponsoring cultural events that involved national figures; arranging lecture tours primarily of black college campuses; and involving the committee in local and racial matters.

Being an activist was not without cost for Dunbar-Nelson, as is noted in her diary on Saturday, October 1, 1928. She indicated that her trip to Marion, Ohio, to participate in Social Justice Day activities "started consequences in Wilmington that . . . will take years to obliterate," and changed her life.[39] The school district fired Dunbar-Nelson from her teaching job at Howard High School. Although the dismissal plunged Dunbar-Nelson into a financial crisis that was to plague her almost until her death, she still persisted in her activism.

The literature is replete with a litany of other activities in which Dunbar-Nelson engaged. A July 20, 1928, entry in her diary began with the notation "very full day."[40] Dunbar-Nelson then summarized her performances that day, noting that she had been elected an alternate from the Northeastern Federation National Council of the American Inter-Racial Peace Committee, elected ninth vice president from Delaware, made head of a new Inter-Racial Relations department, "wrote a resolution and put over endorsing the American Inter-Racial Peace Committee;" kept Mazie Mossell "from getting through resolution endorsing John R. Hawkins;" helped "write resolutions censoring G.O.P. for indicting" a black man for "sale of offices."[41] Dunbar-Nelson then went home and packed for a lecture trip.

As did Ida Wells-Barnett and Mary Church Terrell, Dunbar-Nelson's activism took her all the way to the White House. According to Hull, "In September 1921, she enjoyed recognition as a member of the delegation of prominent black citizens who presented racial concerns to President Harding."[42]

PUBLICATIONS FOR WHICH DUNBAR-NELSON WROTE

Dunbar-Nelson's literary career began while she was a young woman in New Orleans, where she wrote poetry and short stories. There Dunbar-Nelson began what was possibly her first journalistic endeavor by editing the women's page of the *Journal of the Lodge*, the official organ of the local black fraternal order, the Knights of Pythias. Although she continued to write literary pieces during her thirteen-year marriage to Paul, there is no evidence that Alice was involved in journalistic pursuits during that time.

Dunbar-Nelson was affiliated with black newspapers for almost forty years. "When most other avenues closed, she did manage to get articles and essays published in black newspapers and journals,"[43] Williams wrote. By 1913, Dunbar-Nelson had begun to write for black church publications, as did other black women journalists of the period.[44] Her job as woman's page editor and a writer for the African Methodist Episcopal denomination's *A.M.E. Church Review* cemented her position as a journalist.[45] She became one of those black women journalists who wrote for church papers and became "journalists of consequence"[46] that Wade-Gayles described. The black church "was as political as it was religious" and "through numerous regularly published papers, the black church educated the community on matters relevant to black progress and achievement."[47]

Dunbar-Nelson continued her journalism activities by editing and publishing *Masterpieces of Negro Eloquence*, a two-volume compilation of speeches by blacks, in 1914. Robert Nelson, the man whom Alice would later marry, was president and editor-in-chief for the Douglass Publishing Company, which produced the work. According to Hull, both *Masterpieces* and the *Dunbar Speaker and Entertainer,* which Dunbar-Nelson later published, were unprofitable, but they capitalized on the Dunbar name and Alice's literary-journalism training. Ministers, educators, and those who engaged in public speaking distributed the works widely.[48]

Alice's marriage to Robert Nelson provided the impetus for a venture that would provide her with a steady venue for her journalistic writing.[49] From 1920 to 1922, the couple co-edited and published the *Wilmington Advocate,* a "liberal black newspaper . . . substantially financed by the Republican Party interest"[50] and published in Delaware. Williams stated that the *Advocate* was an excellent outlet for Dunbar-Nelson because "she could be more than creative, she would have a forum for some of her political and racial ideas."[51]

For that publication, Dunbar-Nelson reviewed novels, poetry, plays and art, and she wrote editorials. The *Advocate* was her principal preoccupation because the man the Nelsons hired to manage it was incompetent.[52] Dunbar-Nelson was involved not only in writing, but also in "raising money to keep it afloat,"[53] Williams offered. The editor cooked for the staff and participated "in the all-night sessions necessary to get it on the street by Friday afternoon, even folding and addressing the out-of-town mailings,"[54] Hull explained. The *Advocate* ceased operations two years after its debut.

For the next four years, Dunbar-Nelson submitted articles, reviews, essays, and columns to the black press while she continued her activism on behalf of Democratic political candidates, black women, and young people. She continued to work for the *AME Church Review,* and she wrote for the *New York Age* and *Southern Workman* magazine.

The beginning of 1926 saw the debut of Dunbar-Nelson's column, "From A Woman's Point of View" for the *Pittsburgh Courier,* a respected black newspaper.[55] Dunbar-Nelson changed the name of the column to "Une Femme Dit" shortly after its debut because, as she wrote, other editors and writers had begun to use her title in their publications.[56] Dunbar-Nelson continued the column for nine months, when she began to write a column for the *Washington Eagle,* a general circulating weekly that her husband managed and the official organ for the Improved Benevolent and

Protective Order of Elks.[57] From September 1926 to 1930, Dunbar-Nelson's "As in the Looking Glass" columns were also syndicated for the Negro Press Association. She returned to the *Pittsburgh Courier* in January 1930 with a column titled "So It Seems to Alice Dunbar-Nelson." From the end of 1930 until her death in 1935, she wrote a column, "Little Excursions Week by Week," for the black syndicated press.

During her career, Dunbar-Nelson was a contributor to *The Messenger*, as well as the *Journal of Negro History*, *The Negro History Bulletin*, the NAACP's *Crisis*, and the Urban League's *Opportunity*. Dunbar-Nelson submitted and had articles published in white newspapers, including the *Wilmington Journal Every Evening* and the *Delmarva Star*. The writer generally was not paid for those articles. [58]

Although she directed some of her writings to a white audience, Dunbar-Nelson generated the vast amount of her work for the black press and thus a black audience. While existing literature indicates that some of the early female journalists wrote for an uneducated populace, it is clear that Dunbar-Nelson wrote for the educated, developing black middle class of the early 1900s.[59] Her columns were "of general interest and for a literate audience" that warmly received her reviews of plays and other literary works, Hull wrote.[60]

THEMES

The examination of approximately thirty of Dunbar-Nelson's columns, essays, and articles revealed the multidimensional nature of the issues that she addressed. As with the other black women journalists in this book, Dunbar-Nelson addressed racial issues and simultaneously provided insight and information she believed would help advance blacks. Like the other women, she often wrote about the plight of black women and the denial of rights for all women. Topics that appeared in her writings included the work of black club women, war, declining birthrates of black women, education, racial progress and lack thereof, black productivity and elevation, race relations, and the misrepresentation or lack of acknowledgement of blacks in the press and history books. Culture was another theme, as illustrated by a number of reviews of books, art, music, and poetry Dunbar-Nelson did.

The review primarily of Dunbar-Nelson's columns for this chapter confirmed Williams' assertion that the writer's subjects were literary, sociological, historical, religious and racial, and that she also addressed women's rights and the woman's point of view.[61] In a chapter devoted to Dunbar-Nelson's literary writing, Hull described the themes the woman addressed, noting that her journalism showed her as a literary critic, political analyst, social commentator, race theorist, humorist, stage, and film critic.[62]

WRITINGS ON RACE

Dunbar-Nelson wrote primarily for the black press, a medium known for its protest and advocacy functions. In her first "From a Woman's Point of View" column for the *Pittsburgh Courier*, Dunbar-Nelson tackled the race issue immediately. She equated the black man's plight to a puppy that had been trained from birth to believe that he could not jump over hurdles or overcome obstacles. Dunbar-Nelson wrote that the black man only needed to exert himself, "lift his huge racial might," and "brush aside" the obstructions.[63]

Dunbar-Nelson returned to that same theme a week later when she criticized blacks' reaction to President Herbert Hoover's State of the Union message. The columnist queried,

> Why is it that the American Negro always feels somehow that if he hasn't a special paragraph in the president's message, calling attention to his wonderful progress since emancipation (that's about all any president can say, there is nothing else)—if such a paragraph does not appear, somehow the party has slipped up, and the occupant of the White House will bear close watching.[64]

In a sarcastic tone, Dunbar-Nelson asserted: "Segregation and scant recognition, and Sweet trials and Rhinelander cases, and exclusion from colleges, and student strikes" did not seem to matter when the "Man and Brother" is given just a few sentences "tacked on at the end of the message."[65] Clearly, Dunbar-Nelson was dismayed that blacks were not giving sufficient attention to issues and actions that had a greater impact on the race.

In that same column, she criticized the state of Florida for carrying out and broadcasting a lynching. She wrote,

> Northern visitors are called out of their beds to see the horror, and to taste well of the sweetness of a murdered man's cries. The microphone records and transmits the victims dying moans, and the Floridians far and near, who are unable to be among those present to turn on Station S-A-V-A-G-E, and have their cup of cruelty filled to its poisoned brim.[66]

A few months after she wrote that column, Dunbar-Nelson unleashed her displeasure over a ruling by the Missouri Supreme Court that held that the Fifteenth Amendment to the United States Constitution "has been the source of more plague to the body politics that the legends tell us were visited upon by pharaoh by the God of Israel."[67] To illustrate the subjugated position in which blacks found themselves in America, Dunbar-Nelson pondered what blacks could do to protest the ruling. She queried:

> Write bitter editorials in all of our Negro papers? Write long and scholarly letters to such white papers as will publish them gratis? Let loose a flood of excellently prepared and authenticated statistics to show that the whole country has benefited by the passage of the Fifteenth Amendment. Deluge the members of that Missouri Supreme Court with letters from individuals, organizations, scholars, Negroes and friends of the Negro? What good will it all do?[68]

Adding that the court had spoken and its decisions would not be revisited, Dunbar-Nelson concluded that "a precedent has been set" and "the bitter editorials in our own paper will not be read by members of the Supreme Court of Missouri, nor by the lawyers of Missouri, Mississippi, Georgia or elsewhere, who might be influenced by this statement."[69]

Political parties also were the targets of Dunbar-Nelson's wrath. In an October 26, 1928, editorial for the *Washington Eagle*, the columnist chastised the assistant to presidential candidate Herbert Hoover for the man's vehement and strident reaction to an assertion by Governor Theodore G. Bilbo that Hoover had danced with a black woman. Dunbar-Nelson characterized George Arkerson's wrath as "Jovean," when he called the statement "unqualifiedly false" and said it was "the most indecent and unworthy statement in the whole of a bitter campaign."[70] The columnist wrote that such statements hurled "the vilest insults in the face of every Negro in the United States," and "wiped mud in their teeth."[71] Dunbar-Nelson concluded that such statements destroyed "whatever lingering belief in the decency of the Republican Party remained."[72]

A 1928 column also criticized both the Democratic and Republican parties for race baiting. Writing that again the black person was the "spectacle of the domination of the United States," Dunbar-Nelson continued with the following observation:

> He is the greatest factor in the life of the nation, and here in the most interesting, hardest fought, bitterest, and most unconventional campaign for the presidency that has been waged since the Civil War, we have the injection of the Negro, overruling and overtopping many of the real issues of the campaign. In effect, the United States is being told: "Vote for Al Smith, and you will have Negroes taking an active part in the government, and social equality all over the nation," or, "Vote for Hoover," and you'll have parties of white men and colored women all over the nation."[73]

Dunbar-Nelson took issue with those statements the opposing camps made in order to sway the votes their way by associating the other camp with blacks. Dunbar-Nelson was disturbed that the parties would behave in what she characterized as a callous and disrespectful manner.[74]

She vented her antipathy on groups as well as individuals. One person who was at the receiving end of her criticism was a Democratic candidate for U.S. senator who used the label "darkie" for people Dunbar-Nelson identified as "some of the most outstanding colored national leaders."[75] The negative characterization was even more appalling and confusing, Dunbar-Nelson suggested, because Coleman du Pont, the candidate who made the remark, might have been confused with Pierre du Pont, a philanthropist who had given more money to educate blacks "than any single individual in a specific state."[76]

Like other crusading black women journalists, Dunbar-Nelson was not afraid to criticize society and lambaste whites for their actions that harmed blacks. In a five-line blurb in one of her columns, she ridiculed the North Carolina Inter-Racial Committee for its appointment of "a committee to investigate traveling conditions in the Jim Crow car, and to insist upon better Jim Crow cars." Dunbar-Nelson's disparagement was subtle, as illustrated by the style in which she concluded her entry. In all capital letters, she wrote: "TO INSIST UPON BETTER JIM CROW CAR!" She then queried: "Can you beat it?"[77] In a not so subtle manner, Dunbar-Nelson criticized what she called a "race-segregation ordinance" that the Indianapolis City Council passed. A provocative Dunbar-Nelson offered: "The only thing needed now to make the ghetto of Indianapolis complete ... will be a ton of barbed wire, strung around the prescribed district, guaranteed to keep colored people in, day and night, and white men out at night."[78]

Continuing to attack racial intolerance, Dunbar-Nelson poked fun at a prominent white Georgia pastor who preached that white Christians were not spending enough money to educate and evangelize blacks. The columnist agreed with the minister, but she suggested that white Christians of Georgia were "not spending enough money to educate and evangelize white men and women." Dunbar-Nelson proffered the following:

> White Christians of Georgia could do nothing better than raise a huge fund to educate their own kind in learning the Golden Rule, and applying it, for instance, to: The Georgia legislature; the Georgia Ku Klux Klan; the Georgia Stone Mountain Committee; the Georgia white barbers; the Georgia legislators; lynchers.[79]

Dunbar Nelson continuously returned to the theme of black elevation and lack of black productivity. She often pointed out to blacks the need to become involved in affecting their own destiny and the fruitlessness of some of the actions in which they engaged. An extremely long column was devoted to futile actions of black men during election campaigns. Criticizing the males for opposing suffrage for women, Dunbar-Nelson outlined the notions and strategies in which the men engaged, the numerous discussions they had, and their desire to be important participants in the process of electing candidates to office. The columnist concluded that the effort was for naught "because the Man and Brother is such a nonessential in the picture."[80]

A column written for Thanksgiving highlighted things for which blacks should be grateful, including growing wealth built up by "subtle and polite forms of gambling."[81] The main thrust of the column, however, focused on the things for which blacks should not be thankful, including growing discrimination and segregation in northern cities. In biting sarcasm, Dunbar-Nelson wrote about the things for which her race members should be thankful, including, "life on this continent until the whole race has put its shoulder to the wheel to help adjust some pitiful inequalities" and "any crumbs or sops thrown to him from the dominant group; and any lowering of his standards."[82] This column seemed to posit that blacks–and not just the society—were responsible for the plight of the race.

On December 28, 1928, Dunbar-Nelson criticized blacks for behaving as whites expected them to. To illustrate her disgust with such blacks, she presented a vignette about a "large colored man" who had "clambered aboard a trolley"[83] with a paper bag in his hands. A description followed of how the man "attacked the bag avidly," pulled out "part of a pig's foot," ate it, and "threw the bone on the floor."[84] Dunbar-Nelson declared:

> White passengers smiled knowingly; colored ones looked disgustedly away. Another piece of pig's foot; another bone, and another and another, until the contents of the brown paper bag were all distributed—with meat within the capacious maw of the large colored gentleman, the bones upon the floor of the platform. That done, he wiped his mouth on the back of his hand, and his hands on the brown paper bag, which followed the bones on the floor of the car, and sat back with a look of supreme satisfaction on his face.[85]

While it may appear the writer spent considerable time criticizing her fellow brethren, that was not the case. In an effort to uplift the race, Dunbar-Nelson used a February 6, 1926, column to caution blacks that their artistic works would never be viewed as creative until they let go of the notion that they should be "propagandists" for the race. Writing on a theme about which she deeply cared—culture and art—Dunbar-Nelson bemoaned the fact that the black community insisted that every black artist be a propagandist. The journalist stated:

> We want our pictures to be painted with an eye single to the exploits of the race. We want our poets to sing of the fame of the Negro. We want our novels, short stories to have a bludgeon, none too cleverly

concealed within the narrative, hitting the Nordic and exalting the Negro.[86]

Using Shakespeare as an example, Dunbar Nelson concluded her piece with a reminder:

> The real novel about, by and for the Negro will be written only when blacks can see clearly the sharp cleavage between the work of art and the propaganda pamphlet; when we learn to tell a story for the sake of the artistry and the sheer delight of a good tale, without an eye for the probable effect of the story on the consciousness of the white man.[87]

Another instance in which Dunbar-Nelson used her columns to caution her race as well as to chastise fellow blacks appeared in the May 15, 1926, "Une Femme Dit." Dunbar-Nelson addressed the fact that noted Harlem Renaissance poet Countee Cullen had been denied entrance to a hotel. She stressed that "the Negro" should not demand of Cullen that he "break down discrimination, insults to the Negro, Jim Crowism, the practice of making engagements with artists without finding out local conditions, and all other evils of being a Negro."[88] Dunbar-Nelson appeared to be concerned that blacks would expect Cullen to boycott the hotel or take similar actions that might have jeopardized his career. With this accommodationist perspective, Dunbar-Nelson differed from both Wells-Barnett and Jacques Garvey, who felt that race members should not tolerate any form of discrimination and that blacks of Cullen's stature should be leaders in that effort.

In much the same way that she touted the accomplishments of blacks, Dunbar-Nelson often used her columns to praise the actions of whites and blacks. In the May 15, 1926, column, she further acknowledged a Georgia clergyman who had spoken out against discrimination; and she saluted the Columbus, Georgia, *Enquirer-Sun*, which had won the 1925 Pulitzer Prize for speaking against the Ku Klux Klan, racial and religious prejudice, and an anti-evolution law.[89] Dunbar-Nelson wrote: "To be in Columbus, Georgia, to live there, to be a white Southerner there, and to take so fearless and advanced a stand, merits not only the Pulitzer Prize for journalism, but the Carnegie medal for heroism."[90]

In still another column, Dunbar-Nelson criticized legislators for stirring up controversy on the issue of reading the Bible in school. She declared,

> When legislators haven't anything else to do, they jump on the poor teachers about reading the Bible or not reading, as the case may be.
>
> If one could just get hold of one of these backwoods solons and make him take charge of a school room for a week, it might be wonderfully illuminating to said solon.

> He might find out, for instance, that when Dear Teacher stands up to read the Bible, dear little Johnny and Mary and Betty and Lizzie and Andy fold their little hands, and their dear little faces go absolutely blank, as do their dear little minds.[91]

The misrepresentation of the race was a theme that Dunbar-Nelson discussed often in her column. She criticized whites whom she wrote had neglected to acknowledge that Crispus Attucks, the first person killed in the American Revolution, was a black man. Dunbar-Nelson lamented at the beginning of a column that people did not see "any mention of Crispus Attucks in a school history written by Nordic authors."[92] Noting that because blacks had started writing about Attucks and erecting monuments to him, white historians found they could prove beyond a doubt that while it was true that "the first blood of the Revolutionary War was shed by Crispus Attucks—that he was not a Negro!"[93] Continuing, Dunbar Nelson quipped,

> But a negro? A historical error.
> Let us draw a deep breath of relief. The supremacy of the white race has been saved, and the courage of the early Continentals rescued from the black man, and placed on the breast of the proud Puritan. Hurrah![94]

The writer inserted a blurb in her March 13, 1926, column that pointed out that the "vehement denials" of King Tut's "Negroid descent" had tapered off when people discovered that the youthful king had died of tuberculosis. Dunbar-Nelson quipped, "That tubercular taint just settled things."[95]

Writings on Gender

While writing about racial issues, Dunbar Nelson also addressed gender themes. In her debut column for the *Pittsburgh Courier*, she commented on the dreary lifestyle of women of the day and the lack of appreciation or recognition they received both inside and outside the home. In what can be called a salute to women, Dunbar-Nelson wrote that women had little time to attend to themselves because of the constant demands of being wives and mothers. Of the woman, Dunbar-Nelson wrote,

> She had not had time to bob her hair; the babies came too fast. She did not know much about international affairs, and the latest agony story in the howling tabloid was unread by her. Her gingham frocks were comfortable looking and she was able to hold a cooing bit of soft loveliness in the hollow of her arm, while she cut bread and butter for two others clinging to her skirts. Like Werter's Charlotte, when the artists

begged to be allowed to sketch her she "went on cutting bread and butter." Nothing marred the serenity of her broad brow.[96]

Dunbar-Nelson addressed the aftermath of passage of the Nineteenth Amendment and the extent to which black men opposed suffrage for women on the grounds that the "woman's place" was in the home.[97] The columnist equated that argument with the one that justified lynching as a response to "the crime of rape."[98] Satirically, Dunbar-Nelson suggested the inference was that

> woman would get up early in the morning, Monday morning, and vote steadily all day, Monday, Tuesday, Wednesday, Thursday, Friday, Saturday and twice on Sunday. There would be no time for washing, ironing, cooking, scrubbing, sewing, baking, wiping the children's noses or getting them ready for Sunday school.[99]

Dunbar-Nelson suggested that once women got "in the game," they found out that "men obtained that conception of the ballot. Right from themselves." Accordingly, men "knew all along that it takes them about three weeks to vote, and that for about ten days before election they are not fit for anything else, and they simply judged the poor women by themselves."[100]

In a previous column, Dunbar-Nelson commented on suffrage when she wrote that people were "howling about the danger of the obliteration of the sex line."[101] With chagrin, she wrote,

> Humph! Might not be so bad in obliterating it, the single-standard of sex morality took its rightful place in the life of the nation. Time was when any worn out old rake felt cheated and defrauded if he could not marry a pure young innocent girl. But the innocent young thing is learning to demand equal chastity from her spouse to be, and in turn to feel herself cheated and defrauded if she gets shop-worn goods.[102]

The manner in which Dunbar-Nelson concluded the column provided insight into the depth of her feelings about the role women played in society. She wrote, "Basic womanhood. The backbone of the world."[103] On March 6, 1926, Dunbar-Nelson addressed the question posed by one of her contemporaries regarding whether the United States dishonored women. The columnist answered with a resounding "hardly," and she added: "No one can dishonor a woman but herself, in the first place. She may be insulted, reviled, even raped, but dishonor cannot be put upon her, except in so far as she is a consenting party to the aforementioned proceedings."[104] With the charge that "Uncle Sam has been a silent party to the rape of black women for over three hundred years," Dunbar-Nelson concluded that section of the column with the words, "Think about it."[105]

The accomplishments of black club women was a frequent theme. In one column, Dunbar-Nelson saluted the former principal of a renowned high school where she had once worked. Edwina A. B. Kruse's accomplishments included, raising "the intellectual standard of a community," contributing to the "education of thousands of boys and girls," and leaving "the enduring monument of a splendid school." Dunbar-Nelson wrote Kruse's "worthwhile," achievements and concluded that the educator's life had "been finely worth living."[106]

Again focusing on the achievement of black women in February 1926, Dunbar-Nelson's column included an account about a woman who had built a school in Summit, New Jersey. According to the columnist, in building the school, Violet Johnson had

> brought to the little town the best that we have and presented them at the leading churches so that the white population—their entire conception of the Negro too often gleaned from the kitchenry—might know and see our contribution to the literature, music, and history of America.[107]

Dunbar-Nelson observed that "a deeper respect for the Negro permeated the atmosphere of the haughty little town, and the Negro in the town held his own head higher for having gained the respect of his white neighbor."[108]

A Mrs. Eva G. Monroe received accolades from Alice at the beginning of another column. Dunbar-Nelson said Monroe had been "doing yeoman service for the children of our race for the past 26 years," and that she "saw her duty and, without any flinching, went ahead and did it."[109] The duty about which Dunbar-Nelson wrote was Monroe's establishment of an orphanage. In glowing terms, Dunbar-Nelson stated:

> How Mrs. Monroe has weathered the storm of the past quarter of a century; how her orphanage has thrived; how her children have grown up, gone through schools, 'made good,' and returned many a time and oft to bless the great-hearted mother, is a story that some day we hope she will tell herself.[110]

Again writing about club women in 1928, Dunbar-Nelson proclaimed it "would be a sheer waste of time and energy so far as colored women were concerned" to talk about anything but the National Federation of Colored Women meeting in Washington, D.C., that week.[111] Dunbar-Nelson pointed out that the federation was doing great work, including opening a national headquarters in the nation's capital and dedicating a caretaker's cottage at the (Frederick) Douglass Home and Shrine at Anacostia.[112]

A month later, the columnist commented on a conference on interracial cooperation, asserting that black women were the ones who

> kept the discussion on frank and open plane; who struggled hardest to prevent the conference from degenerating into a sentimental mutual admiration society; and who insisted that all is not right and perfect in this county of ours; and that there is a deal to be done by the right thinking church women of both races.[113]

Such frank discussions contributed to interracial cooperation, Dunbar-Nelson believed. She once pointed out that cooperation was first "sneered at, but was growing" as illustrated by "the historic meeting of white and colored women at Tuskegee in 1920, and the furor it created."[114]

The economic plight of black women and their entry into the workforce was also a theme Dunbar-Nelson addressed. One of her contributions to the *Messenger* put in focus her concern about black women joining the workforce to gain the "thrill of pride in her new economic status."[115] While Dunbar-Nelson did not believe that black women's involvement in the political arena would have a negative effect on the race, she was distressed that their entry to the labor force would lead to a disintegration of the race. She maintained that the race was "faced with a startling fact,"[116] as evidenced by a declining birth rate and an increase in infant mortality. Dunbar-Nelson lamented that the black "educated and intelligent classes" were "refusing to have children" and that black women were "going into the kind of work that taxes both physical and mental capacities."[117]

With the assertion that "churches, social agencies, schools and Sunday schools cannot do the work of mothers and heads of families," Dunbar-Nelson averred that no race would "amount to anything economically, no matter how high the wages it collects nor how many commercial enterprise it supports, whose ownership of homes has not kept proportionate pace with its business holdings."[118]

CULTURE

Dunbar-Nelson was not just consumed with issues of racism and sexism; as her career progressed, she appeared to address more cultural themes. She covered the arts in many columns, and in doing so, highlighted the accomplishments of blacks. Almost all of her "As in the Looking Glass" columns for the *Washington Eagle* included at least one review of a play, book, poem, or other literary work.

On April 3, 1926, she reviewed the portraits of Laura Wheeler, a young black artist.[119] The January 11, 1929, issue of the *Washington Eagle* saw Dunbar-Nelson reviewing a new book, *An Autumn Love Cycle*, by Georgia Douglas Johnson. A month later, Dunbar-Nelson commented on the opening installment of *An African Savage's Own Story*.[120] Of the work, she wrote: "It ought to be pretty racy reading as it is pretty good."[121] A week after that, Dunbar-Nelson wrote that "those who love the stage" would have thoroughly enjoyed the NAACP's twentieth anniversary dance.[122]

Clearly Dunbar-Nelson was writing about the Harlem Renaissance when she addressed the complaint by blacks that literary works were not stressing the "cultured, refined, educated Negro."[123] The critic expressed her enthusiasm about a writer, DuBose Heyward, who had found a way to "treat the best of the Negro" in novels, plays, and songs "without showing off or patronizing."[124] According to Dunbar-Nelson, Heyward accomplished the task "by the very simple expedient of telling the story, describing the scenes in an easy, natural manner."[125] Of Heyward's writing, Dunbar-Nelson explained:

> We see the church service in the fashionable Episcopal colored church in Charleston; we attend musicals at the home of one of the leaders of the "blue vein" group; we go in the automobile of the wealthy banker; we discuss Negro artists at the club meeting.[126]

A year later, Dunbar-Nelson reviewed Langston Hughes' new book, *Not Without Laughter*. Asserting that the day had past "when any book about Negroes is hailed as a masterpiece," Dunbar-Nelson noted that Hughes had "done well." Continuing, she wrote, "If his book is more objective than subjective as some have asserted, the objectivity is of a high order, holding the interest, and containing within it the appeal of the individual and not the race."[127]

What Dunbar-Nelson called "Race shows"[128] was an item in yet another column. The piece cautioned that "one cannot be struck with the thought that in this golden harvest which the Negro is reaping on the stage, he will be improvident indeed if he does not make hay while this auriferous sun is shining." Dunbar-Nelson added, "racial fads on the stage are intense while they last, but all too short-lived. And once dead it is many a lean year before they revive."[129] She provided examples of fads that had ended, such as the Hawaiian craze "when everyone was wearing grass skirts and dislocating their hips trying to do the hula-hula." Stating that people called their children to "Poi" instead of dinner, Dunbar-Nelson offered, "Now when the inevitable beach-comber strolls in, and the quartette off stage begins to wail about Oloha, we yawn and climb over the feet of our next neighbor in a wild effort to get out of the theatre."[130]

OTHER THEMES

Perhaps because of a desire to add levity to her columns, Dunbar-Nelson often wrote about seemingly insignificant topics. A very short piece in her

February 6, 1926, column questioned the ban on radios that the U.S. President and a college in Baltimore were proposing.[131] Dunbar-Nelson highlighted that the college president blamed radio for "loss of pep, lowered efficiency, stupidity in class and general non-scholastic attainments." And the writer asked, "Who is to be commended, Prexy for his innocence in placing the blame on the radios, or for his insularity in banishing a modern invention? Or the fair maidens for their sweet childish love for the dear radio, or their cleverness in making poor Prexy place the blame on the loud speaker?"[132]

On May 29, 1926, Dunbar-Nelson wrote about the traditional end-of-school field day, calling it "a day for healthful sports, for taking stock of the physical well-being of the young people."[133] Just a week earlier, Dunbar-Nelson penned a short piece about a chain letter she had received in the mail and discarded. The columnist informed her readers that, after falling and spraining her ankle a week later, she now felt about chair letters –"not affection—but respect."[134] In an earlier column, she described the lengths whites were going to learn the Charleston. She noted that white "writers rush eagerly into print to prove that the dance was not invented by Negroes, but is the legitimate brain-child of a pure Nordic."[135] She added that whites were engaging in "exhaustive discussion" that were "rife for proving that the colored boy or girl does not dance it right."[136] Dunbar-Nelson offered that blacks just "look on and listen placidly to all these mental and physical gyrations" because they had been dancing the Charleston for five years and were "pretty well tired of it."[137] She added sarcastically, "Perfectly willing to let Mr. White Man take his leavings from the dance hall, and do as best he can with his undeveloped sense of rhythm."[138] And as if to drive her point home, Dunbar-Nelson concluded her column with the following:

> For it is the history of dance and song in America, that the white man takes up where the Negro leaves off. And just as aforesaid White Man is getting quite excited over his rare discovery the Man and Brother, and Woman and Sister have hied them to fresh fields and pastures in the musical world.[139]

WRITING STYLE

The tone of Dunbar-Nelson's writing showed a no-nonsense, yet sometime humorous approach to life. Wit and sarcasm characterized her humor. This was illustrated in the Thanksgiving Day column cited earlier in which Dunbar-Nelson chided both blacks and whites for the black's dire circumstances.[140] Her humor and acerbity were also evident when she chastised members of her race for not doing enough to plan for their future. Pointing to the success of the play, *Porgy and Bess*, Dunbar-Nelson said that the Negro had become the "fad" in theater and music. Dunbar-Nelson wondered "what the hundreds of young men and women who are high in the public favor are doing now to improve themselves and make the passing more than a brief candle–like existence soon to be snuffed out and forgotten."[141]

In this column, the writer did not preach. Rather, Dunbar-Nelson drew the reader into the story by first talking about fads. She asked, "Then do you remember the Hawaiian fad? When everyone was wearing grass skirts and dislocating their hips trying to do the hula-hula? When the home that did not have at least three ukuleles was felt to be on the verge of bankruptcy?"[142] Only after Dunbar-Nelson's readers had probably chuckled about the picture her description created did the writer present her message for consideration–that the Harlem Renaissance was a passing fad that was not of lasting benefit to blacks.

Dunbar-Nelson's wit and sarcasm were also evident when she gave her reasons for changing the name of her column. She did so because other newspapers had begun using the same name for their columns. She remarked:

> The title, *A Woman's Point of View*, got to be so popular that it cropped up in all sorts of places and the writer found herself reading articles that bore her title, but not her imprint . . . Am almost tempted to hunt up some of these battered old dictionaries and wordbooks, left over from the crossword puzzle craze, and distribute them to the fraternity of the Fourth Estate. So, the English language not being large enough to accommodate all the female columnists extant, recourse must be made to the French. So–"One Woman Says" in French is the future caption of these burning thoughts.[143]

Although she was highly critical of black males on many occasions, Dunbar-Nelson couched her denunciation in well-woven stories. Her May 22, 1926, column on the "Man and Brother" during election campaigns was full of humorous examples of the males' behavior.[144]

As already noted, Dunbar-Nelson wrote about multiple issues in single columns. That technique in all likelihood prevented her columns from becoming oppressive. On the same day that she praised a woman who had been working with young black children for twenty-six years, Dunbar-Nelson also criticized the Missouri Supreme Court for a decision it rendered on the Fifteenth Amendment, bemoaned the fact that blacks could not get their messages across to whites, and criticized a white man who wanted retribution after his wife and daughter had been raped while partying in "Tia Juana," Mexico.[145]

In the February 20, 1926, column where she announced her reasons for changing its name, Dunbar-Nelson reviewed the play, *Lulu Belle*. The same column also described the massive amount of information school teachers tried to "cram in the heads of students" during Negro History Week. Dunbar-Nelson pointed out, "What that little month lacks in chronological length, it amply makes up in historical depth."[146]

Dunbar-Nelson sometimes interjected blurbs into her columns. Nestled between a book review and her reflections on a positive *Time* magazine review of a play, Dunbar-Nelson wrote about the horrors of war or the challenges her race faced.

CONCLUSION

Alice Dunbar-Nelson used her writing abilities to uplift her race during a dark period in their history. In addition, she sought to elevate women. In the process, Dunbar-Nelson became a journalist, fulfilling the roles of providing information, persuading, entertaining, and advocating. Beginning as a teenager and continuing for approximately 40 years, Dunbar-Nelson wrote hundreds of articles, columns, and essays for the black press and for some white publications. She did not limit herself to writing; she was also an editor, publisher, and co-owner of various publications. She gave her black audience information they needed to have to live better lives. She exposed all of her audiences to the arts. She criticized and cajoled. Sometimes she merely stated or summarized facts. Other times, she only gave opinion. She tackled serious issues, but she also sprinkled her columns with bits of information that her audience did not *need* to know, but probably enjoyed reading anyway.

While Dunbar-Nelson addressed a variety of themes, she overwhelmingly devoted her columns to providing information and advice that would strengthen her race. Even if a column dealt primarily with the arts, Dunbar-Nelson also included in the same column information that might help blacks to make better decisions. She highlighted the hypocrisy and bigotry of whites, and in many columns, Dunbar-Nelson pointed to the futility of certain actions in which blacks engaged. Sometimes she chastised both blacks and whites, but other times, the writer also praised members of both races. In what may have been an effort to motivate her race, Dunbar-Nelson frequently used her column to highlight the accomplishments of blacks individually and collectively and to criticize destructive behavior. Dunbar-Nelson's columns gave her audience a sense of the black person's place in society, as well as insight into what blacks could and should do to improve their condition.

Similarly, Dunbar-Nelson's work probably served as topics for consideration for a broader audience. Within the wider context of elevation and equality, Dunbar-Nelson addressed weighty themes that touched upon politics, education, the economy, and social issues. Her work as a journalist is especially noteworthy because she used her columns and articles to tackle conditions that rendered her race second-class citizens during the Jim Crow era. Often with biting satire and wit, Dunbar-Nelson confronted oppression, economic deprivation, and social and political inequities. Dunbar-Nelson did so both as the co-owner of a newspaper and as a columnist and writer. Many of the issues to which she called attention and the themes she sounded are still being discussed today, almost seventy years since her death.

Chapter Five

Amy Jacques Garvey
Mouthpiece For A Movement

> The Negro of fifty years ago might have been satisfied with a cabin and plenty of hog-meat, but this New Negro wants everything that the civilized white man wants. The New Negro wants nice homes, and the means to protect them. . . . And since this New Negro knows that the white man has only such luxuries as a cabin and hog meat to offer him, he is planning and working toward establishing a government and a nation of his own, where he can satisfy his needs and ambitions as a MAN.[1]
>
> *Amy Jacques Garvey*

As she prepared for a television interview in 1968, Amy Jacques Garvey identified herself for the program's host as the "widow of Marcus Garvey—Jamaica's First National Hero" and as the "author of four books on the life of this remarkable man."[2] From the time she met and married Black Nationalist Marcus Mosiah Garvey until she died in 1973, Jacques Garvey carried that mantra of companion, wife, and "main propagandist"[3] for the Garvey Movement. Her role as Garvey's wife, and later, his widow, surpassed all others in her view. She, therefore, dedicated her life to advancing her husband's views while Garvey served as head of a movement that sought to repatriate blacks to Africa, while he was in prison for alleged mail fraud from 1925 to 1927, and after his death in 1940.[4]

Although Jacques Garvey has received acclaim for her works about Marcus Garvey and as a racial activist, her career as a journalist rarely is acknowledged. Nevertheless, during the 1920s, Jacques Garvey served as an associate editor and women's page editor of *The Negro World*, the weekly newspaper her husband published. From February 1924 through

November 1927, Jacques Garvey wrote some one hundred fifty editorials and articles for *The Negro World*. The editorials were the means through which she advocated the Garvey Movement's philosophy of black self-help, race pride, nationalism, black repatriation to Africa, and the dire effects of what she saw as white exploitation of weaker nations. Jacques Garvey also spoke throughout the United States to champion Garveyism and to crusade for her husband's release from prison.

This chapter provides a brief overview of Jacques Garvey's life and examines her journalistic work. This analysis allows for the discovery of insight into how a black woman who is virtually invisible in the literature on the history of the press used journalism to advance the agenda of a movement that had an impact on perhaps millions of people in the early 1900s. By analyzing the themes in Jacques Garvey's writings in *The Negro World* from 1924 through 1927, I ascertained the values this militant activist espoused and the meaning she ascribed to being a black person, a woman, and a black woman during a volatile time in the history of blacks and the history of this country. During this period the United Negro Improvement Association, the umbrella organization for the Garvey Movement, had a membership of what has been estimated as between one half million and six million.[5] Thousands of UNIA members in almost every Caribbean and sub-Saharan African country read *The Negro World*.[6]

BIOGRAPHICAL INFORMATION

Although this study found scant information about Amy Euphemia Jacques Garvey's early life, it is known that she was born on December 31, 1896, in Kingston, Jamaica, to Samuel and Charlotte Jacques, members of the Jamaican middle class and educated property owners.[7] Samuel, who had lived in Cuba and Baltimore, Maryland, before moving to Jamaica, West Indies, greatly influenced his only child, kindling in her a love for reading and exposing her to world affairs. Jacques Garvey wrote that her mother prayed for a son and heir, "but I came along and my Dad trained me as if I were a boy."[8] Samuel collected his foreign newspapers on Sunday afternoons and directed Amy to get a dictionary and read editorials and news items to him. He then explained what Amy had read and answered her questions. This routine benefited Amy, she later recalled, because it made her "learn to think independently on world affairs and to analyze situations."[9]

A year after graduating from the Wolmer's Girls' School in Jamaica, Amy migrated to the United States in 1917 to seek further education. However, she almost immediately became involved with the UNIA, and she became Marcus Garvey's private secretary and office manager at UNIA headquarters in New York. Garvey and Jacques married in July 1922 after his divorce from Amy Ashwood Garvey.[10] Garvey's union to Jacques produced two sons, Marcus Garvey, Jr., who was born in 1931; and Julius Winston Garvey, whose birth was two years later. Both children were born in Jamaica after Garvey was deported there following his release from prison in November 1927.[11]

Amy Jacques viewed her marriage to Garvey as an arrangement. She told an interviewer in 1971, "Marcus Garvey never married me for love. No, sir. That was not the proposal. He needed me. That was all. He needed someone he could trust. It wasn't a personal matter. He knew that the life of the organization "'was at stake.'"[12] Documents in the Marcus Mosiah Garvey Memorial Collection at Fisk University in Nashville, Tennessee, confirmed the arrangement between the UNIA, the African Communities League, Marcus Garvey, and Amy Jacques Garvey. The arrangement gave Jacques Garvey "the right and privilege to inspect, audit and investigate at any and all times the records and books or accounts" of the UNIA. Garvey and Jacques Garvey obtained equal rights to the proceeds of all books, pamphlets, and pictures of which they were the authors and subjects.[13]

Garvey scholars conjecture that Jacques Garvey may have been the power behind both *The Negro World* and the UNIA.[14] Calling Jacques Garvey "an amazing woman," Tony Martin said she ran the UNIA "almost singlehandely [sic] when Garvey was either imprisoned or otherwise unavailable."[15] Honor Ford-Smith called her an important activist and one of the most important organizers for the UNIA who "worked tirelessly to keep the organization going" while Garvey was imprisoned.[16] In 1968, an interviewer for *Ebony* magazine came away from her session with an elderly Jacques Garvey believing that "this little lady could very well have been the fuel that fed the powerful Garvey machine for so many years."[17]

Jacques Garvey was steadfast in her belief in and commitment to her husband's philosophy. She deemed her advocacy necessary, especially at that point in the history of the black race. The Harlem Renaissance did not affect the majority of blacks during the early 1920s, for it was a time when African Americans were constrained by the economic, social, and political impediments society placed in their paths. Blacks found little work beyond the homes and fields of white employers. Black children rarely attended the few schools open to them; therefore, they were far more illiterate than white children.[18]

The anxiety that accompanied blacks' discovery that they would not be recognized as equals "was marked by the rise of a series of revitalizing movements," that included Marcus Garvey's United Negro Improvement Association, Lawrence W. Levine argued[19] "With its insistence on race history, race pride, and an autonomous race development," the movement reached its zenith during the 1920s, according to Levine.[20] African-

American historian John Hope Franklin wrote that Garvey was very popular "at a time when Negroes generally had so little of which to be proud."[21] Adding that Garvey "exalted everything black," Franklin noted that Garvey "insisted that black stood for strength and beauty, not inferiority," and that "Africans had a noble past" of which blacks should be proud.[22] Sociologist E. Franklin Frazier argued that blacks in America were "fertile soil" for the Garvey movement for they were "repressed and shut out from all serious participation in American life."[23] Frazier added that the black intellectual also felt "this repression," therefore, blacks "took refuge in the belief that in an autonomous black Africa they would find their proper place."[24]

It was within that context that a fiercely militant Jacques Garvey worked as a journalist and advocated through her editorials in *The Negro World*. In the introduction to one of her books, Jacques Garvey wrote that her husband "whipped Negroes into the consciousness of race pride, and consequently made them grow in power and stature. He quickened their initiative to do, kindled their imagination and lifted them out of the lethargy of inferiority."[25] Likewise, Jacques Garvey used her editorials to elevate her race, especially the black masses, despite a hostile environment that dominated, demeaned, and devalued them.

PUBLICATIONS FOR WHICH JACQUES GARVEY WROTE

Unlike other black women journalists who wrote for a variety of black publications and some white publications at the beginning of the twentieth century, Jacques Garvey appears to have written exclusively for *The Negro World*. There is no indication that the black press of the day carried her articles. It is also not clear exactly when she became an editor of *The Negro World*, however, she is listed as associate editor in March 1925, the earliest copy of the complete paper that was available for this study. T. Thomas Fortune of the *New York Age* was listed as editor, but whether he fulfilled that role is not evident. Jacques Garvey assumed the role as editor of *The Negro World's* woman's page, "Our Women and What They Think," and she wrote her "first editorial"[26] on February 2, 1924.[27]

THEMES

In her editorials that ran through November 29, 1927, two days after her husband's release from prison, Jacques Garvey addressed themes pointing to the necessity of blacks gaining economic independence, especially at that point in the history of the black race. Framing her writings in what was happening in the international arena, the columnist advocated racial advancement and productivity via self-determination, self-reliance, productivity, and economic independence. Other themes included the role of women in the home and society, and the lack of motivation on the part of black men. Jacques Garvey's articles revealed that she consistently and passionately espoused the Garveyist goals and philosophy, seeking "to arouse a unified race consciousness in all peoples of African descent;" to strengthen the united race by organizing black-owned and managed, large-scale business enterprises and shipping lines; and to create a "black-governed nation in Africa that would host the creation of a renewed black civilization and stand up for the rights of black people everywhere."[28]

Jacques Garvey articulated the black nationalism view that has been defined as "a loss of hope in America" and a belief that white people would never "place black people on a par with them."[29] Hence, Jacques Garvey not only revealed what she termed instances of white domination and oppression, but she sought to arouse in blacks zeal to turn to themselves for their salvation. Her writings on race were laden with powerful language that denounced whites. She stridently chastised blacks as she sought to motivate them to take charge of their lives.

Exploitation of people of color and how they should rise above such misuse was the common thread that ran through Jacques Garvey's editorials. In addition, almost all of her editorials advocated the Garvey doctrine of racial solidarity and self-reliance. Similarly, Jacques Garvey focused on empowerment of blacks in not only America, but also in Africa and what she sometimes called the "darker" nations.[30]

INTERNATIONAL AFFAIRS AND WHITE EXPLOITATION

The first editorials that Jacques Garvey wrote in February 1924 illustrated her steadfast belief in and commitment to her husband's philosophy of proposing solutions to what scholars have called "the twin problems of racial subordination and colonial domination."[31] The writings also portended the protest, agitation, and advocacy role Jacques Garvey would adopt in subsequent writings during the next three years.

As if to illustrate that blacks were part of an international community and that the actions of dominant countries affected them negatively, Jacques Garvey, on February 2, 1924, noted that a new premier had taken the helm of the British Labor Party and had planned to continue the government's oppressive policy toward India.[32] Jacques Garvey quoted the premier's message to the Indian people that clearly conveyed that England would not tolerate interference from locals. The government leader asserted that England would not be "cowed by threat of force or by policies designed to bring the Government to a standstill." Furthermore, "if any Indian sections are under the delusion that this is not so, events will sadly disappoint them."[33]

The same editorial also contained a four-paragraph blurb in which Jacques Garvey mentioned the death of Nickolia Lenin and called him "the great Russian emancipator" and "the wonder man of Russia, who, with one blow, deposed the Czarist despots and set up a form of government in Russia."[34]

In her third editorial, Jacques Garvey returned to the topic of the British Labor government, this time criticizing its bombing of villages in Mesopotamia that were delinquent in paying their taxes to England. Jacques Garvey also chastised the editor of the *New York American* newspaper who had praised the British action and had stated that "dropping explosives from the sky" was an appropriate way to suppress and regulate "savage nations."[35] Jacques Garvey pondered whether the editor and his family would like the British "raining bombs" on them. She further noted the hypocrisy of the editor who devoted "his precious daily columns to denouncing the killing of Jews in Poland and Russia as inhuman and savage," but believed killing innocent black people was acceptable.[36]

These topics which Jacques Garvey addressed during her first month as an editorial writer signaled the content and tone of what was to be a steady offering of how white exploitation in the international community affected blacks and other oppressed peoples.

Moreover, her continuous commentaries on international affairs revealed her belief that dominant nations, intent on amassing great wealth, subjected people by enslaving their minds. According to Jacques Garvey, "The oppressed are always made to believe they are inferior" and once they acquire "that state of mind, they become willing tools of others" and "their ambition dies in them."[37] The writer maintained "the oppressive system is maintained because anyone who dares to think independently and seeks to expose the system is dubbed a RADICAL and agitator, a dangerous fellow to be gotten rid of."[38]

Editorials that denounced white subordination of the darker races or "darker peoples"[39] invariably carried appeals for blacks to take charge of their destinies and seek to create opportunities in Africa and worldwide. Furthermore, Jacques Garvey praised her husband and others who opposed the tyrants. One such editorial commended the premier of Egypt, who despite being seized by the British and being sent to Suez, had vowed to once again make his country independent of England. Jacques Garvey held that Zaghloul Pasha was "an active politician and an aggressive forceful character," and a "born statesman" who could "match wits with English intrigue and diplomacy."[40] The deposed leader had written a manifesto accusing the British of breaking its promises to both leave Egypt after initial occupation and to recognize the country's independence. The premier argued that England justified its action because it held that Egypt was "indispensable to British common interests."[41]

Jacques Garvey expressed a similar view about whites in a September 13, 1924, editorial titled "Work of Oppression in North Africa." The column proffered that the Spanish were unable to conquer the Moroccans even with the help of French and British fighting forces. Jacques Garvey wrote that the "scattered sons and daughters of Africa pray" that their "gallant brothers may be strengthened physically and spiritually to hold that portion of Africa, their native home, against all invaders and usurpers."[42] Six months later, the writer explained that white men wanted Africa in order to exploit the raw products and minerals "for their home consumption and comfort."[43]

A month after that editorial, Jacques Garvey called on "Mr. White Man" to stop the "centuries of injustice and brutality meted out to unorganized peoples."[44] She stressed that if the "white dominant powers" continued "their oppression and exploitation of the weaker, darker peoples of the world," aided by "wind shifts and evolution," would "retaliate in no uncertain terms."[45] Further citing tyrannical action by certain countries, Jacques Garvey informed readers that some Mexicans had lost their citizenship simply because they fought for the Moors.[46]

Returning to the theme of exploitation on July 5, 1925, Jacques Garvey noted that the yellow and white races were preparing for what she called "Armageddon," and she demanded to know what blacks were doing to create an "independent homeland."[47] Somewhat satirically, Jacques Garvey asked, "Mr. Colored Man, who does not want to be called a Negro, for whom will you fight? . . . Mr. Negro, who loves his race, what preparation are you now making to preserve your race when the human slaughter starts?"[48] As if to ignite a spark in blacks, Jacques Garvey stressed that Japan, China, and "discontented groups" in all parts of the world were "rising up in an effort to throw off the shackles of oppression and come into their own."[49] Clearly, the writer believed that the black race should do the same.

Jacques Garvey viewed the work of white missionaries as another form of exploitation. In his book, James Cone offered that black Christians believed white Christians would one day "see the truth of the gospel and thereby accept them into their churches and society."[50] Cone explained: "Many black Christians believed it was only a matter of a little time before Jesus revealed the gospel truth to whites and slavery and segregation would come tumbling down."[51] Jacques Garvey held no such view. She did not trust white missionaries who were working in foreign countries. She argued that the missionaries did not adhere to Christian teachings. Equating their work with misuse, Jacques Garvey wrote: "The principle of self-determination coming from the lips of the white man is applicable only to members of his race, but when it is spoken to men of other races, it loses its original form, and its application resembles 'the principle of exploitation.'"[52]

According to Jacques Garvey, the "Eastern Giants" were now moving on China and Morocco; and for that reason, she called on "black Mohammedans" and "black Christians" to recognize that their interests were identical, to understand that they were all "struggling under the same yolk," and to join forces to "throw off the common oppressor."[53]

Jacques Garvey believed that World War I was the ultimate form of white exploitation of weaker nations. In an editorial titled "Be Prepared," Jacques Garvey pointed out that wars would always occur because European countries kept Asiatic and African populations "in poverty and ignorance."[54] According to the writer, this was done to allow England, France, Holland, Belgium, and Portugal to "use and misuse" the populace while they extracted "the wealth of these peoples' countries, in order to rebuild and support the countries of Europe, and thus maintain European superiority."[55] Pointing out that the dominant countries' "very existence" depended "on Colonies," Jacques Garvey pondered, "Is it any wonder that they even disregard the laws of man and God in their anxiety to 'live good'?"[56]

Editorials such as the aforementioned postured that economic gain was the primary reason that white nations subjugated weaker nations, especially African countries. Writing in the September 12, 1925, issue of *The Negro World*, Jacques Garvey charged that American rubber manufacturers that were unable to grow rubber and were having difficulty obtaining it from England at reasonable prices, turned to the "little black Republic of Liberia" where rubber trees thrived.[57] Jacques Garvey wrote that despite the protest of Marcus Garvey and the UNIA, the Liberian government engaged in negotiations with Harvey Firestone and conceded "one million acres of land or more . . . to be exploited for rubber or any other development." Noting that her husband saw the danger to Liberian autonomy, Jacques Garvey lamented:

> The American rubber man has got what he wanted—rubber lands, and all mineral under the ground, also cheap labor [sic]. All at the expense of poor black natives in Liberia, who will be compelled to toil for white American Capitalists [sic] for a mere pittance.[58]

Jacques Garvey regretted that the Liberian government, because it owed money to America, had not "kept its word to allow the black men of UNIA to enter the country to cultivate rubber plantations, and participate in other developments of the country."[59] For the years that it was a viable movement, Garveyism sought, without success, to establish such relationships in order to advance blacks in America and Africa. According to Jacques Garvey, had such an economic agreement become a reality between Liberia and the UNIA, the Liberian government would have been able to repay its debt to America, corner the rubber market through the UNIA, and "restore her finances to par." More importantly, according to Jacques Garvey, the Liberian people would have been on "equal terms with the blacks from America, and their wages standardized to allow them to live like men, not peons." With a conclusion that charged that Liberia had "been bartered away," Jacques Garvey queried, "Who has received the thirty pieces of silver?"[60]

Jacques Garvey's vigorous pronouncements against white domination continued in September 1925, when she discussed the debt the French had incurred from the United States in France's quest to "purchase guns, bombs, poison gas and armored cars with which to kill 'the brutal Hun,' and make the world safe for democracy."[61] The article also professed that the United States, intent on becoming the "greatest colonial empire," might trade her debts from European countries for "some of their ill-gotten territory."[62]

The progress of World War I appears to have given Jacques Garvey the idea that oppressed people were close to ending white domination. In one piece, the columnist was strong in her pronouncement that the white race had "had its day" and was about to be eclipsed by "dark humanity."[63] The writer wrote two months later that selfish nations which "thrive on the sweat and life blood of oppressed peoples never flourish for long, because their prosperity is not built on righteousness."[64] To buttress this argument, Jacques Garvey cited as examples the fall of the Roman and Greek empires.

Throughout 1926 and 1927, Jacques Garvey continued to emphasize the havoc white imperialism wreaked. In May 1926, she warned that whites had planted the "germ of the future Armageddon"[65] through their quest for power and wealth. A month later, Jacques Garvey explained that whites were in Italy to exploit the country for economic gain,[66] and that they were finding natural resources in Africa.[67] September 1926 found Jacques Garvey again pointing out that Africa, which she described as "the treasure-house of the world,"[68] had been partitioned by every white nation.

While she concentrated overwhelmingly on her husband's imprisonment, as well as black empowerment, during 1927, Jacques Garvey continued to share her opinions on white oppression in other countries. For what she indicated was her "last editorial"[69] on April 30, 1928, Jacques Garvey wrote that the white race would not "voluntarily change its cruel attitude toward the darker races," and that it was useless to appeal to "their conscience or religious protestations."[70]

Although Jacques Garvey ceased her woman's page with that issue, she continued to write articles that ran as editorials in *The Negro World*. Those articles contained references to white domination. For example, in August, she informed readers that Italy had gone "sabre [sic] rattling."[71] October again saw Jacques Garvey writing about the powers that would control

Africa in the future, the suffering that resulted from Indian independence, and happenings in Afghanistan and Ceylon.[72]

As she had begun her work as an editorial writer with discourse on and reaction to international affairs, Jacques Garvey ended on the same note. These editorials and others showed her knowledge of world affairs, as well as her determination to energize her race with continuous calls for blacks to join the UNIA and the Garvey Movement. Jacques Garvey once stated that although "the road to liberty" was "a rocky one," blacks must have faith in themselves and a grim determination."[73]

RACIAL PRODUCTIVITY THROUGH SELF-DETERMINATION

Jacques Garvey held firm to the view that grim self-determination would lead to productivity, which, in turn, would bring about economic independence for black people throughout the world. This stream of reasoning was another theme on which Jacques Garvey dwelled during the four years that she wrote her editorials. In almost all of the editorials reviewed for this chapter, Jacques Garvey stressed that the black race must be productive and engage in economic development initiatives, seek to become involved in business ventures, make sound judgements regarding how to invest and spend their money, and assist fellow blacks. Only then would blacks be able to take charge of their destinies.

In her scrapbook housed in the Marcus Mosiah Garvey Memorial Collection at Fisk University, Jacques Garvey's handwritten notation, "important editorial,"[74] reflected the extent of her belief in the need for blacks to become motivated and to organize themselves. Throughout the year, while focusing mainly on the theme of white exploitation, Jacques Garvey also encouraged her race members worldwide to be self-reliant, self-directed, and productive.

In January, she told her readers to weigh "the year's misfortunes," find out the reasons for their failures, and resolve in their minds "to conquer the cause." She added, "When this is done you will be on the way to success in the New Year."[75] Under a subhead titled, "What Are You Doing with Your Money?," Jacques Garvey emphasized that spending money "foolishly" amounted "to criminal negligence." [76] "Such squandering not only hurts us personally, but hurts the race," she advised, adding, "Money accumulated can be invested in business, which would not only bring profit to the investors, but give employment to members of the race, thereby serving a two-fold purpose."[77]

The next week, Jacques Garvey urged her readers to back up their talk with action and to refrain from ending the year by remarking that they could have been productive but something had prevented them from being so. The woman offered,

There are not buts' [sic] that you cannot remove. The things that you plan to aid in need your help, and are neglected while you talk about it. Get into action so that you will be able to say to yourself at the close of the year "Thank God, I was able to better my condition and help my race in its struggle for manhood rights." Herein lies the joy of living.[78]

The need to take action was still on Jacques Garvey's mind on April 18, 1925, when she issued the following impassioned directive: "Wake up, Mr. Black Man, and go up and possess the land."[79]

Five months after that pronouncement, Jacques Garvey penned an editorial that questioned what the League of Nations had accomplished following World War I, she and specified ways in which blacks could become productive and elevate themselves. The columnist challenged the men of her race to "get all the implements of protection that the other fellow has, and if possible improve on it so that the very knowledge of your preparedness will cause other races to think twice before they attempt to seize your land and wealth."[80]

At the end of 1925, Jacques Garvey returned to her January admonishments when she told readers to ask themselves whether they had "been slipping back or advancing," whether they were "merely observers of the accomplishments of others or active participants in the march for human attainment."[81] She then called upon them, whom she described as "son, wife, husband, patriot or race lover," to "make their contributions of good deeds."[82]

The need for race consciousness was illustrated when Jacques Garvey argued that because the black race no longer had a history, its members were "scattered all over the world, laying claim to alien nationalities."[83] She then wrote that the UNIA was "working and praying" for the day when her people would be united in Mother Africa."[84] Stressing the benefit of service to each other that was inherent in race consciousness, Jacques Garvey a month later quoted her husband. She said his belief was that "the man or woman who essays to work for the betterment of the Negro race must forget self in the struggle upward, so that in the end all will enjoy life more abundantly."[85] Again in August, Jacques Garvey pointed out that race members must be prepared to make sacrifices in order to enjoy rewards for themselves or others. "He can see opportunity through adversity and good in everything exemplifies that faith in self and faith in God that make of him a successful and contented person,"[86] Jacques Garvey wrote.

Returning to the theme in a November 28 editorial, she again pleaded for blacks to assist each other. The writer pointed out that Christmas was about more than parties and "getting intoxicated and overeating" in the name of "celebrating." In a tone of familiarity, Jacques Garvey added,

Friends, this is a mistaken idea, and gets us nowhere, but in bed with a bad headache or indigestion the morning after the night before. But the fellow who remembers his fellow man and shares his "cheer" with them, whether financially or otherwise, is he who feels happy.[87]

RACIAL PRODUCTIVITY THROUGH ECONOMIC INDEPENDENCE

The need for blacks to obtain economic independence by becoming business owners and supporting black businesses was the creed of Marcus Garvey and the UNIA. Focusing on that issue, Jacques Garvey, on February 7, 1925, called blacks their "own worst enemy" because of their attitude "toward business conducted by members of the race."[88] She referred to the failure of blacks to build businesses in the United States and Africa, as well as the neglect of blacks to patronize businesses that did exist.

Despite her negative declaration about blacks, it was clear from the rest of Jacques Garvey's editorial that the failure to build businesses did not rest solely with blacks. Jacques Garvey provided a list of circumstances that prevented blacks from becoming successful, including inexperience and a lack of capital. Of the black businessman and the business acquisition process, Jacques Garvey explained,

> He belongs to a pauper race; he is himself poor compared to the men of the other race who compose his business environment. He goes to the white bank in which he places his money, and lays his plans before the manager, who will listen attentively, lean back in his chair, scratch his head, cough a little, and then remark, "Well, that's a very good idea, and you ought to make money in that line, but it is the policy of our office not to make loans of that sort to colored people."[89]

Although it was a common practice for white lenders to refuse to lend money to blacks during the period, that was not the only problem the potential black entrepreneur faced. His plight was exacerbated by the lack of support from fellow blacks, Jacques Garvey explained. In this editorial, she may have been referring to her husband who had collected money to buy the Black Star Line Steamship Company in order to engage in foreign commerce and to take blacks back to Africa.[90] Ula Y. Taylor pointed out that the shipping and passenger fleet "was the UNIA's main venture to offset" the "injustice" of black people the world over living as "second-class citizens."[91] Taylor explained: "Unfortunately, this capitalistic enterprise sowed the seeds of the organization's demise and Garvey's downfall. Mismanagement of the Black Star Line gave the U.S. government legal justification to entangle Garvey in a web of innuendo and fraud."[92] Garvey was imprisoned for alleged mail fraud in connection with that venture.

Jacques Garvey charged in her editorial that as soon as funds for the black business trickled in, "five or ten dollars at a time," the black press began to harass the entrepreneur. According to Jacques Garvey, the black newspapers "malign the five thousand dollars he has collected into five hundred thousand dollars," and they ask, "What has he done with the money? Where is the business he promised?"[93] Jacques Garvey declared that black ministers, fearful of a drop in collections, urged their congregations not to contribute to black business ventures, "but to lay it (their money) on the altar."[94] Stockholders next became distrustful and, consequently, the businessman "is at a loss to know what to do," Jacques Garvey explained, adding

> Mr. Colored Man is so harassed that he is compelled to buy the first business he can lay his hands on, in order to satisfy his critics. The result is that he has not enough money left to equip the business to meet the white competitor in his line. His patrons have no sympathy for his efforts. They refuse to buy from him if he cannot sell cheaper than Mr. Ginsberg, whose brother is a wholesale dealer; whose uncle is his landlord; and who gets a loan from his bank to properly stock his store or equip his business.[95]

Jacques Garvey ended her discourse with the revelation that the black business inevitably failed, and the black newspapers "trumpet the demise" with headlines that read, "Mr. Colored Man failed." The black preacher, likewise, "gets up in the pulpit and says, 'I told you so, sisters and brothers; colored folks just can't do anything right,'" Jacques Garvey concluded.[96]

While the exhortation for blacks—especially black men—to elevate themselves was a constant refrain of Jacques Garvey, an equally frequent pronouncement was her view that the UNIA and Marcus Garvey were the avenues for black resurrection. On November 14, 1925, Jacques Garvey clarified that her husband had studied the political and economic life of blacks and America and that he was convinced blacks could not rise above their present status in the United States because of white prejudice and intolerance. Jacques Garvey made the case that blacks were entirely dependent on the white man for mainly menial work for which they were underpaid. After pointing out that the invention of labor-saving devices was further eroding the ability of blacks to earn a living, Jacques Garvey warned,

> It is imperative that the Negro create his own job, or face unemployment and consequently starvation. The black consumer is short unless he starts out immediately to produce essentials of everyday life, [sic] which will take him out of the servant class and at the same time ensure his livelihood, [sic] but the question of protection lies in the establish-

ment of a government of his own in Africa strong enough to protect him in any part of the world he may reside.

Truly the Negro has served well the white man's purpose for bringing him to America; and the enlightened wide-awake Negro is now determined to serve his own purpose, [sic] that of living and enjoying life as any other man, without limitations and without barriers against his development and progress.[97]

Jacques Garvey believed that the poverty of her race equated to slavery and that blacks were the poorest of all peoples, despite the richness of Africa. Acknowledging that poor people would never be independent because they had to work for money, she wrote, "To be truly independent, one must have money invested, so that whether one wants to play golf or play the fool, that money will be earning enough interest to meet all expenses."[98]

The new year saw Jacques Garvey aggressively urging blacks to rise above their dependency and to take charge of their destinies by becoming entrepreneurs. Jacques Garvey's editorials in 1926 reflected her dismay about the lack of racial productivity in that area. The February 27, 1926, editorial, "Don't Avoid, But Seek Responsibility," pointed out that the white race had advanced because of "the readiness of its individual members to shoulder responsibilities."[99] The column called the black race a "child race" and lamented that it was "the most backward, measured by the material standards of progress," because "it has been accustomed to be led by others."[100] Again, Jacques Garvey stressed her husband's and the UNIA's quest to teach blacks "the spirit of independence," and she told her readers to have faith in themselves. She believed that such faith would save the race and would "enliven" its members to stand on their own feet, instead of doing "the white man's bidding."[101]

The need to engage in commerce to build nationhood was the subject of Jacques Garvey's supplication to "learn the value of industry and commerce."[102] Despite Jim Crow and other impediments during the period, blacks were becoming educated and making advances in medicine, nursing, teaching, and other areas.[103] Jacques Garvey pointed out that it was fine to have a profession, but she believed "the basic foundation of a people's existence must be the means whereby they shall eat bread."[104] In support of this view, Jacques Garvey noted that those who were in the professions still depended on other blacks to patronize their businesses; therefore, they had little control of their livelihood.

Still preaching economic independence, Jacques Garvey asserted in October 1926, that only when the black man stopped "hunting a job" and created one would he prosper.[105] In a condescending tone, Jacques Garvey charged that blacks were "the greatest job hunters in the world."[106] The following passage reflected her complaint about the attitude of blacks toward entrepreneurship and explained why business development was necessary. She wrote:

> The opportunities for doing business does not interest him; [sic] the light of slavery being still on him, he is afraid of responsibilities and clings to the idea of working under a white man and saying, 'Thank you boss' for a pay envelope, no matter how small it is. That's the reason why the race is so poor and backward. When a people of any race cannot employ themselves [sic], they must be prepared to be dictated to by those who employ them, and subjected to their whims and fancies. Naturally white men are not going to the trouble of opening up their industries, and give Negro the best positions, nor are they disposed to build their governments for Negroes to legislate for them. Knowing the strength of the Negro race, they are not going to give them big sticks to break their heads.[107]

The familiar refrain in this editorial was that the solution rested with blacks themselves. Moving away from holding Jews as examples of entrepreneurship, Jacques Garvey explained that financier J.P. Morgan and industrialist Henry Ford were not going to assist blacks through the financial world or hire them for any of their industries. Jacques Garvey implored blacks who wanted to be bank presidents to open their own banks and "experiment" until they reached "the standard of a Morgan." As if to illustrate that the poverty of blacks should not prevent them from being entrepreneurs, Jacques Garvey observed that Ford "started out with only a few dollars" and had "worked his way up to the top—the richest man in the world."[108] The writer then asked, "why, therefore, should he make a berth for Negroes, when his own race needs his help." Returning to another ongoing theme, Jacques Garvey pointed out that there was "plenty of iron ore and coal in Africa;" and she again posed the question, "Why can't Mr. Black man go there and do for that great continent what Ford has done for America?"[109]

In this lengthy editorial, Jacques Garvey sought to educate her readers as to how self-reliance worked and why it was so important. She maintained that one race should not have to provide for another, "either industrially or economically." Instead, the race should provide for its members. A pessimistic Jacques Garvey wondered whether blacks would pick up the gauntlet when she wrote, "it remains to be seen whether they will continue to be, or will make an effort to become independent, and thereby claim the respect of their white neighbor."[110]

As she continued to write into the next year, Jacques Garvey was fervent in her desire to invigorate blacks to be self-reliant. The headline on her May 14, 1927, column, "It All Depends on You," summarized Jacques Garvey's view.[111] While the columnist advocated racial self-help and reliance at home, she also advocated racial solidarity and entrepreneurship among blacks and minorities worldwide. One editorial illustrated her concern about economic conditions in the West Indies. Jacques Garvey maintained that British control, its failure to invest in industries that benefited natives, and its discouragement of American investment robbed West Indians of their ability to find employment or earn a living. Because of such repressive practices, natives had been forced to immigrate to other countries, but popular places were beginning to bar their entrance. West Indians who remained had to pay exorbitant prices for imported goods, thereby enriching the government and further impoverishing the natives.[112]

After outlining a situation, Jacques Garvey proposed a solution. She called upon the "elected members of the legislative councils of their respective colonies" to enact laws that would encourage outside capital and local commercial ventures. She observed that tropical countries had the most delicious fruits, but because they had no jam or preserve factories, the fruit rotted on the ground. Jacques Garvey proposed that factories be built in the tropics where the natives could construct them and where jobs would be produced.

Not only was Jacques Garvey dismayed about the lack of entrepreneurial spirit and business acumen, she was chagrined that West Indian housewives, whom she said had "so much citrus fruits in their garden that even hogs refuse it," still sent to the grocery for a jar of marmalade made in England.[113] Such actions accounted for lack of achievement and economic empowerment, Jacques Garvey believed. Of the housewives, she wrote,

> They don't stop to consider that they could gather their own citrus fruits and make marmalade to be used in and out of season. They also fail to observe that oranges do not grow in England, and the fruit used in making the marmalade was bought for a small amount from some tropical country, shipped to England and preserved in factories there, then reshipped to the tropics and sold at an enormous price.[114]

Jacques Garvey, therefore, suggested that the women could "help materially by using good judgment in the regulation of their purchase for their homes."[115]

JEWISH EXAMPLE OF RACIAL SOLIDARITY AND ECONOMIC INDEPENDENCE

In seeking to motivate her fellow race members, Jacques Garvey's entreaties often cited the Jewish people as an example of an oppressed group that had risen above obstacles and elevated itself. Her writings revealed that she clearly embraced the negative stereotypes of Jews as shrewd, wealthy, money-grubbers. In an editorial titled "Will the Jews Conquer the World?," Jacques Garvey argued that Jews were not trying "to conquer the world religiously, and rule it spiritually" because they knew that "the spirit of hate would vent itself even above the ideas of Judaism."[116] Jacques Garvey stressed that the Jew had instead "shown the good sense in the choice of leadership when he chose to become the financial leader of the world. He has emancipated himself without bloodshed."[117] A few months after that editorial, Jacques Garvey related efforts to solve the "Jewish problem in Russia" by a proposal to give them a "special section" in the Ukraine. The columnist explained that blacks, unlike the Jews, could not envision a "national home," nor could they "forget their factional differences and work toward that end."[118] In what was clearly a reference to the UNIA, Jacques Garvey wrote that some people were "working with might and main" to "secure to themselves and to their posterity the independence and glory that was once their forebears."[119] May 1924 saw Jacques Garvey explaining that the "Jew employs himself," and "thinks always in terms of race," while "the Negro always thinks in terms of self."[120] The approach of the Jews allows them to conquer prejudice, Jacques Garvey wrote, while the "Negro bemoans his fate and prays to God for relief." She concluded pointedly, "God only helps those who help themselves."[121]

Jacques Garvey did not relent in invoking the stereotype of Jews when she compared blacks to them. In June, she related that New York Jews had raised more than six million dollars for a cause, and she asked what blacks were doing.[122] On September 18, 1926, Jacques Garvey used her editorial to stress the need for blacks to put themselves in a position where they could gain respect, just as Jews had done. She offered that "the wandering Jew" had compelled the "hostile Gentile" to "respect him because he monopolizes trade everywhere he goes and thereby becomes rich and dictatorial. He employs his own people and prevents them from being servants to others."[123] Jacques Garvey continued expressing her views on the differences between blacks and Jews when she noted that some Jews only went to synagogue twice a year, but went to their businesses every day. Further elaborating, Jacques Garvey maintained that Jews did not keep the Sabbath because it fell on a Saturday, "the day when Gentiles spend the most money." On the other hand, Jacques Garvey professed, "Negroes go to church every Sunday and spend the other six days of the week hunting a job. There lies the difference between a thinking and unthinking group of people."[124] The columnist urged activism as she ended her piece with the admonishment that if whites kicked blacks around in the western world, "it is all our fault."[125] She added, "we are too darn lazy, [sic] and lack the pluck and ambition that cause men of other races to go out and to make themselves independent and respected."[126]

Reflecting her animosity toward Jews, Jacques Garvey used a January 8, 1927, editorial to make yet another comparison. She equated persecution of Jews in Romania with the maltreatment of blacks, and noted that "both groups" were "wanderers without protection of a government of their own, no flag and aeroplanes."[127] Again embracing the stereotype by pointing to Jewish wealth, Jacques Garvey offered: "Yet Jews are treated better than Negroes in all countries because they control big finance and are huge producers while Negroes are poor consumers, dependent on other races for employment."[128] And Jacques Garvey criticized Jews for what she called their "opposition to African redemption."[129] She pointed out that both blacks and Jews were "striving for nationalism," and working "for their respective homelands," while "programs in Europe and lynchings in America continue to take their toll," yet "the Jew is heartless enough to persecute the Negro."[130]

Propagandizing for the Movement

The overarching theme of Jacques Garvey's editorials was economic independence via self-help and productivity as a means of overcoming white domination. Significantly, the common thread that ran through her messages was that blacks could achieve their goal of independence by adhering to the teachings of Marcus Garvey and through their involvement in the UNIA. Hence, Jacques Garvey devoted considerable space to encouraging, beseeching—almost willing—blacks to join the UNIA and to be confident in her husband's ability to lead.

She once explained that Marcus Garvey was the one person who could counter the negative stereotypes that whites had ascribed to blacks. She wrote that "white men the world over have been propagandizing that every Negro was low and good-for-nothing."[131] Even more detrimental, she added, was the fact that blacks "themselves were taught that they were only fit for servants of and that white men were their natural masters." Alluding to her husband, Jacques Garvey then offered,

> It rested with someone bold and courageous enough to launch counter propaganda to educate whites and blacks to the fact that the black man first gave civilization to the world and it is because of the sinister acts of suppression and oppression why Negroes are unable to achieve much in this age as a people.[132]

A March 3, 1924, column by Jacques Garvey noted that blacks "in every quarter of the globe" had endorsed the UNIA's objective of organizing "the scattered and dispersed members of the race and prepare them for the conflict," and were, therefore, joining the UNIA.[133] Jacques Garvey then accused the blacks who did not join the UNIA in its quest for African redemption of being "criminally negligent" of their future."[134]

Over the years, Jacques Garvey kept up a steady drumbeat for the UNIA and the movement. On January 2, 1926, Jacques Garvey asked members "to make every effort to do something real and tangible to further the work of this great organization."[135] She was concerned about the lack of involvement of UNIA members, as the following comment illustrates:

> Just to attend your local meetings and clap your hands at big moments will not get us very far, as we are now well established throughout the world, and must demonstrate our ability by deed, not words—[sic] the orator must make way for the business man, and the smart uniform must clothe a man of worth and ability, or our cause will stagnate.[136]

At this point, Garvey had been in prison for more than a year, but his wife was intent upon keeping the movement going and fending off dissenters. Pointing out that the work of the UNIA was "African redemption and Negro uplift," Jacques Garvey told readers: "Let no swell-headed egotist in your locals tell you about 'his plan' and 'his program.'"[137] She added that the only strategy was "the one laid down by Marcus Garvey." Jacques Garvey exhibited her militancy when she invited members who disagreed with Garvey to leave the UNIA. With both an invitation and a challenge, Jacques Garvey wrote,

> We will be broadminded enough to "wish him luck," and put no obstacles in his way; but when it comes to changing the UNIA into something else in order to put over some selfish scheme for personal gain, here is where we call a halt, and warn that brother that he will have trouble on his hands.[138]

In 1927, Jacques Garvey was trying to reassure followers that the Garvey Movement was still viable although her husband was still imprisoned. In her appeal for blacks to become involved in the UNIA, Jacques Garvey recognized that some blacks said they were waiting to join when the organization's troubles were over. To that she responded,

> Let us be serious with ourselves and about our future, and realize this, that the U.N.I.A. or any liberation or reform movement is bound to have troubles, because the oppressor is not going to sit quietly and allow his vicious system, out of which he grows fat, overthrown. He is bound to fight back, and in the most subtle manner. That is why leaders are framed up and imprisoned; organization officials bribed, and made to betray their trust; spies planted within the ranks and members are harassed. These opposition tactics should be expected, and the proper spirit maintained to offset them.[139]

During the years she wrote for *The Negro World*, Jacques Garvey never grew weary of promoting the UNIA as the means of helping blacks to become self-reliant. In an editorial titled "Racial Achievements," she lauded the efforts and achievements of the organization and enthused that it was "the only organized body of Negroes that employs a large number of Negroes all over the world," endeavored to go into big business, and encouraged its members to do so.[140] Moreover, Jacques Garvey believed that black women were picking up the mantra.

WRITINGS ON GENDER

Jacques Garvey's writings on gender indicated that she held black women in higher esteem than she did black men, and she believed her fellow race women were making valiant contributions to the race. Jacques Garvey's editorials revealed her deep disappointment in black men whom she believed had not taken hold of the vision espoused by Garvey and had not done enough to elevate their status. The columnist could not abide what she believed was the black male's failure to shoulder responsibility. Therefore, her editorials often praised black women while denigrating black men for not doing enough for their wives, children, and race. Overall, Jacques Garvey heaped accolades on women, regardless of race.

She felt a need to re-emphasize her views about women in December 1925. In an editorial titled "Woman's Function in Life," Jacques Garvey maintained that she was convinced that "woman, lovely woman," was making her presence "felt in every walk of life."[141] Acknowledging the ambivalence of men toward women's roles, Jacques Garvey highlighted accomplishments of women in various arenas. She wrote that eastern women were being "emancipated and educated to the point where they no longer consider themselves human incubators, and slaves to do the bidding of their husbands, but intelligent, independent human beings that assert and maintain their rights in co-partnership with their men."[142] Turkish women had cultivated their minds and had become the "most virtuous and the most serious ladies in the world," Jacques Garvey wrote.[143]

She devoted a portion of her second editorial to defending the honor of women and pointing out sexism. In highlighting sexism, Jacques Garvey criticized a judge who pointedly ignored that the two women before him had fought over a man. Straightforwardly, Jacques Garvey postulated,

> The class of women who resort to fisticuffs usually do not fight for the fun of it, nor to display their pugilistic ability, but for the ephemeral possession of some man. Magistrate Doyle instinctively knew that there was a man at the bottom of it, and in protection of his sex was "mum" on the CAUSE of the fit, but loud on the EFFECT.[144]

On another occasion, Jacques Garvey took note of the abilities of women by declaring that "no line of endeavor" remained "closed for long to the modern woman." Of the modern woman, Jacques Garvey stated,

> She agitates for equal opportunities and gets them; she makes good on the job and gains the respect of men who heretofore opposed her. She prefers to be a bread-winner [sic] than a half-starved wife at home. She is not afraid of hard work, and by being independent, she gets more out of the present-day husband than her grandmother did in the good old days.[145]

Women were successful, Jacques Garvey believed, because they were more "versatile than men," had "more staying power than the he-male," had "more charm, wit, intuition, humor, and ingenuity," and could "balance a home budget on a few dollars, and make the food 'stretch' to feed her hungry household."[146] November 27, 1926, saw Jacques Garvey reacting to a prediction that women would one day rule the world if they continued to wear scanty clothing. She rebuked the sexist comment when she suggested that if women would assume such a role, "the world would be a better place to live, for women have a conscience, while men have not, and even-handed justice will be more likely meted out."[147] Offering that women were "practicing medicine, pleading in the courts, and preaching in the pulpits," Jacques Garvey wrote a few days after Christmas in 1926 that large businesses were also adding women to their executive boards because they were realizing "that women are born to control and order things systematically and economically."[148]

Especially proud of the accomplishments of black women, Jacques Garvey was like other black women journalists and activists who highlighted the tenacity of their fellow race women. Jacques Garvey wrote in January 1926, that they had toiled on the plantation during slavery, been "subjected to vicious propensities" of the "white slave-master,"[149] worked hard after emancipation to rear children, and made sure their offspring received an education. Jacques Garvey then offered, "Look at her today, educated, independent and well-equipped along all lines to compete with her men and in many instances outclass them."[150]

Black thought in the late nineteenth and early twentieth century posited that the black woman's most valuable role was one of molding and guiding the young, who were the hope of the race. In that regard, Jacques Garvey was no different. In her initial editorials, Jacques Garvey contended that women should "be given every opportunity to develop intellectually, so that their off-spring may inherit such a quality."[151] In October 1925, she wrote, "Women of all climes and races have a great part to play in the development of their particular group as the men."[152] Such was Jacques

Garvey's conviction that she added, "Even before birth a mother can so direct her thoughts and conduct as to bring into the world either a genius or an idiot."[153] In yet another piece, Jacques Garvey described "woman power" as "love, care, and training in a home" that could mold a child's character. The columnist added that what the child "inherits from its father can be overcome or enhanced by an intelligent, disciplined mother." [154]

On the question of whether the woman should be confined to the home or enter politics, Jacques Garvey acknowledged that "rich and poor men alike"[155] were concerned that children would be neglected if women decided to do the latter. On June 14, 1924, Jacques Garvey observed that men did not realize the value of women in the home until the female decided to enter politics. Nevertheless, Jacques Garvey lauded women's entry into politics because she believed they "realized that if they remained at home and trained their children without having some knowledge of outside affairs, the children (especially the boys) would have a rude awakening on stepping out into the world."[156]

A few months later, in an editorial titled "Women as Leaders Nationally and Racially," Jacques Garvey provided reassurance for men. To those who argued that the home would "be broken up" and women would become "coarse and lose their gentle appeal" if they entered the public arena, Jacques Garvey said "everything can be done with moderation:"

> Some women are good cooks, yet because of the call to other duties they rarely ever cook a meal; but when the necessity presents itself they know how. Others were good business women, yet they would not neglect their children and homes to attend business with their husbands, but if the hubby dies or becomes incapacitated, they can fit in his place and save a situation. The doll-baby type of woman is a thing of the past and the wide-awake woman is forging ahead, prepared for all emergencies, and ready to answer any call, even if it be to face the cannons on the battlefields.[157]

Jacques Garvey also believed that the decision to enter the political arena rested solely with the individual woman, because women were "rational and reasonable enough to give as much time to the home as the exigencies of the hour demand. Woman's inherent self-sacrifice and love will influence her decision in this direction."[158] The writer took up the issue of women in the home again in July 1924, pointing out that the home and school were "the two great forces" that influenced "the minds of children" due to the mothers and teachers.[159] Jacques Garvey used her editorial to call for more money for teachers and to present opinions from three readers who agreed that teachers had tremendous influence on young people. Jacques Garvey also believed that while fathers were supposed to provide the "means of existence, women made the homes, reared the children, shaped the minds of young people, and prepared them for contact with the outside world."[160]

While consistently praising black women, Jacques Garvey sometimes compared white and black women. White women, the columnist pronounced, were "bolstering up a decaying white civilization," and "yellow and black" women were "slowly, but surely imitating them."[161] In some instances, black women often did not measure favorably, in Jacques Garvey's estimation. She once noted that a "lone white woman" had spent eleven months in Africa collecting "a wealth of information to be used by members of her race to further exploit and rob Africa."[162] Jacques Garvey then asked,

> What in the name of all that is reasonable is the matter with Negro women that they cannot return to the land of their ancestors, and cooperate [sic] with our brothers over there to realize the value of minerals and the rich products of the country?[163]

As was her practice in a significant number of editorials, Jacques Garvey admonished her fellow race of women not to wait for the black man "to carry the gospel of African nationalism," because she said black men were not going to do it.[164]

CHASTISEMENT OF BLACK MEN

Jacques Garvey's writings about gender overwhelmingly focused on the strength and accomplishments of women and the failure of black men. Hence, the latter group frequently incurred Jacques Garvey's wrath. She was incensed that black men were not living up to their potential or the expectations of the Garvey Movement. Early in 1924, she exhorted black men to "beware" of their "listless attitude toward" the progress of their race.[165] The columnist chided:

> Your women are tired of menial jobs and being abused by men of other races; your children want care and provisions made for their future if they are to live. Your race wants a first class rating according to present day standards. Your country calls. Will you answer?[166]

"Negro men," Jacques Garvey wrote in May 1925, had "contributed in a large way to the backward condition of the race by failing to provide for their children."[167] Calling black men "selfish," Jacques Garvey said that because they did not get an education or other necessities of life in their youth, they "did not worry themselves to give to their children."[168] Jacques Garvey reflected her optimism when she explained that the black race was coming into its own and that as a result, it was necessary for black men to "forget all selfish, ignorant reasoning, and think along new lines, in keeping with the progress of the age in which we live, and for the benefit of our posterity."[169]

Jacques Garvey returned to the theme in her October 1925 editorial. She maintained that white women had greater opportunities to excel because "of the standing of both races," and because black men were "less appreciative of their women than white men."[170] Jacques Garvey complained that white men "more readily" praised their women than did black men. The columnist was infuriated that black males failed to pay homage to their women, especially because she believed her race of women had persevered through slavery and had withstood "the deprivation consequent on a pauperized race and the indignities heaped upon a weak and defenseless people."[171] Jacques Garvey encouraged black women not to be troubled, despite what she perceived as the lack of initiative and the failures of black men. Resolutely, she wrote,

> A race must be saved, a country must be redeemed, and unless you strengthen the leadership of vacillating Negro men, we will remain marking time until the yellow race gains the leadership of the world, and we be forced to subserviency [sic] under them or extermination.
>
> We are tired of hearing Negro men say, "There is a better day coming," while they do nothing to usher in the day. We are becoming so impatient that we are getting in the front ranks and serve notice to the world that we will brush aside the halting, coward Negro leaders, and with prayer on our lips and arms prepared for any fray, we will press on and on until victory is ours.[172]

Stressing that the black race needed trained men, Jacques Garvey wrote in July 1926, that black men were not keeping abreast with "yellow and white races, but lingering and weak," dependent on the support of others.[173] Jacques Garvey indicated that no one had ever become "independent and respected by being a beggar, nor can anyone become powerful and strong by depending on the charity of others."[174] Charging that many blacks were "content" as long as they had something to eat, clothes to wear and somewhere to sleep, Jacques Garvey pronounced that such "lethargy" would "doom the race."[175]

Commenting that there were four hundred million blacks in the world, Jacques Garvey then queried,

> Where are our statesmen? They are the trained men we need to protect our interest in the council chambers of the people, and to direct our destiny in the mother country, [sic] where are our commercial magnates and industrial giants to secure outlets for trade and open up plants and factories to manufacture goods, and thereby provide

employment for millions of young men and women just out of school? Where are our big laboratories and experimenting stations? Where and oh, where, are our patriots, living for race and country, and ever ready to die for same if the sacrifice is required? Survey the intellectual, political and industrial groups of other races, and ask yourself if black men are measuring up to present day standards.

In April 1927, Jacques Garvey was still praising women and denouncing black men when she wrote,

> Negro women are the acknowledged burden bearers of the race. Whether this is due to the innate laziness of Negro men, or to their lack of appreciation for their noble women, we are not quite sure. Perhaps both these reasons are contribution factors, yet the results are the same—an overburdened woman hood, and a backward race. We hope our male readers will in defense of the sex supply us with a plausible excuse; that is, if they can summon enough energy to do so.[176]

In the lengthy article, Jacques Garvey expressed her concern for the men of the race. She maintained that because they lacked faith in themselves, they had to "be driven to accomplish anything." She theorized that the "oppression of slavery" had contributed to that state of mind, and Jacques Garvey asserted that, as a result, "The achievement of any Negro man can always be traced to the push and perseverance of a good woman."[177] Jacques Garvey was even more strident in that editorial as she accused the black male of having no love for his women, no incentive to achieve, and being too lazy to go out and make a job for himself. All of these factors, she declared, made the race poorer.

Just a few months before formally discontinuing her editorial and women's page, Jacques Garvey lambasted black men with the following stinging commentary:

> Negro men—who, by the way, detest any sort of responsibility—contend that the reason they do not care to become husbands is because they are not fit for the task economically. But we feel that since they make very little effort to lift themselves to the standards of economic independence, they really have not the proper appreciation or love for their women, and this is the basic reason for the low status of the race and the insults heaped on Negro women by white men.[178]

The editorial concluded with the hope that male readers, especially the younger ones, would "see the far-reaching effects of their attitude toward marriage and wives, and so act as to prevent a continuation of their existing conditions, and exhibit the sterling qualities of real manhood that go to make up a progressive race and a powerful nation."[179]

The headline on her May 14, 1927, column, "It All Depends on You," summarized Jacques Garvey's view. She often cited God in her references to self-reliance, and this time she pointed out that the black man, "God's masterpiece," had "the power to order his life according to his own likes and dislikes."[180] She elaborated,

> He can change his surroundings, his manner of dress, eating or sleeping; he can be a superman or an underdog; either a saint or a devil, [sic] like a rank weed, he can choke the growth and progress of those around him, or, like a useful tire, he can give food to the hungry . . . God gave us power and we owe it to our Maker . . . to keep us as near perfection as possible.[181]

Some Garvey scholars argue that Jacques Garvey's criticism was aimed at such black intellectuals and leaders as the NAACP's W. E. B. DuBois, whose views for racial advancement were diametrically opposed to Marcus Garvey's. While Garvey's movement appealed to and focused on the "unlettered and inexperienced Negro urban element,"[182] DuBois originated the concept of the talented tenth, which postulated that the top ten percent of the black race, by demonstrating their talents, skills, and education, would debunk the negative stereotypes of blacks and, thereby, gain for the race acceptance by and respect from whites.[183] DuBois was a vocal critic of Garvey because he believed the black nationalist's focus on economic objectives did not contribute to the total development of the race and was "bombastic and impracticable."[184] The views expressed in Jacques Garvey's editorials coincided with Marcus Garvey's opinions that DuBois and other blacks, rather than expressing pride in their race, wanted to "become white by amalgamation."[185]

Scholars also note that Jacques Garvey's disillusionment with her husband's inability to provide for her may have contributed to her castigation of black men.[186] Jacques Garvey does not mention either factor in her editorials. Rather, she compared the initiative and zeal of race women to race men, and concluded that in the majority of instances, black women were more self-reliant and were doing more to advance the race that the males.

Jacques Garvey may have had some conflict regarding her husband, as when she told the interviewer from *Ebony* magazine that her marriage to Garvey was an arrangement. Nevertheless, Jacques Garvey never criticized her husband in any of the 150 editorials examined for this chapter. Instead, she held Marcus Garvey as virtually the lone black man who had the vision and capability to lead the race of blacks throughout the world to independence. She pointed out that her husband's UNIA was "the only organized body of Negroes that employs a large number of Negroes all over the world. It is also the only organization that endeavors to go into big business and that encourages its membership to do so."[187]

Bolstering her husband while he was facing problems in attempting to make the Black Star Line successful, Jacques Garvey complained that some blacks who were "jealous, selfish and narrow" had frustrated "the noble ambition of the promoters, and forced them to suspend operations."[188] The writer complained: "Today the petty Negro traitor, guilty of this crime, boast that they caused the setback to the Black Star Line and were instrumental in having Marcus Garvey imprisoned.[189]

Jacques Garvey further blamed blacks for the role she said they played in the federal government's attempt to imprison Garvey. In an August 16, 1924, column, Jacques Garvey argued that opposition to her husband was based on his being of West Indian descent, and she charged that blacks were "moving heaven and earth to remove Marcus Garvey."[190] Calling her husband the "genius of the race," the columnist said blacks had done everything in their power "to hinder and embarrass" Garvey as he tried to implement "the program of this great organization."[191] Jacques Garvey, on a mission to bolster Garvey's reputation, continued to castigate the opposition. She wrote:

> They started with the Black Star Line, thinking thereby to convince Negroes, [sic] Marcus Garvey was a crook and a thief, but they discovered that the people will not stand for that kind of propaganda. Marcus Garvey was arraigned before the court and the world to shake from him the support of millions of Negroes whom he had lined up, and today they are using every means in pursuit of the same vindictive ends.[192]

OTHER THEMES

Undoubtedly, Jacques Garvey devoted her editorials to proselytizing against whites and for racial productivity and the goals and objectives of the Garvey Movement. Nonetheless, she sometimes inserted blurbs in her editorials about other themes. For example, in November 1926, Jacques Garvey addressed clothing styles. She noted that the modern woman was wearing "less and less clothing each year."[193] Contrary to the view of middle class black women who embraced the cult of true womanhood and stressed modesty for black women, Jacques Garvey pointed out that "scantily clad women need not be vulgar. They can be modest and innocent looking even in an abbreviated garment, while fully clad women can be suggestively vulgar."[194]

Advice for parents found its way into several editorials over the years. Jacques Garvey suggested that mothers and fathers listen to their children and fulfill a duty to them.[195] In yet another article, she queried whether family members who were away from home had written back, noting that "it is the little thoughtful acts that make us happy and bring joy to those with whom we come in contact."[196]

Despite her criticism of black men, Jacques Garvey still expressed pride in her race and in some men. In December 1923, she penned an editorial that praised Booker T. Washington and Tuskegee Institute, the school he founded. Jacques Garvey offered that Washington built the institute "on a foundation of inspiration," backed by his "courage and perseverance."[197] She asserted that Washington's faith in God and in his race enabled him to struggle against "hardships and criticisms" to produce "what is today the greatest educational centre in the country for technical and general training for Negroes."[198]

The need for black women to share their views was another theme that appeared in Jacques Garvey's columns. Because she believed so strongly in the power of black women to influence black men, throughout the years, Jacques Garvey invited women to let their voices be heard. She provided the pages of *The Negro World* as their forum. On August 2, 1924, Jacques Garvey appealed to all black women to send their views in English, French, and Spanish. She wrote that expressions from the women would "help the race materially" and inspire "our men" who read of "our lofty ideals and aims."[199] In September, Jacques Garvey appealed to women to send in their contributions. She noted that the newspaper had allotted a page to the women to give them an opportunity to express their views on all questions affecting the home and public life. Jacques Garvey had an even nobler goal, for she believed the contributions would also "enlighten other races of the merits of black womanhood."[200] Again in February 1926, Jacques Garvey asked women to send in their articles.[201]

CONCLUSION

Jacques Garvey's editorials afforded a unique analytic opportunity to gain insight into another aspect of the Garvey Movement by one of its premiere unsung proponents, and they provided perspective on the role and voice of a segment of the black press during the early 1920s. The more than one hundred fifty editorials analyzed in this chapter indicate that Jacques Garvey raised the consciousness of blacks on social and economic issues that impacted their human dignity and well being. She placed the black experience for the black masses in context by providing lessons on world affairs and insight into the negative impact of international activities on blacks and people of color worldwide. Calling for a oneness of blacks, she crafted messages that beseeched, chastised, encouraged, demanded—almost willed—that blacks worldwide act in their race's interest and rely on themselves to achieve racial freedom. In providing courses of action for her readers, she challenged blacks to have pride in their race and to look toward Africa for their future. She argued that black empowerment could only occur by bringing together American blacks, Caribbean people and Africans.

Believing, as did her husband, that white people would never treat blacks as equal, Jacques Garvey trusted no white people and affixed the label of imperialists and exploiters to the United States and European countries. In addition, she negatively stereotyped Jews as she held them up as an example of racial productivity and accomplishments. In this respect, she came from a different ideological position than the black press and other black activists of her day that fostered interracial cooperation as an avenue of black empowerment. Jacques Garvey's racial ideologies centered on detachment from anything American in favor of repatriation to Africa. Therefore, her editorials mainly ignored what was happening in the United States—Jim Crow, lynching, disfranchisement—while focusing exclusively on Pan-Africanism. It may be surmised that her reason for not placing those issues on the agenda for her readers and for not seeking changes at home to better their conditions was her desire for blacks to turn to her husband and his movement to ameliorate their plight.

Jacques Garvey advocated on behalf of blacks. Like other black women journalists, she sought to elevate her race and gender, albeit, through a different path. Her editorials were informative, persuasive, insightful, bold, and at times, uplifting. Although her tone was often harsh, critical, and even demeaning, Jacques Garvey endeavored to convey the values of the Garvey Movement as she shared her opinions, urged, enlightened, and educated her race. With an urgency, fierceness, and militancy, she challenged blacks to take charge of their lives; and she pointed out that a race that did not have the means to create employment was, therefore, always dependent upon others.

In sum, this chapter revealed that Jacques Garvey was a journalist who used straightforward, unadorned language to report on and convey the values and racial ideologies of a major movement in this country during an especially dark period in black history. As she instructed, cajoled and criticized, she articulated the Black Nationalism view that had been defined as "a loss of hope in America."[202]

CHAPTER SIX

Synthesis

The preceding chapters have presented an overview of the journalistic careers of four black women who wrote for newspapers, magazines, and other media during the late nineteenth century. All of the women wrote at the beginning of the twentieth century, and Mary Church Terrell wrote well into the twentieth century. With the goal of lifting the veil of obscurity and placing these women into journalism history, I have looked at the lives of the women, the publications for which they wrote, their audiences, and the themes in their writings within the context of the period in which they lived.

My research leaves no doubt that these women were journalists, despite their prior invisibility in journalism literature. Collectively, they worked for dozens of black publications, owned newspapers, were editors, correspondents, columnists, and editorial writers. Ida B. Wells-Barnett, Mary Church Terrell, and Alice Dunbar-Nelson wrote for and submitted articles and letters to white publications, while Amy Jacques Garvey did not.

Thus far, I have focused on the women individually. I found that while the women were alike in many ways, and although all of them used journalism to bring about racial solidarity, racial self-reliance, race pride, and an end to discrimination, Wells-Barnett, Terrell, Dunbar-Nelson, and Jacques Garvey were not monolithic in their ideology or their approaches to accomplishing their objectives. I now look at the women as a group and examine the commonalities among the women, common threads that ran through their lives and journalism careers, and the extent to which the women differed on issues and other factors that affected blacks. Moreover, I present how the women, through their writings, shaped black thought and had an impact on history.

Common Threads

Perhaps the greatest common denominator was the state of the black race in America during the periods in which the women lived and worked. The period I covered in this book included the last two decades of the nineteenth century through the Civil Rights era in the twentieth century. Continuing efforts to turn back the gains blacks had made during Reconstruction defined the last decades of the nineteenth century. During the early decades of the new century, racial segregation became the law of the land. The post-World War I years also witnessed the dashing of black expectations after the soldiers returned from the battlefields to face racism at home. Later years saw more of the same for blacks.

Nevertheless, race members exhibited a spirit of agitation and protest as they sought to hold on to the rights they had won after slavery. Many became involved in seminal movements that included the Great Migration of blacks from the South to the North, the cultural and literary awakening of the Harlem Renaissance, and Marcus Garvey's black liberation quest. Although vastly different, the movements were the vehicles through which blacks sought to improve their lot.

Patricia Hill Collins wrote in her book on black feminist thought that the position of the race in the political economy shaped black women's subordination and their activism.[1] The four women in this study did not allow the dominant society, racism, sexism, or other impediments to subjugate them. Instead, they became activists.

The black press was a medium that helped to shape black thought by serving as a vehicle of protest and elevation for blacks during the decades I addressed in this study. As consummate racial activists, these black women journalists promoted their views primarily through the black press. Wells-Barnett and Dunbar-Nelson wrote during the 1890s through the 1930s. Terrell began to write during the last decade of the nineteenth century and continued almost until her death in 1954. Jacques Garvey wrote mainly during the 1920s. Together, the women made the press their bully pulpit.

Historians have noted that black women played an active role in the struggle for black liberation during the late nineteenth century and into the twentieth century. Wells-Barnett, Terrell, Dunbar-Nelson, and Jacques Garvey were not merely participants in that fight, they were vocal leaders. They not only reacted to, but they were in the forefront of precipitating actions aimed at ending discrimination, lynching, segregation, and other conditions that negatively affected their race and gender. Like other black women activists, the four women I studied were involved in labor, religious, political, and social spheres.

They enlightened readers about what it meant to be black, female, and black females in America. Their writings conveyed to a downtrodden race the need to seek to improve its position in society, live moral and upstanding lives, to seek an education, be self-reliant, and work together toward accomplishing goals of racial, political, and social equality. Moreover, through their columns and articles, Wells-Barnett, Terrell, Dunbar-Nelson, and Jacques Garvey told white America and the world that blacks had made contributions to both their country and the world. They told their readers that blacks should be treated fairly. They told the world that black women were not sexually promiscuous, but were wives, mothers, leaders, and examples of true womanhood. The women journalists told the world about the accomplishments of the race as well as of individual race members. In doing so, the journalists corrected the misrepresentation of blacks and gave them a feeling of pride.

The writings of these women had an impact on American society. For example, Wells-Barnett's muckraking exposes were the impetus for anti-lynching legislation. Jacques Garvey's newspaper and editorials helped the Marcus Garvey Movement to galvanize thousands, perhaps millions, of blacks. Terrell's and Dunbar-Nelson's articles about black involvement and accomplishments in the arts, society, and travel provided a view of the race that the dominant society did not commonly hold. With the press as their vehicle, and through lecturing extensively, Wells-Barnett, Terrell, Dunbar-Nelson, and Jacques Garvey were militant agitators for the race. They not only were the voices of blacks; they also gave blacks a voice.

As did many black women of the period, all of the journalists in this study had dual roles. Wells-Barnett, Terrell, and Dunbar-Nelson were mothers, teachers, lecturers, wives, community activists, and members of the black elite. Although consummate activists who were involved in a whirlwind of activities, the women took their role as wives and family members seriously. Jacques Garvey had no children during the period explored in this study; hence, I do not discuss her role as a mother. Wells-Barnett postponed her education to help raise her siblings, and she gave up her active public work while her children were young. When she resumed her activities and as she traveled, a nanny often accompanied her with the children. Dunbar-Nelson cared for her mother and sister who lived with her for most of their lives, while also tending to her children and stepchildren. Terrell's economic status allowed her to have attendants that included nannies and housekeepers.[2]

There is no indication that Jacques Garvey considered herself a member of the black middle class, although her parents were part of the Jamaican educated and propertied class. The Garvey Movement disavowed all semblance of a black class system, and instead shaped its message to appeal to blacks of lower socio-economic status. Terrell was born to wealth and status, and her marriage to Robert Terrell, a highly educated and influential attorney, activist, and public official, further ensconced her as a leader in the black upper class. Although Dunbar-Nelson was considered a part of the middle class, her diaries indicated that she faced a constant struggle of balancing her budget and keeping afloat financially. Dunbar-Nelson "had the breeding, education, culture, looks, and manners of the 'higher classes' (and thought of herself in this way), but . . . none of the money to back it up," [3] according to the editor of her diary. Wells-Barnett was always near poverty early in her life, but her marriage to businessman and attorney F. L. Barnett elevated her financially. Jacques Garvey struggled financially in her personal life, as did the UNIA, the organization her husband formed and she helped to guide.

All of the women except Jacques Garvey attended college. Terrell and Dunbar-Nelson studied at the post-baccalaureate level. Wells-Barnett, who never graduated from college, constantly sought to educate herself by becoming an avid reader and availing herself of college courses and those offered in the communities in which she taught. I uncovered no evidence that Jacques Garvey received any formal education after she came to the United States, yet her editorials conveyed that she had as strong a grasp of issues and world affairs, not unlike the other women.

Black women who lived during the late nineteenth century and early twentieth century had few avenues of employment available to them beyond teaching. Hence, while educated and qualified for many fields of endeavor, Terrell and Dunbar-Nelson became teachers. Wells-Barnett, likewise, taught for many years before becoming a full-time journalist. Jacques Garvey did not teach, but like the other women, she educated the masses of black people through her writings.

Wells-Barnett, Terrell, Dunbar-Nelson, and Jacques Garvey were fiercely independent. None of them allowed the Jim Crow practices in the country to prevent them from giving a voice to blacks, seeking to correct the misrepresentations of the race, or advocating on behalf of blacks. They did not shy away from being vocal race and gender advocates, in that order. Just as Wells-Barnett had brought suit against discriminatory practices in public transportation, Terrell, later in her life, also looked to the courts as she successfully spearheaded the campaign to end segregation in public eating places in Washington, D.C.[4] As Wells-Barnett had chronicled her case with accounts in the press, so, too, did Terrell use journalism to aid her cause, as her letters to the editor of the *Washington Post* illustrated. Similarly, through her lectures and columns, Dunbar-Nelson was like Wells-Barnett and Terrell in criticizing Jim Crow and racial injustice.

All of these women except Dunbar-Nelson pointed to the influential role their fathers played in shaping their views of the world, yet Dunbar-Nelson and Jacques Garvey, at times, wrote disparagingly about black men.

Jacques Garvey credited her father with helping her to understand world affairs and to think critically by discussing articles in the Sunday newspapers with her. Wells-Barnett noted that Jim Wells was a racial, political, social, and educational activist. Moreover, Wells-Barnett explained how her father set up his own business rather than do the bidding of his white boss. Likewise, in her autobiography, Terrell related that her father was shot simply because he was a black businessman. Terrell also gave an account of how Robert Church stood up for her on a train when the conductor tried to remove her from a coach because she was a black.

There is no doubt that these and other instances of discrimination shaped the women's ideology, their worldview, and led them to become activists. This was especially the case with Wells-Barnett and Terrell, whose careers ran parallel courses. Wells-Barnett, as a very young woman, reacted in a manner similar to Robert Church when a conductor told her to leave a first class railroad car. Defiantly, she refused to move and sued the Chesapeake Ohio Railroad because she was ejected from the coach. The train incidents planted the seeds of advocacy for both Wells-Barnett and Terrell. However, for both Wells-Barnett and Terrell, the lynching of one man, Thomas Moss, precipitated their activist zeal. Such was the effect of the lynching on them that both women wrote about it in their diaries and autobiographies. Moss's death led Wells-Barnett to launch the anti-lynching campaign through her exposes in the press, and the lynching convinced Terrell to give up her life of leisure to work on behalf of her race.

The manner in which these women in this study interacted with whites also may have stemmed from their early contact and relationships with caucasians. Both Wells-Barnett and Terrell recalled vividly the white slave owners who had fathered their parents. In page one of her autobiography, Terrell remembered fondly the regular Sunday visits she and Robert Church made to Captain C. B. Church, noting that he "always welcomed me cordially to his beautiful home, would pat me on the head affectionately, and usually filled my little arms with fruits and flowers when I left."[5] Despite racism she faced during her life, the visits and Captain Church's relationship with her father had a lasting impact on Terrell, for she wrote decades later, "as for myself, I simply adored him."[6] Terrell's belief in the innate goodness of some whites may also have stemmed from the example Captain Church set. Terrell knew that he sent her father to work on his merchant ships rather than allow Robert to work on the plantation. She also recollected a conversation that she and her father had during which he explained that Captain Church had always been kind to him, had raised him from a baby, taught him to defend himself, and told him that he would always stand by him.[7]

Wells-Barnett also acknowledged in her autobiography that her grandfather had treated her father better than the other slaves. But she could not forget that his widow, Miss Polly, had ordered Peggy Wells, Jim's mother, stripped and whipped on the very day the master died. According to Wells-Barnett, although her grandmother had forgiven Miss Polly, Jim Wells refused the woman's request that he visit her during her old age and declared that he was never going to forgive her for what she had done. Jim Wells stated that Miss Polly "could have starved to death" if he had his "say-so."[8]

Although Terrell never forgot the experience of her fellow classmates laughing at her because she was black, she was able to move beyond those experiences to work cooperatively with whites. Terrell wrote in her autobiography that she did not forget the slight she felt when her teachers slated her to be a character who "killed the king's English,"[9] in the school production, although Terrell was one of the most articulate and intelligent students at the school. Seared in Terrell's memory also was the laughter of her white schoolmates who ridiculed her because of her skin color.[10] Because Terrell was committed to interracial cooperation, she used diplomacy and tolerance to accomplish her aims. Wells-Barnett found little room for diplomacy in her dealings with whites—or blacks. She was like her father in her unwillingness to forgive and forget.

Virulent racism in the South and political, economic, and social discrimination throughout the nation spurred Wells-Barnett, Terrell, and Dunbar-Nelson to activism. For Jacques Garvey, racism in America was less a focus than what she believed was the exploitation of weak and dark people by the United States and European countries. Her desire to expose and fight against imperialism was the impetus for Jacques Garvey's agitation.

Some of the women suffered negative consequences because of their criticism and their activism. Wells-Barnett was fired from her teaching job after she wrote articles about discrimination in the Memphis public school system. Similarly, Dunbar-Nelson was not rehired to her teaching job at Howard High School in Delaware after she traveled to Marion, Ohio, to participate in Social Justice Day activities. Dunbar-Nelson wrote in her diary on Saturday, October 1, 1928, that her participation "started consequences in Wilmington" that would "take years to obliterate and changed the course"[11] of her life. Wells-Barnett's newspaper office was destroyed and her life was threatened after her scathing editorials that followed the lynching of Moss and his business partners. However, there is no indication that Terrell faced reprisal as a result of any of her activities or writings. It does not appear that Jacques Garvey experienced retribution for the scathing condemnations she made or because of her worldview. A contributory dynamic may have been that Jacques Garvey largely denounced whites worldwide rather than individuals or specific institutions in America. These women held American government, institutions, and individuals accountable for social injustices. Moreover, Jacques Garvey's advocacy of black repatriation to Africa may have also been embraced, although not publicly, by the larger society. Hence, they simply ignored her pronouncements. The other three women wanted equality for blacks, as well as interracial cooperation. Jacques Garvey wanted nothing from American society. Therefore, America rebuked two of these agitators, while ignoring or willingly sparing the other two.

Gender Issues

Their writings reflected that the four women were overwhelmingly alike in their views of black women. Their ideology was apparent in their writings, for none of the women placed gender above race. Their views coincided with beliefs of other middle class black women of the period while in sharp contrast with those of the dominant society. Scholars such as Gloria Wade-Gayles argued that "according to nineteenth century racist definitions, black women were inferior members of the sex whom God himself had colored a distasteful hue and imbued with insatiable sexuality, phenomenal strength and limited intelligence."[12]

Historians and other scholars who have written about nineteenth-century black women maintain that the black press and many black activists established that black women conformed to a strict moral code and aspired to be noble and refined, just as white women of the same standing adhered to the cult of true womanhood.[13] Hull explained that Dunbar-Nelson "was conservative, stiff, uptight, and accommodationist" as "part of the attempt to counter negative racial stereotypes and put the best racial foot forward."[14] Like the other middle class and activist women, Dunbar-Nelson was "always mindful of their need to be living refutations of the sexual slurs to which black women were subjected, and, at the same time, as much as white women, were also tyrannized by the still-relevant cult of true womanhood," Hull wrote.[15] Dorothy Sterling maintained that activist black women "who worked with whites were caught between two worlds. Only a generation or two removed from slavery themselves, hemmed in by the same discriminatory laws that poor blacks faced, they nevertheless strove to live up to the standards of their white associates."[16] Wells-Barnett, Terrell, Dunbar-Nelson, and Jacques Garvey not only fit Hull's and Sterling's paradigm, they used their writings to convey that black women were moral, decent, educated, and refined. Moreover, despite the twin obstacles of racism and sexism, the four women were like fellow black women activists Adella Hunt Logan, Charlotte Forten, Francis Watkins Harper, and others whom Paula Giddings argued "asserted their spirit in social and economic matters"[17] that also included protection of their families, protection of their daughters from continuing exploitation by white men, and building community institutions and church and civic organizations.[18]

They sought to counter the negative perceptions of black women while defining their roles as not only essential to the race, but as leaders in the home and public arena. The journalists wrote about black women in glowing terms, using such words as "woman, lovely women,"[19] as Jacques Garvey did, or calling them "the backbone of the world,"[20] as Dunbar-Nelson did. Terrell devoted columns and articles to highlighting the work of clubwomen, as did Dunbar-Nelson, although to a lesser extent. Jacques Garvey filled several columns with accolades to black women, and her editorials credited her fellow race sisters for the progress the black race was making and would make to the Marcus Garvey Movement and to black women, in that order. In writing about the progress of black women, the four journalists often attributed the race's successes in social reform, in the home, and in the workplace to their fellow race sisters. They argued through their articles and columns for universal suffrage, and they traveled throughout the country to seek enfranchisement for their sex, despite racism in the white woman suffrage movement.[21] Both Terrell and Wells-Barnett took their messages and causes to Europe.

In their writings about gender, Jacques Garvey and Dunbar-Nelson expressed similar sentiments about black males. Dunbar-Nelson primarily criticized black men for their views on suffrage, their political ineffectiveness, and their preoccupation with trivial matters that in no way affected the race. Jacques Garvey focused on what she saw as the failure of black men to be productive and liberate their race. Dunbar-Nelson's diaries indicated that she experienced financial troubles throughout both of her marriages. Likewise, scholars suggest that Jacques Garvey was left to fend for herself during the years she was married to Garvey.[22]

Disappointment in their spouses may have contributed to the negative portrayals that Dunbar-Nelson, sometimes, and Jacques Garvey, often, conveyed in their writings about and to black men. Both women criticized black men who congregated on street corners in idleness while their wives worked. However, historian Jacqueline Jones wrote in 1985 that the societal structure of the time, which limited availability of work to blacks, especially black men, created such a phenomenon.[23] Jones pointed out that black women in urban areas who "were their families" only providers, found relatively steady employment as domestic servants and laundresses. Noting that black men "were deprived of the satisfaction of providing for their families with a reliable source of income,"[24] Jones explained that black males were hired "sporadically for specific contract jobs." This practice "guaranteed husbands and sons low wages and long periods of enforced idleness," Jones argued.[25]

The journalistic writings of Wells-Barnett and Terrell, both of whom were affluent and soundly ensconced in the black middle class, coincided with the characterization that Jones made. They did not communicate the same view of black males that Jacques Garvey continually offered. Terrell, indeed, praised black men and often explained the obstacles they faced as they tried to thread the rocky terrain that was America during the time. Terrell wrote several articles about blacks who assumed white identities in order to obtain jobs but were terminated when their racial backgrounds were revealed. The journalist elaborated on cases where blacks who had obtained education and special skills were refused employment. All of these women, likewise, addressed the low wages and menial jobs that even highly trained men had to take. Therefore, any criticism of black men may have reflected the frustration that black women felt as they pushed their race men to be more aggressive in seeking remedies to their economic and social plight.

Differing Perspectives and Approaches

While these women journalists agreed on gender issues, and although they wrote primarily about racial issues, they differed in their approaches to tackling the race problem in the United States. Their writings, both in tone and content, often reflected those differences. It is important to note that one of the objectives of this book was to explore the themes the women addressed. To do that, race and gender became specific categories for examination. Those two groupings were expanded to reflect specific interests or concerns. Hence, the thematic groupings in the chapters are not uniform, although race was the common thread that ran through all of these women's writings.

Themes in Terrell's and Dunbar-Nelson's writings were more multidimensional than those of Wells-Barnett and Jacques Garvey. Terrell and Dunbar-Nelson not only wrote about racial issues, politics, and economics; they also covered the arts, society, and travel. Wells-Barnett's articles focused primarily on anti-lynching. Jacques Garvey's dealt overwhelming with white exploitation, racial productivity or lack thereof, the need for blacks to own businesses to eventually attain self-sufficiency, and black repatriation to Africa as the means to obtain economic independence and, ultimately, nationhood.

Scholars identify Wells-Barnett as a militant, defiant agitator. Those categorizations also fit the other women, for all of them protested, chastised, criticized, and agitated on behalf of blacks. The tone of their protest, however, sometimes differed. But, Jacques Garvey was much more strident than the other women in this study. For example, Wells-Barnett, Terrell, and Dunbar-Nelson castigated whites and the dominant political and social structure in America. While Wells-Barnett sometimes criticized the black race for its inactivity on certain issues, both she and Terrell more often offered encouragement to blacks. Wells-Barnett produced a stream of anti-lynching literature in which she castigated whites for their failure to condemn or halt the barbaric practice. She did not blame blacks for their situation, yet she did not shy away from criticizing race members and leaders. She leveled criticism on black ministers, politicians, and business owners. Wells-Barnett condemned Booker T. Washington for his emphasis on industrial education for blacks, and she parted ways with W.E.B. DuBois and the NAACP for what she perceived as their slowness to advance the cause of blacks.[26] In contrast, Jacques Garvey attacked whites in America and Europe for what she called their exploitation of weaker countries, especially African countries.

Nonetheless, Wells-Barnett more often than not laid blame for the plight of blacks squarely at the feet of whites. On the other hand, Jacques Garvey focused her criticism not just on the white imperialists, but also consistently on the black race for what she called its lethargy and black men for what she called their laziness and slothfulness. While, Wells-Barnett reserved her harshest tones for whites, Jacques Garvey appeared equally strident when referring to whites and when writing to and about blacks.

Another difference between the women was evident in the emphasis they placed on the South in their writings. While Wells-Barnett, Terrell, and Dunbar-Nelson, all born in the South, leveled harsh criticism at the region. However, only one of Jamaican-born Jacques Garvey's editorials contained references to Jim Crow, the South, or discrimination in America.

Although Jacques Garvey began her writing career decades later than the other three women began, all of the women were writing during the 1920s, when Jim Crow was the accepted law of the land and practiced with impunity in the South. Jacques Garvey also differed from the other women in the degree to which she stressed economic issues in her writings. Economic independence, Jacques Garvey believed, was the *only* way for blacks to elevate themselves. In seeking to motivate blacks to be self-reliant and to establish their own businesses, Jacques Garvey displayed a lack of understanding or a refusal to acknowledge the constraints that prevented blacks during the 1920s from being successful in business. In all of her editorials except one, Jacques Garvey blamed black people for the dearth of black businesses. She singled out the black press, black ministers, and the black masses. Several of her editorials told blacks to stop seeking jobs and create them.

While Jacques Garvey leveled criticism at blacks, and only highlighted their achievements in two of the one hundred and fifty editorials reviewed for this study, the other women devoted many columns and articles to the accomplishments of the black race and individual members of the race. Terrell saw it as one of her missions to correct the misrepresentation of her race, and she, therefore, submitted articles on black achievement to both the black and white press. Dunbar-Nelson did the same. Wells-Barnett's articles on lynching debunked the myth of black male immorality as the need for lynching. Jacques Garvey did not focus as much attention to misrepresentation of blacks, because Garveyists did not care what whites thought about blacks. Instead, Garveyists believed that blacks should have a country of their own "where they should be given the fullest opportunity to develop politically, socially, and industrially."[27]

While Jacques Garvey's editorials reflected that view, on two occasions she addressed misrepresentation of blacks. In one editorial, she used words almost identical to those used by Terrell when she wrote about the attitude of the white press toward blacks. Terrell wrote in her autobiography that the mainstream press ran stories that portrayed blacks as bums and hoodlums, while refusing to run articles that showed blacks in a positive way. Jacques Garvey expressed the same sentiment in a November 18, 1924, editorial. She said, despite the fact that freed black people had "been taking advantage of every opportunity to measure up to the standards of other men in science, art, literature," it was "not the policy of white people to give publicity to the achievements of Negroes."[28] Sounding like Terrell, Jacques Garvey wrote, "On the contrary the most colorful articles are written about the failings of a single Negro, and the race suffers because of such exaggerated tales."[29] Two years later, Jacques Garvey wrote about the "efficiently organized and highly financed . . . anti-negro propaganda"[30] that white newspapers expressed. Again sounding like Terrell, Jacques Garvey added that the newspapers' "method" was "to portray the Negro as a rapist, thief, gambler," and "for these deeds he gets a front page location and glaring headlines."[31]

Jacques Garvey accused blacks of being content as long as they had a place to eat and sleep, and Wells-Barnett, soon after the East St. Louis riot, told blacks not to be content to march and protest, as they so often did. Dunbar-Nelson also implied that blacks were overwhelmingly concerned with symbolism rather than issues that affected the welfare of the race—such as when race members complained about not being mentioned in a presidential state of the union message. Again, I discovered no instance in which Terrell criticized her race. As noted, she illustrated how blacks were successful, despite obstacles. Terrell even used herself as an example when she wrote about the tactics she employed to purchase a home despite the fact the white realtors were not showing her the type of residence she wanted.[32]

The women's views on interracial cooperation revealed a significant difference in approaches to solving the race problem. Wells-Barnett, Terrell, and Dunbar-Nelson believed such cooperation was necessary, and they worked with whites to bring about changes in American society. Wells-Barnett may not have been successful with her anti-lynching crusade without the cooperation she obtained from whites in England. Terrell and Dunbar-Nelson were members of interracial committees. All three worked with white women in the woman suffrage movement. In contrast, Jacques Garvey believed that whites worldwide would never accept blacks. Hence, interracial cooperation could never exist. Jacques Garvey articulated the view that blacks should be proud of their race and their color; therefore, she detested the practice of blacks passing for whites. Conversely, as has been noted in this chapter, Terrell explained why blacks engaged in the practice.

Jacques Garvey made only fleeting references to morality, suffrage, or politics in her writings. Instead, economic independence and the means to accomplish it dominated her writings. In keeping with the Garvey doctrine, Garvey believed and wrote that the condition of the race hinged not on politics or social factors, but on her race members' lack of economic independence, which in turn was caused by their lack of motivation, vision, and failure to embrace Garveyism.[33] Therefore, Jacques Garvey continually pointed out that a race that did not have the means to create employment was always dependent upon others for its livelihood and survival.

Jacques Garvey rarely mentioned black society, and when she did, it was in negative terms. For example, in August 1925, she criticized what she labeled the "class of 'want-to-be' Negroes one finds everywhere."[34] Jacques Garvey said that blacks who believed themselves unworthy bleached their skins, straightened their hair, and tried to look like whites in order to get better jobs or be admitted to "moneyed circles."[35] She called such actions a "slavish concept."[36] Those words illustrated the tone Jacques Garvey used in her editorials. While she urged her race to be proud, the tone and language she used demeaned the black race. The beginning of the chapter on Jacques Garvey related her comment that her husband sought to whip the black race out of its lethargy. The tone of Jacques Garvey's editorial indicated that she, too, shared in her husband's mission. Contrary to Jacques-Garvey's views, the other women in this study clearly believed that full participation in the political and economic life of America was essential for black progress in America. As activists, they worked toward those ends. As journalists, they wrote about those goals. Therefore, although Dunbar-Nelson and Wells-Barnett sometimes criticized the race, they did so less stridently.

Unlike both Wells-Barnett and Jacques Garvey, and even Terrell, to some extent, Dunbar-Nelson appeared to have avoided situations that might have alienated whites—although she chastised them in her columns. The September 1928, entry in her diary provided a glimpse of her thought process. Dunbar-Nelson wrote that she refused to advise her former pupil who had become the first black lawyer in Delaware. According to Dunbar-Nelson, the young man had sought her input regarding whether he should continue to work for someone who might have required him to compromise his "own soul"[37] or renounce his ideals. Dunbar-Nelson offered:

"Told him that was something he would have to fight out for himself. Don't want old man Redding thinking I have interfered in his affairs." This former teacher and mentor further acknowledged, without a hint of regret, that her husband admonished her by saying that the "boy came to his old teacher asking for bread" and she "gave him a stone."[38]

RELATIONSHIPS AND INTERACTION

The four women worked toward similar goals and used comparable avenues to accomplish their aims. Nevertheless, I unearthed no evidence that Wells-Barnett, Terrell, Dunbar-Nelson, and Jacques Garvey collaborated on issues or formed cohesive relationships with each other. All of the women lectured extensively, however, they did not appear to do so cooperatively or in the same locales. Although they wrote for some of the same publications, I located no evidence that they ever conferred with each other on issues they addressed in those organs or others.

The black club women movement, with its aim of uplift and assistance to less fortunate blacks, was an avenue through which the women could have formed personal and professional bonds. To some extent, that occurred when Dunbar-Nelson, at Terrell's request, supplied columns for *National Notes*, the NACW's official organ. However, Wells-Barnett and Terrell did not have an amicable relationship, even as both pursued almost identical activist agendas. Linda McMurry, who did exhaustive research on Wells-Barnett, characterized the relationship between the two women as a rivalry.[39] Wells-Barnett's biography indicated that she was alienated from Terrell and other women.[40] As a young woman in Memphis, Wells-Barnett respected Terrell,[41] and as Well-Barnett was embarking on her anti-lynching crusade, Terrell introduced her when she spoke in Washington, D.C.[42] Believing Terrell blocked her election to the presidency of the NACW in 1899,[43] Wells-Barnett called the woman's failure to put her on the program "a staggering blow," that was hard to understand "because it was the woman whom I started in club work, and to whom I had given all the assistance in my power."[44] Terrell, according to McMurry, "considered Wells-Barnett an ingrate" who "claimed to be a friend." Furthermore, Terrell confided to friends that she had done "everything" she could "for that lady when she had very few friends."[45] Terrell had been among the women who honored Wells-Barnett when she moved to New York from Memphis. Moreover, Terrell's father, Robert Church, had given money to a struggling Wells when she was a teacher in Memphis.[46]

Despite the friction between the two women, I found no instance in which Wells-Barnett wrote or spoke derogatorily of Terrell. On the contrary, Wells-Barnett referred to Terrell in several places in her diary. She took note of Terrell's background, pointing out that Terrell was a graduate of Oberlin, had married a prominent attorney, and was considered "to be one of the most highly educated woman we had in the race."[47] Even when referring to the incident at the NACW convention, Wells-Barnett did not speak harshly of Terrell. Wells-Barnett indicated that the incident "seemed to kill" Terrell's influence, and that it "was a great loss, because Mrs. Terrell was by all odds the best educated women among us."[48]

Dunbar-Nelson also appeared to hold Terrell in high esteem. She thought enough of Terrell to write in her diary that she had seen her at a meeting and that "Mrs. T" was "in close and earnest confab with J. W. J. [James Weldon Johnson]"[49] of the NAACP. Jacques Garvey never mentioned Terrell or any of the other women in her writings. In fact, her editorials and other works gave no indication that she ever interacted with the three other journalists.

Differing Strategies

Although the four women journalists were much like other black women activists of the period, their strategies and tactics diverged. In writing about southern black women activists, Gilmore pointed out that they successfully adapted "progressive programs to their own purposes, even while they chose tactics that left them invisible in the political process."[50] Arguing that the women's "invisibility was often deliberate," Gilmore further stated that "black women reformers depended on their not being seen at all by whites who would thwart their programs and not being seen as political by whites who would aid them."[51] Furthermore, they "used their invisibility to construct a web of social services and civic institutions that remained hidden from view and therefore unthreatening to whites."[52]

The four women journalists and activists in this book, likewise, formed networks that established kindergartens, homes for delinquent girls, health and civic programs, and a host of similarly progressive programs. While Jacques Garvey shunned the club women movement, as one of the guiding forces in the UNIA, she, too, was involved in a similar network to elevate her race. Hence, although Gilmore's characterization may be applicable to southern women and to other women activists, it is not reflective of the black women journalists profiled here. These women were not invisible, nor did they seek to be. Their journalism assured them visibility. They used it as a means of accomplishing the same ends about which Gilmore wrote, to advocate for blacks, and significantly, to highlight the work that black women were doing through a host of voluntary organizations.

Gilmore also maintained that black women reformers were successful because while white political leaders "kept their eyes on black men's political presence, black women organized and plotted an attack just outside of their field of vision."[53] Whites' preoccupation with keeping the black man in his place may have, indeed, cleared the way for the black women in this study to not only write, but to speak as they pleased. It should be further noted that the women, even after suffering repercussions such as being fired from their jobs, or having their businesses destroyed, continued to write, speak, and engage in other activities aimed at racial progress.

Moreover, these four journalistic activists, rather than trying to appear apolitical, were very much involved in the political process. Wells-Barnett, Terrell, and Dunbar-Nelson met with United States presidents, campaigned for candidates, and wrote about politics. Clearly, their ideological perspective was one of activism as opposed to gradualism.

In sum, the aim of this book has not been to make heroes of these women, although published works about them have sometimes recognized them in this manner. The goal here has been to authenticate the women as journalists and to posit that they should be acknowledged as such. All of the women lived during dark years for blacks in this country. During their lifetime, the racial order consigned blacks to second-class citizenship, yet the work of these pioneering journalists assured that the country knew about the injustices against the race. Without their efforts, lynching may have continued, black people may never have achieved pride in their race or confidence in themselves, and black women may not have been included when women won the right to vote with passage of the Nineteenth Amendment.

Hence, although Wells-Barnett, Terrell, Dunbar-Nelson, and Jacques Garvey differed in style and sometimes in substance and ideology, they were journalists and activists who used their pens and their voices to champion causes, call attention to the ills in society, elevate their race, and bring about change in American society. These women performed the functions of the press of their day. Their writings informed, entertained, educated, advocated, and persuaded generations of blacks—and whites—during the late nineteenth century and well into the twentieth century.

Paula Giddings noted that in striving against both racism and sexism, black women in the nineteenth century "became the lynchpin between two of the most important social reform movements in American history: the struggle for black rights and women's rights."[54] The black women journalists in this book were among the women leaders about whom Giddings wrote. Their roles as newspaper owners and editors, reporters, columnists, and writers qualified them to join the ranks of journalists, yet they are obscure in journalism history. Scholars who study African-American, women, and journalism history maintain that racism and sexism account for black women's invisibility in history. That, of course, is the case. However, the absence of the women in this book from journalism may also derive from the fact that, except for Wells-Barnett, they did not perceive themselves as journalists.

Wells-Barnett called herself a journalist, but the other women did not. Although Dunbar-Nelson and Jacques Garvey managed newspaper operations, they defined themselves differently. Dunbar-Nelson called herself a poet, author, and literary figure. Jacques Garvey viewed herself as the promoter of her husband's philosophy during the days of the Garvey Movement. During the 1920s, Jacques Garvey clearly used journalism to do this, yet in her books and interviews that followed, she did not refer to herself as a journalist. Terrell called herself an educator, suffragist, and activist, but never a journalist.

Another factor that may account for the women's obscurity in journalism history may be that they were never reporters. Wells-Barnett performed in the traditional role of journalists, traveling to the scene of lynchings to gather facts and observe first-hand the events she covered, conducting background research that gave her writings credibility, and interviewing subjects. When looking at journalists, scholars may have not included columnists and reviewers as categories for investigation and documentation. Terrell, Dunbar-Nelson, and Jacques Garvey functioned primarily in those journalistic roles.

Notwithstanding how the women viewed themselves or what categories that journalism historians have used, this work confirms that Ida B. Wells-Barnett, Mary Church Terrell, Alice Dunbar-Nelson, and Amy Jacques Garvey were journalists. They fulfilled the advocacy role of the black press, and they gave voice to the voiceless. Therefore, the veil of obscurity should be lifted and these pioneering black women journalists should be included in the history of the press.

Notes

CHAPTER 1 NOTES

1. See, for example, Robert C. Koschersberger, Jr., *More than a Muckraker: Ida Tarbell's Life in Journalism* (Knoxville, TN: University of Tennessee Press, 1996); Mignon R. Rittenhouse, *The Amazing Nellie Bly* (Freeport, NY: Books for Libraries Press, 1956).

2. See, for example, I. Garland Penn, *The Afro-American Press and Its Editors* (New York: Arno Press, 1891), 367–427.

3. Although most works commonly make reference to Ida B. Wells, the woman's maiden name, I use Ida B. Wells-Barnett, as she was known for most of her adult life. I also herein use Amy Jacques Garvey when referring to Marcus Garvey's second wife, thus distinguishing her from Amy Ashwood Garvey, his first wife. I refer to Mary Church Terrell on second reference only as Terrell because I found no evidence of her using Church Terrell. Alice Dunbar-Nelson used the hyphenated name, hence I do so in this work.

4. Harvard Sitkoff, *A New Deal for Blacks: The Emergence of Civil Rights as a National Issue: The Depression Decade* (New York: Oxford University Press, 1978), 3–5.

5. W. R. Lawton, "Our Present Situation," The *Colored American Magazine*," 14 (1908): 230.

6. Ibid., 231.

7. Gloria Wade-Gayles, "Black Women Journalists in the South, 1880–1905: An Approach to the Study of Black Women's History," *Callaloo* 4 (1982): 138.

8. Ibid.

9. Sitkoff, *New Deal for Blacks*, 5.

10. See, for example, Rayford W. Logan, *The Betrayal of the Negro: From Rutherford B. Hayes to Woodrow Wilson* (New York: Collier Books, 1965), originally published as Rayford W. Logan, *The Negro in American Life and Thought: The Nadir, 1877–1901* (New York, Dial Press, 1954). Logan developed the concept of the "Nadir" in his book.
11. Dorothy C. Salem, "Black Women and the NAACP, 1902–1922: An Encounter with Race, Class, and Gender," in Kim Marie Vaz, ed., *Black Women in America* (Thousand Oaks: Sage Publications, 1995), 54.
12. Ibid.
13. Lawrence W. Levine, *Black Culture and Black Consciousness: Afro-American Folk Thought from Slavery to Freedom* (New York: Oxford University Press, 1977), 260.
14. Ibid.
15. Salem, "Black Women and the NAACP," 54.
16. August Meier and Elliot Rudwick, Introduction to Emma Lou Thornbrough, "Segregation in Indiana during the Klan Era of the 1920s," in August Meier and Elliot Rudwick, eds., *The Making of Black America: Essays in Negro Life and History* (New York: Atheneum, 1969), 184.
17. Salem, "Black Women and the NAACP," 54.
18. Sitkoff, *New Deal for Blacks*, 31.
19. Ibid.
20. Ibid.
21. See, for example, Edward Peeks, *The Long Struggle for Black Power* (New York: Charles Scribner's Sons, 1971), 222; Nathan I Huggins, *Voices from the Harlem Renaissance*, (New York: Oxford University Press, 1995), 3–11. Huggins wrote that the "New Negro," (as blacks dubbed themselves), was "a man and a citizen in his own right—intelligent, articulate, self-assured."
22. Edward Peeks, *Long Struggle for Black Power*, 226.
23. Sitkoff, *New Deal for Blacks*, 32.
24. Gerder Lerner, Introduction to *Black Women in White America: A Documentary History* (New York: Vintage Books, 1973), xvii; Paula Giddings, Preface to *When and Where I Enter: The Impact of Black Women on Race and Sex in America* (New York: William Morrow and Company, 1984), 6; Rosalyn Terborg-Penn, *African American Women in the Struggle for the Vote, 1850–1920* (Bloomington, IN: Indiana University Press, 1998), 1–12.
25. Marjorie Spruill Wheeler, ed., *One Woman, One Vote: Rediscovering the Woman Suffrage Movement* (Troutdale, OR: New Sage Press, 1995), 13; Rosalyn Terborg-Penn, "African American Women and the Woman Suffrage Movement" in Wheeler, ed., *One Woman*, 135.
26. Wade-Gayle, "Black Women Journalists," 138.

Notes

27 Dorothy Sterling, ed., Introduction to *We Are Your Sisters: Black Women in the Nineteenth Century* (New York: W. W. Norton and Company, 1984), ix.

28 Paula Giddings, *When and Where I Enter*, 2.

29 Cynthia Neverdon-Morton, Introduction to *Afro-American Women of the South and the Advancement of the Race, 1895–1925* (Knoxville, TN: University of Tennessee Press, 1989), 2.

30 See, for example, W. C. Matney, "Black Women in America," Introductory essay to Marianna W. Davis, ed., *Contributions of Black Women to America*, vol. 1 (Columbia, S.C.: Kenday Press, 1986), iii–ix.

31 See, for example, Dorothy Sterling, Introduction to *Black Foremothers: Three Lives* (New York: The Feminist Press and the McGraw-Hill Book Company, 1979), xvi.

32 Lerner, *Black Women in White America*, xvii–xviii.

33 Sterling, *Black Foremothers*, xvi.

34 Glenda Gilmore, Introduction to *Gender and Jim Crow: Women and the Politics of White Supremacy in North Carolina, 1896–1920* (Chapel Hill, NC: The North Carolina Press, 1996), xvi, xxi.

35 Darlene Clark Hine, ed., Preface to *Black Women in United States History*, vol. 1 (Brooklyn, NY: Carlson Publishing Inc., 1990), xi.

36 Alfreda Duster, ed., *Crusade for Justice: The Autobiography of Ida B. Wells* (Chicago: The University of Chicago Press, 1970).

37 Roland E. Wolseley, *The Black Press, U.S.A.* (Ames, IA: Iowa State University Press, 1990), 40.

38 Rodger Streitmatter, *Raising Her Voice: African-American Women Journalists Who Changed History* (Lexington, KY: The University of Kentucky Press, 1994), 1–2.

39 Darlene Clark Hine, ed., Preface to *Black Women in American History: From Colonial Time through the Nineteenth Century*, vols. 1–8 (Brooklyn, NY: Carlson Publishing Inc, 1990), xi; Rosalyn Terborg-Penn, *African American Women*, 35, 163.

40 Streitmatter, *Raising Her Voice*, 2.

41 Ibid., 2–3.

42 Ibid.

43 See, for example, Streitmatter, *Raising Her Voice*, 1–4.

44 Bernell Tripp, "Black Women Journalists, 1825–1860," Abstract to (Ph.D. diss., The University of Alabama, 1993).

45 Michael Emery and Edwin Emery, *The Press and America: An Interpretive History of the Mass Media*, 7th ed. (Englewood Cliffs, NJ: Prentice Hall, 1992), 228.

46 Rodger Streitmatter, "Economic Conditions Surrounding Nineteenth Century African-American Women Journalists: Two Case Studies," *Journalism History* 18 (1992): 45 cites Jean Folkerts and Dwight L. Teeter,

     Voices of a Nation: A History of the Media in the United States (New York; MacMillan, 1989).
47. Wm. David Sloan and James D. Startt, eds., *Media in America: A History*, 4th ed. (Northport, AL: Vision Press, 2000).
48. Armistead S. Pride and Clint C. Wilson, *A History of the Black Press*, (Washington, DC: Howard University Press, 1997), 93–95.
49. Gayle Hardy, *American Women Civil Rights Activists, Bibliographies of 68 Leaders, 1825–1992* (Jefferson, NC: McFarland and Company, 1992), 134–142; 378–384; 403–408.
50. Ibid., 20, 53, 59, 345, 378.
51. Marion Marzolf, *Up from the Footnote: A History of Women Journalists* (New York: Hasting House Publisher, 1977), 24–25.
52. Penn, *Afro-American Press*, 367–427.
53. See, for example, Gerda Lerner, *A Majority Finds Its Past: Placing Women in History* (New York: Oxford University Press, 1979); Paula Giddings, *When and Where*, 75–82, 119; Jacqueline Jones, *Labor of Love, Labor of Sorrow: Black Women, Work, and the Family from Slavery to the Present* (New York: Basic Books Inc., 1985).
54. Frankie Hutton, *Early Black Press in America: 1827–1860* (Westport, CT: Greenwood Press, 1993), 57.
55. Wade-Gayles, "Black Women Journalists," 139.
56. Ruby O. Williams, "An In-depth Portrait of Alice Dunbar-Nelson," (Ph.D. diss., University of California, Irvine, 1984), 25.
57. Penn, *Afro-American Press*, 367–427.
58. Wade-Gayles, "Black Women Journalists," 140.
59. Pride and Wilson, *History of Black*, 53–54.
60. Robert Skinner, "Lucy Wilmot Smith," In Jessie C. Smith, ed., *Notable Black American Women* (Detroit: Gale Research Inc., 1992), 1047.
61. Penn, *Afro-American Press*, 413.
62. Ibid.
63. See, for example, Mildred Thompson, *Ida B. Wells-Barnett: An Explanatory Study of an American Black Woman, 1893–1930* (Brooklyn, NY: Carlson Publishing, 1990); Darryl M. Trimieu, *Voices of the Silenced: The Responsible Self in a Marginalized Community* (Cleveland, OH: Pilgrim Press, 1993); Linda O. McMurry, *To Keep Waters Troubled: The Life of Ida B. Wells* (New York: Oxford University Press, 1998).
64. Sterling, *Black Foremothers*, 62.
65. Penn, *Afro-American Press*, 408.
66. Sterling, *Black Foremothers*, 73–74.

Notes

67 Barbara Christian, Foreword to Dorothy Sterling, *Black Foremothers: Three Lives*, 2nd ed. (New York: The Feminist Press at The City University of New York, 1988), x.
68 Lerner, *Black Women in White America*, 197–198.
69 Streitmatter, *Raising Her Voice*, 49–50.
70 Ibid., 50.
71 Clark Cook, "Ida B. Wells," Available at the Black Excellence in World History site, http://www.csusm.edu/Black_Excellence/documents/pg-i-b-wells2.html.
72 Ibid., 2.
73 Lerner, *Black Women in White America*, 198.
74 Christian, Foreword to Sterling, *Black Foremothers*, x.
75 See, for example, Phillip B. Davis, "Mary Church Terrell (1863–1954)," Available at http://www.csusm.edu/Black_Excellence/documents/pg-m-c-terrell2.html; Rosalie Massery Sanderson, "Mary Church Terrell: A Black Woman's Crusade for Justice" (master's thesis, The University of Arkansas, 1973); Margaret Nell Price, "The Development of Leadership by Southern Women through Clubs and Organizations"(master's thesis, The University of North Carolina at Chapel Hill, 1945).
76 Darlene Clark Hine, Elsa Barkley Brown, Rosalyn Terborg-Penn, eds., *Black Women in America: An Historical Encyclopedia*, vol 2 (Bloomington, IN: Indiana University Press, 1994), 1158.
77 See, for example, Rosalie Massery Sanderson, "Mary Church Terrell;" Margaret Nell Price, "Development of Leadership."
78 Terrell, *Colored Woman*, 221–237.
79 Ibid., 222.
80 Ibid.
81 Articles can be found in issues of *The Voice of the Negro* from 1904–1907.
82 See, for example, Williams, "In-depth Portrait;" Gloria T. Hull, ed., *The Works of Alice Dunbar-Nelson*, vol. 2 (New York: Oxford University Press, 1988); Gloria T. Hull, *Color, Sex, and Poetry: Three Women Writers of the Harlem Renaissance* (Bloomington, IN: Indiana University Press, 1984); Violet Bryan, *The Myth of New Orleans in Literature* (Knoxville, TN: The University of Tennessee Press, 1993).
83 Hull, *Works of Alice*, 89.
84 Williams, "In-depth Portrait," 87.
85 Ibid.
86 Ibid., 89.
87 Ibid.
88 Ibid.
89 Ibid., 87.

90 Ula Taylor, "Garvey, Amy Euphemia Jacques (1896–1973)" in Hine, Brown, and Terborg-Penn, eds., *Black Women in America*, 482.

91 References can be found in the Marcus Mosiah Garvey Memorial Collection, 1887–1940, Boxes 1–4, Fisk University, Nashville, TN; Tony Martin, "Women in the Garvey Movement," in Rupert Lewis and Patrick Bryan, eds., *Garvey, His Work and Impact* (Trenton, NJ: African World Press, Inc., 1991), 71; "Amy Jacques Garvey," Available at www.kasnet.com/heroesofjamaica/mg/g11/g11.htm.

92 "Amy Jacques Garvey," Available at www.kasnet.com/heroesofjamaica/mg/g11/g11.htm.

93 References can be found in the Marcus Mosiah Garvey Memorial Collection. Boxes 1–12. Fisk University, Nashville, TN.

94 For reference see notation for an August 25, 1968 television show in Marcus Mosiah Garvey Memorial Collection, 1887–1940, Box 5, Folder 8, Fisk University, Nashville, TN.

95 Beverly Reed, "Amy Jacques Garvey—Black, Beautiful and Free," Manuscript in Marcus Mosiah Garvey Memorial Collection, 1887–1940, Box 5, Folder 8, Fisk University, Nashville, TN.

96 Ibid., Taylor, "Garvey, Amy Euphemia," 482.

97 Martin, "Women in the Garvey Movement, 71.

98 Hine, et al., *Black Women in America*, 483.

99 See notation labeled "Contributions of Editor of *Negro World*" in scrapbook in Marcus Mosiah Garvey Memorial Collection, Box 12, Fisk University, Nashville, TN.

100 Ibid.

101 Pride and Wilson, *History of the Black Press*, 14.

102 For reference, see Bernell Tripp, *Origins of the Black Press* (Northport, AL: Vision Press, 1992).

103 Ibid., 90.

104 Charles A. Simmons, *The African American Press: With Special Reference to Four Newspapers, 1827–1965* (Jefferson, ND: McFarland and Company, 1998), 1.

105 Wade-Gayles, "Black Women Journalists," 140.

106 See, for example, Penn, *Afro-American Press*, 367–427.

107 Ibid., 375.

108 Marzolf, *Up from the Footnotes*, 26.

109 Wade-Gayles, "Black Women Journalists," 141.

110 See, for example, Evelyn Brooks-Higginbotham, *Righteous Discontent: The Women's Movement in the Black Baptist Church, 1880–1920* (Cambridge, MA: Harvard University Press, 1993).

111 Wade-Gayles, "Black Women Journalists," 142.

Notes

112 Streitmatter, *Raising Her Voice*, 62.
113 Ibid.
114 Wade-Gayles, "Black Women Journalists," 142.
115 See, for example, Hutton, *Early Black Press*, 59–78.
116 Shirley J. Yee, "Organizing for Racial Justice: Black Women and the Dynamics of Race and Sex in Female Antislavery Societies, 1832–1860," in Vaz, *Black Women in American*, 38.
117 Hutton, *Early Black Press*, 57.
118 Salem, "Black Women and the NAACP," 54.
119 Nora Darlene Hall, "On Being an African-American Woman: Gender and Race in the Writings of Six Black Women Journalists, 1849–1936," (Ph.D. diss., University of Minnesota, 1998), 155–156.
120 Frederick Detweiler, *The Negro Press in the United States*, (College Park, MD: McGrath Publishing Company, 1968), 79.
121 Streitmatter, *Raising Her Voice*, 141.
122 Wolseley, *Black Press*, 24.
123 Pride and Wilson, *History of Black Press*, 13.
124 Salem, "Black Women and the NAACP," 59.
125 Wade-Gayles, "Black Women Journalists," 143.
126 Streitmatter, *Raising Her Voice*, 1–5.
127 Rosalyn Terborg-Penn, *African American Women in the Struggle for the Vote, 1850–1920* (Bloomington, IN: Indiana University Press, 1998), 58.
128 Simmons, *African American Press*, 1.
129 Duster, *Autobiography of Ida*, 47–67; Terrell, *Colored Woman*, 105, 108.
130 Streitmatter, *Raising Her Voice*, 3–4.
131 Ibid., 54.
132 Christian, Introduction to Sterling, *Black Foremothers*, xxii.
133 Terborg-Penn, *African American Women*, 58.
134 Ibid.
135 Giddings, *When and Where*, 69–71.
136 Hutton, *Early Black Press*, 104.
137 For reference, see Penn, *Afro-American Press*, 413.
138 Hutton, *Early Black Press*, x.
139 Ibid.
140 Detweiler, *Negro Press*, 70.
141 Wolseley, *Black Press*, 39.
142 Detweiler, *Negro Press*, 70.
143 Streitmatter, *Raising Her Voice*, 4–5.

144 See, for example, W. Jawitz, *Understanding Mass Media*, (Lincolnwood, IL: National Textbook Company, 1996).
145 Wolseley, *Black Press*, 24.
146 Wade-Gayles, "Black Women Journalists," 140.
147 Ibid.
148 Streitmatter, *Raising Her Voice*, 3.
149 Wolseley, *Black Press*, xv.
150 Hutton, *Early Black Press*, ix.
151 Wade-Gayles, "Black Women Journalists," 146–147.
152 See, for example, Williams, "In-depth Portrait."
153 Wade-Gayles, "Black Women Journalists," 146–147.
154 Terrell, *Colored Woman*, 212–237.
155 Streitmatter, *Raising Her Voice*, 10.
156 James D. Startt and Wm. David Sloan, *Historical Methods in Mass Communication* (Hillsdale, NJ: Lawrence Erlbaum, 1989), 117.
157 Startt and Sloan, *Historical Methods*, 158.
158 Ibid.

Chapter Two Notes

1 Alfreda M. Duster, ed., *Crusade for Justice: The Autobiography of Ida B. Wells* (Chicago: The University of Chicago Press, 1970), 370.
2 Although most works commonly make reference to Ida B. Wells, the woman's maiden name, I use Ida B. Wells-Barnett, as she was known for most of her adult life.
3 Duster, *Crusade for* Justice, 36–62, 181.
4 Ibid., 181.
5 Ibid., 364.
6 *Indianapolis Freeman*, "Fortune and His Echo," 19 April 1890.
7 Duster, *Crusade for Justice*, 33.
8 Henry Davenport Northrop, Joseph R. Gray, and I. Garland Penn, *The College of Life; Or, Practical Self-Educator: A Manual of Self-Improvement of the Colored Race* (Chicago: Chicago Publication and Lithography Company, 1895), 100, as cited in Duster, *Crusade for Justice*, 33.
9 Ibid.
10 Ibid., 32.
11 See, for example, Mildred I. Thompson, *Ida B. Wells-Barnett: An Exploratory Study of an American Black Woman, 1893–1930* (Brooklyn: Carlson Publishing Inc., 1990); Linda O. McMurry, *To Keep the Waters*

Notes

12. *Troubled: The Life of Ida B. Wells* (New York: Oxford University Press, 1998).
12. Ibid.
13. See, for example, Roger Streitmatter, *Raising Her Voice: African-American Women Journalists Who Changed History* (Lexington, KY: The University of Kentucky Press, 1994), 49–50.
14. Margaret Walker, Introduction to Dorothy Sterling, *Black Foremothers: Three Lives* (New York: The Feminist Press and McGraw-Hill Book Company, 1979), xix.
15. Ibid.
16. Duster, *Crusade for Justice*, 8.
17. Ibid.
18. Miriam DeCosta-Willis, *The Memphis Diary of Ida B. Wells* (Boston: Beacon Press, 1995), 7.
19. Duster, *Crusade for Justice*, 8–9.
20. Ibid., 9, 13, 16, 17.
21. Ibid., 16. It should be noted that Wells-Barnett, born in 1862, was sixteen at the time of her parents' death in 1878.
22. Ibid., xviii.
23. Ibid.
24. McMurry, *Keep Waters Troubled*, 23.
25. Ibid.
26. DeCosta-Willis, *Memphis Diary*, 3.
27. Duster, *Crusade for Justice*, xviii.
28. McMurry, *Keep Waters Troubled*, 17.
29. Duster, *Crusade for Justice*, 239.
30. Ibid., 242–243.
31. Ibid., xxiii.
32. Ibid., 249.
33. Thompson, *Ida B. Wells-Barnett*, 7.
34. Paula Giddings, *When and Where I Enter: The Impact of Black Women on Race and Sex in America* (New York: William Morrow and Company, 1984), 89.
35. Thompson, *Ida B. Wells-Barnett*, 128.
36. Ibid.
37. Duster, *Crusade for Justice*, xxv.
38. Wells-Barnett letter to Joel E. Springarn, 21 April 1911, Joel E. Springarn papers, Moorland-Springarn Research Center, Howard University Library, Washington, D.C.; Duster, *Crusade for Justice*, 327.

39 Duster, *Crusade for Justice*, 327.
40 Ibid., 345.
41 See, for example, Duster, *Crusade for* Justice, 345–347; Thompson, *Ida B. Wells-Barnett*, 105–106; Giddings, *When and Where I Enter*, 130.
42 Rosalyn Terborg-Penn, "African American Women and the Woman Suffrage Movement, In Marjorie Spruill Wheeler, ed., *One Woman, One Vote: Rediscovering the Woman Suffrage Movement* (Troutdale, OR: NewSage Press, 1995), 147.
43 Ibid.
44 Streitmatter, *Raising Her Voice*, 60; Giddings, *When and Where I Enter*, 127–128.
45 "Ida B. Wells-Barnett," Available at www.greatwomen.org/women.php?action=viewone&id=167.
46 Duster, *Crusade for Justice*, 375.
47 Wanda Hendricks, "Ida B. Wells-Barnett," In Darlene Clark Hine, et al., *Black Women in America: An Historical Encyclopedia*, vol. 2 (Bloomington, IN: Indiana University Press, 1993), 1242.
48 Duster, *Crusade for Justice*, 190.
49 Streitmatter, *Raising Her Voice*, 56. Streitmatter cites Lloyd W. Crawford, "Ida B. Wells: Her Anti-Lynching Crusades in Britain and Repercussions from Them in the United States," paper presented to the Association for the Study of Negro Life and History, October 1962, Xenia, Ohio, pp. 17–20, 22–24.
50 Duster, *Crusade for Justice*, 31.
51 DeCosta-Willis, *Memphis Diary*, 20–21.
52 Ibid., 21.
53 Duster, *Crusade for Justice*, 23.
54 Ibid.
55 Ibid.
56 Ibid., 23–24.
57 DeCosta-Willis, *Memphis Diary*, 100.
58 Ibid., 102.
59 Duster, *Crusade for Justice*, 30–33.
60 Streitmatter, *Raising Her Voice*, 51.
61 Duster, *Crusade for Justice*, 19.
62 Ibid.
63 Duster, *Crusade for Justice*, xvi, 18–21.
64 Ibid.
65 Duster, *Crusade for Justice,* 20.

Notes

66 DeCosta-Willis, *Memphis Diary*, 140–141.
67 I. Garland Penn, *Afro-American Press and Its Editors* (New York: Arno Press, 1891), 407.
68 Duster, *Crusade for Justice*, xviii.
69 DeCosta-Willis, *Memphis Diary*, 71, 109, 116.
70 Duster, *Crusade for Justice*, 359.
71 McMurry, *Keep Waters Troubled*, 92–93.
72 DeCosta-Willis, *Memphis Diary*, 110.
73 Ibid., 109–110.
74 Duster, *Crusade for Justice*, 31–32.
75 Duster, *Crusade for Justice*, 32.
76 Ibid.
77 Ibid.
78 Duster, *Crusade for Justice*, 35.
79 Ibid., 41.
80 Ibid.
81 Ibid., 40.
82 Ibid.
83 Ibid., xviii–xix.
84 Ibid., 37.
85 Ibid.
86 Ibid., 41.
87 Ibid., 63.
88 Ibid., 62.
89 Ibid., 61–62.
90 Ibid., 71.
91 Ibid., 63.
92 See, for example, Ann Allen Shockley, "Ida B. Wells-Barnett: Iola, 1862–1931," in *Afro-American Women Writers, 1746–1933: An Anthology and Critical Guide* (Boston: G. K. Hall and Company, 1988).
93 Duster, *Crusade for Justice*, 196.
94 See, for example, Giddings, *When and Where I Enter*, 17–29.
95 Ibid., 18.
96 See, for example, Duster, *Crusade for Justice*, 47–49; Steve Klots, *Ida B. Wells-Barnett: Civil Rights Leader* (New York: Chelsea House Publishers, 1994), 11–15.
97 Klots, *Ida B. Wells*, 12.
98 Duster, *Crusade for Justice*, 50.

99   Ibid., 47.
100 Ibid., 47, 48.
101 Ibid., 55.
102 Wells-Barnett, Editorial in *Free Speech*, cited in Duster, *Crusade for Justice*, 52.
103 Ibid.
104 Ibid.
105 Wells-Barnett, Editorial in *Free Speech*, as cited in Duster, *Crusade for Justice*, 65.
106 Ibid., 52.
107 Ibid., 53.
108 Ibid., 66.
109 Ibid., 69.
110 Ida B. Wells, "Exiled," New York *Age*, 5 June 1892.
111 Duster, *Crusade for Justice*, 71.
112 See, for example, Ida B. Wells, "Lynch Law in All Its Phases," originally published in *Our Story* (May 1893): 333–337, reprinted in Mildred Thompson, *Ida B. Wells-Barnett*, 171–187.
113 Ibid., 171.
114 Ibid., 172.
115 Ibid.
116 Ibid., 176.
117 Ibid., 179.
118 Ibid.
119 Ibid., 236.
120 Ibid.
121 Ibid., 181.
122 Ibid., 183.
123 Ibid.
124 Ibid., 185.
125 Ibid.
126 Ibid.
127 Ida B. Wells, "Lynch Law in America," originally published in *Arena*, (January 1900):15–24, reprinted in Thompson, *Ida B. Wells-Barnett*, 240.
128 Ibid., 240–244.
129 Ibid., 241.
130 Ibid.
131 Ibid., 242.

Notes

132 Ibid.
133 Ibid.
134 Streitmatter, *Raising Her Voice*, 56.
135 Ida B. Wells, *A Red Record: Tabulated Statistics and Alleged Causes of Lynchings in the United States, 1892–1893–1894*. (1895), originally published by Donohue and Henneberry, Chicago, reprinted in Trudier Harris, comp., *Selected Works of Ida B. Wells-Barnett* (New York: Oxford University Press, 1991); and Jacqueline Jones Royster, ed., *Southern Horrors and Other Writings: The Anti-Lynching Campaign of Ida B. Wells, 1892–1900* (Boston: Bedford Books, 1997), 73, 75–78, 80–81, 131–32, 138–40, 146–147, 153–155.
136 Ida B. Wells-Barnett, "Lynching and the Excuse for It," *The Independent*, (May 1901):1133–1136, reprinted in Thompson, *Ida B. Wells-Barnett*, 249.
137 Ibid.
138 Ibid., 250.
139 Ibid., 254.
140 Ida B. Wells-Barnett, *Mob Rule in New Orleans* (Chicago: Self, 1900), 224–225.
141 Ibid., 284.
142 Ida B. Wells-Barnett, "Lynching: Our National Crime," originally published in *National Negro Conference: Proceedings*. New York, 1909, 174–179, reprinted in Thompson, *Ida B. Wells-Barnett*, 261.
143 Ibid.
144 Ibid.
145 Ibid., 263.
146 Ibid., 263–264.
147 Ibid.
148 Ida B. Wells-Barnett, "Our Country: Lynching Record," originally published in *Survey* (February 1913): 573–574, reprinted in Thompson, *Ida B. Wells-Barnett*, 277.
149 Ibid., 279.
150 Ibid.
151 Duster, *Crusade for Justice*, 70.
152 Gilmore, *Gender and Jim Crow*, 83.
153 Ibid., 81.
154 See, for example, Duster, *Crusade for Justice*; McMurry, *Keep Waters Troubled*.
155 Ida B. Wells-Barnett, *New York Freeman*, 1 January 1887.
156 Ibid.
157 Ibid.

158 McMurry, *Keep Waters Troubled*, 308.
159 DeCosta-Willis, *Memphis Diary*, 76.
160 Ibid.
161 McMurry, *Keep Waters Troubled*, 53.
162 Ibid.
163 Gilmore, *Gender and Jim Crow*, 83.
164 See, for example, Duster, *Crusade for Justice*; DeCosta-Willis, *Memphis Diary*.
165 Duster, *Crusade for Justice*, 329.
166 Ibid.
167 Ida B. Wells, "Woman's Mission," *New York Freeman*, 26 December 1885.
168 Ida B. Wells, "The Model Woman: A Pen Picture of the Typical Southern Girl," *New York Freeman*, 18 February 1888.
169 Ida B. Wells, A Story of 1900," *Fisk Herald* (April 1886), reprinted in DeCosta-Willis, *Memphis Diary*, 183.
170 Ibid., 183, 184.
171 Wells-Barnett, "Woman's Mission," *New York Freeman*, 26 December 1885.
172 Ibid.
173 Ibid.
174 Ibid.
175 Ida B. Wells, ed., *The Reason Why the Colored American is Not in the World's Columbian Exposition: The Afro-American's Contribution to Columbian Literature* (Chicago, 1893), reprinted in Thompson, *Ida B. Wells-Barnett*, 193.
176 Ibid.
177 Ida B. Wells, "To Tole with Watermelons," *Cleveland Gazette*, 22 July 1893.
178 Ibid.
179 Ibid.
180 Wells-Barnett, *A Red Record*, 89.
181 McMurry, *Keep Waters Troubled*, 253.
182 DeCosta-Willis, *Memphis Diary*, 38.
183 Ibid., 39.
184 Ibid.
185 Duster, *Crusade for Justice*, 40.
186 Ibid.
187 Ida B. Wells-Barnett, "Booker T. Washington and His Critics," originally published in *World Today* (April 1904): 518–521, reprinted in Thompson, *Ida B. Wells-Barnett*, 257.
188 Ibid., 258.

Notes

189 *New York Age*, 8 August 1891, as cited in McMurry, *Keep Waters Troubled*, 127.
190 Ida B. Wells, "Freedom of Political Action: A Woman's Magnificent Definition of the Political Situation," *New York Freeman*, 7 November 1885.
191 DeCosta-Willis, *Memphis Diary*, 51.
192 Wells-Barnett, "Functions of Leadership," *New York Freeman*, 12 September 1885.
193 Wells-Barnett, *New York Freeman*, 15 January 1887.
194 Wells-Barnett, *Washington Bee*, 8 August 1889, as cited in McMurry, *Keep Waters Troubled*, 127.
195 Duster, *Crusade for Justice*, 38.
196 Ibid.
197 Ibid.
198 *Indianapolis Freeman*, 19 March 1892, as cited in McMurry, *Keep Waters Troubled*, 139.
199 Ida B. Wells-Barnett, Iola on Discrimination," *New York Freeman*, 5 January 1887.
200 Ibid.
201 Ida B. Wells, "The League Is a Lever," *Detroit Plaindealer,* 18 October 1889.
202 Ida B. Wells-Barnett, Letter to the Editor in *Chicago Broad Ax*, 27 October 1917.
203 Ibid.
204 See, for example, McMurry, *Keep Waters Troubled*, 125.
205 Wells-Barnett, Editorial in *Free Speech,* 19 September 1891, cited in McMurry, *Keep Waters Troubled*, 128.
206 Duster, *Crusade for Justice*, 96.
207 Ibid.
208 Ibid., 96–97.
209 Ibid., 96.
210 Ibid., 183–184.
211 Giddings, *When and Where I Enter*, 121.
212 Ida B. Wells-Barnett, "How Enfranchisement Stops Lynchings," originally published in *Original Rights Magazine* (June 1910): 42–53, reprinted in Thompson, *Ida B. Wells-Barnett*, 269.
213 Ibid.
214 Ibid.
215 DeCosta-Willis, *Memphis Diary,* 121.

216 Ida B. Wells, "Afro-American and Africa," originally published in *AME Church Review* (July 1892); 40–45, reprinted in Mildred Thompson, Ida B. Wells-Barnett, 165.
217 Giddings, *When and Where I Enter*, 180.
218 Duster, *Crusade for Justice*, 4–5.
219 Ibid.
220 See, for example, Thompson, *Ida B. Wells-Barnett;* Trimieu, *Voices of the Silenced; The Responsible Self in a Marginalized Community* (Cleveland, OH: Pilgrim Press, 1993); McMurry, *To Keep Waters Troubled*.
221 Carol Cook, "Ida B. Wells," Available at Black Excellence in World History site, www/csum, edu/public/hold-Black_Excellence/pgiwells.html. INTERNET.

CHAPTER THREE NOTES

1 Mary Church Terrell, *A Colored Woman in a White World* (Salem, NH: Ayer Company Publishers, 1986), 230.
2 See, for example, Dorothy Sterling, *Black Foremothers: Three Lives* (New York: The Feminist Press and McGraw-Hill Book Company, 1979), xvii. Sterling wrote that Robert Church became a millionaire by purchasing real estate as landowners in Memphis fled the city during the yellow fever epidemic that ravaged Tennessee and Mississippi in 1878. This is the same epidemic that took the lives of Ida B. Wells-Barnett's parents and one sibling.
3 Terrell, *Colored Woman*, 37–38.
4 See, for example, Darlene Clark Hine, et al., eds., *Black Women in America: An Historical Encyclopedia*, vol. 2 (Bloomington, IN: Indiana University Press, 1993) 1157–1159; Beverly Jones, *Quest for Equality: The Life and Writings of Mary Eliza Church Terrell, 1863–1954* (Brooklyn, NY: Carlson Publishing, 1990); Jessie Smith, ed., *Notable Black American Women* (Detroit: Gale Research Inc., 1992), 1115–1119; Terrell, *A Colored Woman*.
5 Jones, *Quest for Equality*, 88.
6 Rosalie Massery Sanderson, *Mary Church Terrell: A Black Woman's Crusade for Justice* (master's thesis, The University of Arkansas, 1973), 13.
7 Ibid., 13–14.
8 Terrell, *Colored Woman*, 1.
9 Ibid., 18.
10 Ibid., 20.
11 Ibid., 32, 44.
12 Ibid., 221.
13 Ibid.
14 Ibid., 221.
15 Ibid., 35–36.

Notes

16 Ibid., 60.
17 Ibid.
18 Ibid.
19 Ibid., 59–62.
20 Ibid., 63, 66–68.
21 Washington *Bee*, 7 November 1891.
22 Sterling, *Black Foremothers*, 128.
23 Ibid., 120.
24 "Notes," *Journal of Negro History*, (January 1926), 11:223, as cited in Rosalie Massery Sanderson, *Mary Church Terrell*, 12.
25 Ibid.
26 Sterling, *Black Foremothers*, 130–131.
27 Terrell did not indicate the type of business her father had.
28 Terrell, 7.
29 Ibid., 15.
30 Ibid., 22–23.
31 Ibid., 22.
32 Ibid.
33 Ibid., 115.
34 Ibid.
35 Ibid., 98.
36 Ibid.
37 Ibid.
38 Ibid., 128–129.
39 Ibid., 133–134.
40 Ibid., 140–142.
41 Sanderson, "Mary Church Terrell," 17.
42 Hine, *Black Women in America*, 760.
43 Terrell, *Colored Woman*, 150.
44 Ibid., 153.
45 Ibid., 105.
46 Ibid.
47 Ibid.
48 Ibid., 222.
49 Gloria Wade-Gayles, "Black Women Journalists in the South, 1880–1905: An Approach to the Study of Black Women's History," *Callaloo* 4 (1982): 141.

50 Ibid., 222.
51 Editorial, *The Voice of the Negro*, (July 1904): 309.
52 Terrell, *Colored Woman*, 224.
53 Ibid.
54 Ibid., 226.
55 Ibid.
56 Ibid., 227.
57 Ibid., 229.
58 Ibid.
59 Ibid., 227–228.
60 Ibid., 223.
61 See, for example, Frances Detweiler, *The Negro Press in the United States* (College Park, MD: McGrath Publishing Company, 1968),70; Frankie Hutton, Introduction to *The Early Black Press in America, 1827–1860* (Westport, CT: Greenwood Press, 1993), x.
62 Mary Church Terrell, Letter to the Editor, *Washington Post*, Clipping in Mary Church Terrell Papers, Moorland Springarn Collection, Series D, Box 102–3, Folder 78, Howard University, Washington, D.C.
63 Ibid.
64 Ibid.
65 Ibid.
66 Mary Church Terrell, Letter to the Editor, *Washington Post*, 13 March 1947.
67 Mary Church Terrell, Letter to the Editor, *Washington Post*, Clipping in Mary Church Terrell Papers, Moorland Springarn Collection, Series D, Box 102–3, Folder 80, Howard University, Washington, D.C.
68 Articles can be found in issues of *The Voice of the Negro* from 1904–1907.
69 See, for example, Dorothy C. Salem, "Black Women and the NAACP, 1909–1922: An Encounter with Race, Class, and Gender," in Kim M. Vaz, ed., *Black Women in America* (Thousand Oaks, CA: Sage Publications, 1995), 54; Armistead Pride and Clint C. Wilson, *A History of the Black Press* (Washington, D.C., Howard University Press, 1997), 13.
70 Detweiler, *Negro Press*, 79.
71 See, for example Pride and Wilson, History of the Black Press, 13.
72 Mary Church Terrell, "An Ethnologist's Injustice or Ignorance," *Ringwood's Afro-American Journal of Fashion* (April 1893): 1, Clipping in Mary Church Terrell Papers, Series D, Box 102–03, Folder 80, Howard University, Washington, D.C.
73 Ibid.
74 Ibid.
75 Ibid.

76 Ibid.
77 Terrell, *Colored Woman*, 230.
78 Mary Church Terrell, "Up-To-Date," *Norfolk Journal and Guide*, 19 November 1927.
79 Ibid.
80 Mary Church Terrell, "Colored Soldiers Proved Mettle in War of 1776," Washington *Sunday Star*, 24 June 1932.
81 Ibid.
82 Mary Church Terrell, "Outlawing 'Negro,'" Letter to the Editor, *Washington Post*, 27 May 1949.
83 Ibid.
84 Mary Church Terrell, "The International Congress of Women, *The Voice of the Negro* (December 1904): 454–461. See page 459 for specific reference.
85 Ibid.
86 Ibid.
87 Mary Church Terrell, "The Racial Worm Turns," Manuscript in Mary Church Terrell Papers, Moorland Springarn Collection, Series D, Box 102, Folder 92, Howard University, Washington, D.C.
88 Ibid.
89 Ibid.
90 Mary Church Terrell, "Lynching from a Negro's Point of View," *North American Review* 178 (1904): 853–868. Reprinted in Sanderson, Mary Church Terrell, 53.
91 Mary Church Terrell, "Peonage in the United States," *Nineteenth Century* (August 1907), reprinted in Jones, *Quest for Equality*, 255.
92 Ibid.
93 Mary Church Terrell, "Service Which Should Be Rendered the South," *The Voice of the Negro* (February 1905): 182–186.
94 Ibid.
95 Ibid, 186.
96 Ibid.
97 Mary Church Terrell, "Up-to-Date," Norfolk *Journal and Guide*, 3 November 1927.
98 Mary Church Terrell, "Americans Black and White," *The New Student*, 24 February 1923, 1, Clipping in Mary Church Terrell Papers, Moorland Springarn Collection, Series D, Box 149–3, Howard University, Washington, D.C.
99 Ibid.
100 Mary Church Terrell, "Up-To-Date," *Norfolk Journal and Guide*, 21 November (year not legible). Clipping in Mary Church Terrell Papers,

Moorland Springarn Collection, Series D. Box 149–3, Howard University, Washington, D.C.

101 Mary Terrell, "A Colored Woman in the Nation's Capital," Clipping in Mary Church Terrell Papers, Series D, Box 149–3, Howard University, Washington, D.C.

102 Mary Church Terrell, "D.C. Discrimination," Letter to the Editor in *Washington Post,* Clipping in Mary Church Terrell Papers, Moorland Springarn Collection, Series D, Box 102–3, Folder 79, Howard University, Washington, D.C.

103 Ibid.

104 Mary Church Terrell, "Up-to-Date," *Norfolk Journal and Guide,* 23 July 1927.

105 Mary Church Terrell, "Where Black Becomes White," Boston *Herald,* 19 November 1905.

106 Ibid.

107 Ibid.

108 Mary Church Terrell, "Up-to-Date," *Norfolk Journal and Guide,* 11 August 1928.

109 Ibid.

110 Ibid.

111 Ibid.

112 Mary Church Terrell, "Some Aspects of the Employment Problem As It Concerns Colored People," Manuscript in Mary Church Terrell Papers, Howard University, Washington, D.C.

113 Ibid.

114 Ibid.

115 Ibid.

116 Ibid.

117 Ibid.

118 Mary Church Terrell, "A Plea to Colored Race," Washington *Evening Star,* 24 May 1910.

119 Mary Church Terrell, "The Duty of the National Association of Colored Women to the Race," *AME Church Review* (January 1900): 350–354.

120 Ibid.

121 Ibid.

122 Ibid.

123 Mary Church Terrell, The National Association: The Efforts and Aims of Our Noted Negro Women," Indianapolis *Freeman,* 24 December 1898.

124 Ibid.

125 Ibid.

Notes

126 Ibid.
127 Ibid.
128 Mary Church Terrell, "Progress and Problem of Colored Women," Boston *Evening Transcript*, 15 December 1928.
129 Ibid.
130 Ibid.
131 Mary Church Terrell, "Progress of Colored Women," 293.
132 Mary Church Terrell, "Club Work Among Women," New York *Age*, 4 January 1900, 1.
133 Mary Church Terrell, "A Volume of Logic from the Common Place Phrase 'An If or Two,'" Memphis *Weekly Sentinel*, 15 January 1898, Clipping in Mary Church Terrell Papers, Series D, Box 102–03, Folder 8, Howard University, Washington, D.C.
134 Ibid.
135 Mary Church Terrell, "The Progress of Colored Women," *The Voice of the Negro* (July 1904): 292.
136 Ibid.
137 Terrell, "Up-to-Date," *Norfolk Journal and Guide*, 15 October 1927.
138 Ibid.
139 Terrell, *Colored Woman*, 144.
140 Ibid., 144.
141 Ibid., 146.
142 Ibid.
143 See, for example, Rosalyn Terborg-Penn, "African American Women and the Woman Suffrage Movement," in Marjorie Spruill-Wheeler, *One Woman, One Vote: Rediscovering the Woman Suffrage Movement* (Troutdale, OR: NewSage Press, 1995), 147.
144 Marjorie Spruill-Wheeler, Introduction to *One Woman, One Vote*, 12.
145 Terborg-Penn, "African American Women," 147.
146 Mary Church Terrell, "What Women May Do: Suffragists Talk of the Work Which Is Open to Them," *Washington Post*, 10 February 1900.
147 Ibid.
148 Ibid.
149 Ibid.
150 Mary Church Terrell, "The Justice of Woman Suffrage," *Crisis* (September 1912): 243.
151 Mary Church Terrell, "Woman Suffrage and the Fifteenth Amendment," (August 1915): 1991.
152 Ibid.

153 Mary Church Terrell, "Up-to-Date," *Chicago Defender* 1 December 1928.
154 Ibid.
155 Ibid.
156 Ibid.
157 Terrell, "Progress of Colored Women," 292.
158 Mary Church Terrell, "Up-to-Date," *The Chicago Defender*, 3 November 1928.
159 Mary Church Terrell, "Up-to-Date," *Norfolk Journal and Guide*, 26 November 1927.
160 Mary Church Terrell, "Up-to-Date," *Norfolk Journal and* Guide, 19 November 1927.
161 August Meier, *Negro Thought in American, 1880–1915: Racial Ideologies in the Age of Booker T. Washington* (Ann Arbor, MI: The University of Michigan Press, 1966), 239.
162 Mary Church Terrell, "A Son of Howard Scales the Heights," *Washington Post*, Clipping in Mary Church Terrell Papers, Moorland Springarn Collection, Series D, Box 149–3. This article also appeared in the *Washington Post* on 10 February 1929. Just was also the subject of an article titled "Efforts for His Race Brings Dr. Just Honors," found in Terrell's clippings in the Moorland Springarn Collection, Series D, Box 102–3, Folder 65.
163 Ibid.
164 Mary Church Terrell, "Samuel Coleridge-Taylor: The Great Anglo-African Composer. The Two Concerts Conducted by Him in Washington, D.C.," *The Voice of the Negro* (January 1905): 665.
165 Mary Church Terrell, "Writes Negro Symphony," Clipping in Mary Church Terrell Papers, Moorland Springarn Collection, Series D, Box 102–3, Folder 61, Howard University, Washington, D.C.
166 Ibid.
167 Terrell, "Samuel Coleridge-Taylor," 669.
168 See, for example, Mary Church Terrell, "An African Genius," as cited in Beverly Jones, *A Quest for Equality*, 311; Mary Church Terrell, "Phyllis Wheatley: Slave Poetess," Washington *Sunday Star*, 10 March 1929.
169 Mary Church Terrell, "An Appreciation of Frederick Douglass," *National Notes* (February 1923): 4–5.
170 Mary Church Terrell, "I Remember Frederick Douglass," *Ebony* (October 1953): 73–80.
171 Mary Church Terrell, "Up-to-Date," *Norfolk Journal and Guide*, 12 November 1927.
172 See, for example, Mary Church Terrell, "Chemistry Head Means of South's Salvation," Washington *Sunday Star*, 4 October 1931; Mary Church Terrell, "Chemistry Head Means of South's Salvation," *The Dunbar News*, 2 December 1931.

Notes

173 Mary Church Terrell, "Society Among the Colored People of Washington," *The Voice of the Negro* (April 1904): 150–156; "Social Functions During Inauguration Week," *The Voice of the Negro*, (April 1905): 237–242.

174 Terrell, "Christmas at the White House," *The Voice of the Negro* (December 1904): 593–600.

175 Mary Church Terrell, "My Experiences in the Recent Political Campaign," *Howard University Record*, Clipping in Mary Church Terrell Papers, Moorland Springarn Collection, Series D, Box 102–3, Howard University, Washington, D.C.

176 Ibid., 144.

177 Terrell, "Society Among Colored People," 150.

178 Ibid.

179 Ibid., 152–153.

180 Ibid.

181 Mary Church Terrell, "Social Functions During Inauguration Week," *The Voice of the Negro* (April 1905), 237.

182 Ibid.

183 Terrell, "Christmas at the White House," 500.

184 Ibid.

185 Mary Church Terrell, "Convent for Colored Owes Being to French Uprising," *Sunday* (Washington) *Star* 6 (November 1938), clipping in Mary Church Terrell Papers, Moorland-Springarn Collection, Howard University, Washington, D.C.

186 Mary Church Terrell, "Susan B. Anthony, the Abolitionist," *The Voice of the Negro* (June 1906): 411–416.

187 Mary Church Terrell, "Miracles Among Needy Worked by Rosenwald," Clipping in Mary Church Terrell Papers, Moorland-Springarn Collection, Box 149–3, Howard University, Washington, D.C.

188 Mary Church Terrell, "Commends 'Racial' Editorial: Correspondent Says Summing Up in Public Ledger Is One of Finest Statements Ever Read," Letter to the Editor, *Public Ledger* 30 October 1922, Clipping in Mary Church Terrell Papers, Moorland Springarn Collection, Series D, Box 149–3, Howard University, Washington, D. C.

189 Mary Church Terrell, Letter to the Editor, Washington *Evening Post*, 10 May 1910.

190 Mary Church Terrell, "Democracy at Work," Letter to the Editor in *Washington Star,* 17 March 1941.

191 Mary Church Terrell, "District Schools for Colored Preceded Emancipation," Washington *Evening Star* 21 March 1939.

192 Ibid.

193 Mary Church Terrell, "Comments 'Racial' Editorial: Correspondent Says Summing Up in Public Ledger is One of Finest Statements Ever Read," Letter to the Editor in *Public Ledger,* 30 October 1922.

CHAPTER FOUR NOTES

1. Alice Dunbar-Nelson, "From a Woman's Point of View," *Pittsburgh Courier,* 2 January 1926.
2. See, for example, Ruby O. Williams, "An In-depth Portrait of Alice Dunbar-Nelson" (Ph.D. diss., University of California, Irvine, CA, 1974).
3. Gayle J. Hardy, *American Women Civil Rights Activists: Biobibliographies of 68 Women Leaders, 1825–1992* (Jefferson, NC: McFarland and Company, 1993), 273.
4. Gloria T. Hull, ed., Introduction to *Give Us Each Day: The Diary of Alice Dunbar-Nelson* (New York: W. W. Norton and Company, 1984), 16.
5. See, for example, Gloria Wade-Gayles, "Black Women Journalists in the South, 1880–1905: An Approach to the Study of Black Women's History," *Callaloo,* 4:138–142.
6. See, for example, Gloria T. Hull, ed., *The Works of Alice Dunbar-Nelson,* vol. 2. (New York: Oxford University Press, 1988).
7. Wade-Gayles, "Black Women Journalists," 140.
8. References can be found in Williams, "In-depth Portrait;" Hull, W*orks of Alice Dunbar-Nelson*; Violet Bryan, *The Myth of New Orleans in Literature* (Knoxville, TN: The University of Tennessee Press, 1993).
9. Williams, "In-depth Portrait," 85–88.
10. Ibid., 85.
11. Ibid.
12. Hull, *Works of Alice,* xxx.
13. See, for example, Neil R. McMillen, *Dark Journey: Black Mississippians in the Age of Jim Crow* (Chicago: University of Illinois Press, 1990); Glenda Gilmore *Gender and Jim Crow: Women and the Politics of White Supremacy in North Carolina, 1896–1920* (Chapel Hill, NC: The University of North Carolina Press, 1996).
14. Hardy, *American Women Civil,* 273.
15. Hull, *Give Us Each Day,* 14.
16. Hardy, *American Women Civil,* 273.
17. Hull, *Give Us Each Day,* 14.
18. Bryan, *Myth of New Orleans,* 66.
19. Williams, "In-depth Portrait," 13.
20. Hull, *Give Us Each Day,* 14.
21. Ibid., 14–15.

Notes

22. Williams, "In-depth Portrait," 16, 17.
23. Ibid., 16.
24. Ibid.
25. Ibid., 25
26. Ibid.
27. See, for example, Jessie C. Smith, ed., *Notable Black American Women* (Detroit: Gale Research Inc., 1992).
28. Hardy, *American Women Civil*, 25.
29. Gloria T. Hull, *Color, Sex and Poetry: Three Women Writers of the Harlem Renaissance* (Bloomington, IN: Indiana University Press), 42–43.
30. Ibid.
31. Hull, *Give Us Each Day*, 144, 412.
32. Bryan, *Myth of New Orleans*, 66.
33. See, for example, Hull, *Works of Alice*; Gloria T. Hull, *Color, Sex, and Poetry*. (Bloomington, IN: Indiana University Press, 1984).
34. Hull, *Give Us Each Day*, 141–142.
35. Ibid.
36. Ibid.
37. Williams, "In-depth Portrait," 33.
38. Ibid.
39. Hull, *Give Us Each Day*, 87.
40. Ibid., 247.
41. Ibid.
42. Hull, *Works of Alice*, 69.
43. Williams, "In-depth Portrait," 85.
44. Ibid.
45. Ibid.
46. Wade-Gayles, "Black Women Journalists," 141.
47. Ibid.
48. Ibid.
49. Williams, "In-depth Portrait," 63.
50. Hull, *Give Us Each Day*, 42–43.
51. Williams, "In-depth Portrait," 63.
52. Ibid., 64–66.
53. Hull, *Give Us Each Day*, 43.
54. Ibid.
55. Alice Dunbar-Nelson, "From a Woman's Point of View, *Pittsburgh Courier*, 9 January 1926.

56 Alice Dunbar-Nelson, "Une Femme Dit," *Pittsburgh Courier*, 20 February 1926.
57 Hull, *Give Us Each Day*, 143.
58 Ibid., 85–88. Reference can also be found on Hull, *Give Us Each Day*, 142.
59 For reference, see Penn, *Afro-American Press*, 413.
60 Williams, "In-depth Portrait," 87.
61 Ibid.
62 Hull, *Color, Sex and Poetry*, 90.
63 Alice Dunbar-Nelson, "From a Woman's Point of View," *Pittsburgh Courier*, 2 January 1926.
64 Alice Dunbar-Nelson, "From a Woman's Point of View, 9 January 1926.
65 Ibid.
66 Ibid.
67 Dunbar-Nelson, "Une Femme Dit," *Pittsburgh Courier*, 20 March 1926.
68 Ibid.
69 Ibid.
70 Alice Dunbar-Nelson, Editorial in the *Washington Eagle*, 26 October 1928.
71 Ibid.
72 Ibid.
73 Alice Dunbar-Nelson, "As in the Looking Glass," *Washington Eagle*, 2 November 1928.
74 Ibid.
75 Alice Dunbar-Nelson, "Politics in Delaware," *Opportunity*, (November 1924) 23: 339.
76 Ibid.
77 Alice Dunbar-Nelson, "Une Femme Dit," *Pittsburg Courier*, 15 May 1926.
78 Dunbar-Nelson, "Une Femme Dit," 10 April 1926.
79 Alice Dunbar-Nelson, "Une Femme Dit," *Pittsburgh Courier*, 7 August 1926.
80 Dunbar-Nelson, "Une Femme Dit," 10 April 1926.
81 Alice Dunbar-Nelson, "Une Femme Dit," *Pittsburgh Courier*, 30 November 1928.
82 Ibid.
83 Alice Dunbar-Nelson, "As in a Looking Glass," *Washington Eagle*, 28 December 1928.
84 Ibid.
85 Ibid.
86 Alice Dunbar-Nelson, "From a Woman's Point of View" *Pittsburgh Courier*, 6 February 1926.

Notes

87 Ibid.
88 Alice Dunbar-Nelson, "From a Woman's Point of View," *Pittsburgh Courier*, 12 May 1926.
89 Alice Dunbar-Nelson, "Une Femme Dit," 15 May 1926.
90 Ibid.
91 Alice Dunbar-Nelson, "Une Femme Dit," *Pittsburgh Courier,* 13 February 1926.
92 Dunbar-Nelson, "Une Femme Dit," 10 April 1926.
93 Ibid.
94 Ibid.
95 Alice Dunbar-Nelson, "Une Femme Dit," *Pittsburgh Courier*, 13 March 1926.
96 Alice Dunbar-Nelson, "From a Woman's Point of View," *Pittsburgh Courier,* 2 January 1926.
97 Alice Dunbar-Nelson, "Une Femme Dit," *Pittsburgh Courier,* 22 May 1926.
98 Ibid.
99 Ibid.
100 Ibid.
101 Alice Dunbar-Nelson, "From a Woman's Point of View," 9 January 1926.
102 Ibid.
103 Ibid.
104 Alice Dunbar-Nelson, "Une Femme Dit, *Pittsburgh Courier*, 6 March 1926.
105 Ibid.
106 Dunbar-Nelson, "From a Woman's Point of View," 9 January 1926.
107 Dunbar-Nelson, "From a Woman's Point of View," 6 February 1926.
108 Ibid.
109 Alice Dunbar-Nelson, "Une Femme Dit," 20 March 1926.
110 Ibid.
111 Alice Dunbar-Nelson, "As in a Looking Glass," *Washington Eagle,* 3 August 1928.
112 Ibid.
113 Dunbar-Nelson, "As in a Looking Glass," *Washington* Eagle, 28 September 1928.
114 Alice Dunbar-Nelson, "As in a Looking Glass," *Washington Eagle,* 14 December 1928, cited in Hull, *Give Us This Day*, 282.
115 Alice Dunbar-Nelson, "Woman's Most Serious Problem" *Messenger,* 27 March 1927.
116 Ibid.
117 Ibid.

118. Ibid.
119. Alice Dunbar-Nelson, "Une Femme Dit," *Pittsburgh Courier,* 3 April 1926.
120. Alice Dunbar-Nelson, "As in a Looking Glass," *Washington Eagle,* 11 January 1929.
121. Dunbar-Nelson, "As in a Looking Glass," 15 March 1929.
122. Dunbar-Nelson, "As in a Looking Glass," *Washington Eagle,* 22 March 1929.
123. Dunbar-Nelson, "As in a Looking Glass," *Washington Eagle,* 22 February 1929.
124. Ibid.
125. Ibid.
126. Ibid.
127. Dunbar-Nelson, "As in a Looking Glass," *Washington Eagle,* 8 August 1930, cited in Hull, *Give Us Each Day,* 347.
128. Dunbar-Nelson, "As in a Looking Glass," *Washington Eagle,* 22 March 1929.
129. Ibid.
130. Ibid.
131. Dunbar-Nelson, "From a Woman's Point of View," 6 February 1926.
132. Ibid.
133. Alice Dunbar-Nelson, "Une Femme Dit" *Pittsburgh Courier,* 29 May 1926.
134. Dunbar-Nelson, "Une Femme Dit," 15 May 1926.
135. Dunbar-Nelson, "Une Femme Dit," 6 February 1926.
136. Ibid.
137. Ibid.
138. Ibid.
139. Ibid.
140. Alice Dunbar-Nelson, "As in a Looking Glass," *Washington Eagle,* 30 November 1928.
141. Dunbar-Nelson, "As in a Looking Glass," 22 March 1929.
142. Ibid.
143. Dunbar-Nelson, "From a Woman's Point of View," 20 February 1926.
144. Dunbar-Nelson, "Une Femme Dit," 26 March 1926.
145. Dunbar-Nelson, "Une Femme Dit," 20 March 1926.
146. Dunbar-Nelson, "From a Woman's Point of View," 20 February 1926.

Notes

CHAPTER FIVE NOTES

1. Amy Jacques Garvey, "Will the Negro Be Re-enslaved?," *The Negro World*, 15 December 1923.
2. Typewritten notation in Marcus Mosiah Garvey Memorial Collection, Box 12, Fisk University Library Special Collections, Nashville, Tennessee.
3. "Marcus Garvey and UNIA Papers Project," Fact Sheet, University of California at Los Angeles. Available at www.isop.ucla.edu/mgpp/facts.htm.
4. See, for example, Amy Jacques Garvey, *Garvey and Garveyism* (New York: Self, 1923); Beverly Reed, "Amy Jacques-Garvey," *Ebony* (June 1971): 46.
5. John Hope Franklin and Alfred A. Moss, Jr., *From Slavery to Freedom: A History of Negro Americans* (New York: McGraw-Hill Publishing Company, 1988), 321.
6. "Marcus Garvey and the UNIA," 2.
7. Darlene Clark Hine, Elsa Barkley Brown, and Rosalyn Terborg-Penn, eds., *Black Women in America: An Historical Encyclopedia*, vol. 1 (Bloomington, IN: Indiana University Press, 1993), 483.
8. Amy Jacques Garvey, "Role of Women in Liberation Struggles, *Negro World*, 9 February 1924.
9. Ibid.
10. Ibid.
11. See, for example, Hine, et al., *Black Women in America*, 483; "Marcus Garvey and UNIA", 2.
12. Reed, "Amy Jacques Garvey," 48.
13. "Agreement between Universal Negro Improvement Association, Inc., African Communities League, Inc., and Marcus Garvey and Amy Jacques Garvey," New York, May 1923, Box 5, Folder 1, Marcus Mosiah Garvey Manuscript Collection, Fisk University, Nashville, TN.
14. See, for example, Tony Martin, "Women in the Garvey Movement," in Rupert Lewis and Patrick Bryan, eds., *Garvey, His Work and Impact*, (Trenton, NJ: African World Press, Inc., 1991), 72.
15. Ibid.
16. Honor Ford-Smith, "Women and the Garvey Movement in Jamaica," in Rupert Lewis and Patrick Bryan, eds., *Garvey: His Work and Impact*, 78.
17. Reed, "Amy Jacques Garvey," 46.
18. Dorothy C. Salem, "Black Women and the NAACP, 1910–1922: An Encounter with Race, Class, and Gender," in Kim Marie Vaz, ed., *Black Women in America* (Thousand Oaks; Sage Publications, 1995), 54.
19. Lawrence W. Levine, *Black Culture and Black Consciousness: Afro-American Folk Thought from Slavery to Freedom* (New York: Oxford University Press, 1977), 269.
20. Ibid.

21 John Hope Franklin and Alfred A. Moss, Jr., *From Slavery to Freedom: A History of Negro Americans* (New York: McGraw-Hill Publishing Company, 1988), 321.
22 Ibid.
23 E. Franklin Frazier, "The Garvey Movement," *Opportunity* 4 (November 1926): 346.
24 Ibid.
25 Amy Jacques Garvey, Introduction to *Black Power in America: Marcus Garvey's Impact on Jamaica and Africa* (Kingston, Jamaica: Amy Jacques Garvey, 1968), 1.
26 Amy Jacques Garvey, Handwritten notation in Scrapbook, Marcus Mosiah Garvey Memorial Collection, Box 12, Fisk University Library Special Collections, Nashville, Tennessee.
27 Amy Jacques Garvey, "Some Handicaps of the Negro Business Man," *The Negro World*, 7 February 1925.
28 For reference, see, Beryl Satter, "Marcus Garvey, Father Divine and the Gender of Politics of Race Difference and Race Neutrality," *American Quarterly* (1996) 48: 44. Satter cites E. David Gronon, *Black Moses: The Story of Marcus Garvey and the Universal Negro Improvement Association*, (Madison, WI: 1974).
29 James H. Cone, *Martin and Malcolm and America: A Dream or a Nightmare* (Maryknoll, NY: Orbis Books, 1991), 10.
30 Amy Jacques Garvey, "Mankind's Duty to Children," *The Negro World*, 15 March 1924.
31 Horace Campbell in Rupert Lewis and Patrick Bryant, eds., *Garvey, His Work, and Impact* (Mona, Jamaica: Institute of Social and Economic Research, 1988), 191.
32 Amy Jacques Garvey, "Labor at the British Helm," *The Negro World*, 2 February 1924.
33 Ibid.
34 Ibid.
35 Amy Jacques Garvey, "The Civilized Savage," *The Negro World*, 16 February 1924.
36 Ibid.
37 Amy Jacques Garvey, "Enslave the Mind and You Enslave the Body," *The Negro World*, 20 June 1925.
38 Ibid.
39 Amy Jacques Garvey, "Mankind's Duty to Children"
40 Amy Jacques Garvey, "Woman as Cannon Fodder," *The Negro World*, 9 February 1924.
41 Ibid.

Notes

42. Amy Jacques Garvey, "It's Up to You," *The Negro World*, 13 September 1924.
43. Amy Jacques Garvey, "Why White Men Want Africa," *The Negro World*, 18 April 1925.
44. Amy Jacques Garvey, "The Future Portends Evil for the Dominant Posers," *The Negro World*, 16 May 1925.
45. Ibid.
46. Amy Jacques Garvey, "Black Men as Cannon Fodder," *The Negro World*, 11 April 1925.
47. Amy Jacques Garvey, "Yellow and White Races Prepare for Future Armageddon—Mr. Black Man, What about You?," 5 July 1925.
48. Ibid.
49. Ibid.
50. Cone, *Martin and Malcolm*, 7.
51. Ibid., 7–8.
52. Amy Jacques Garvey, "The Tidal Wave of Oppressed Peoples Beats Against the Color Line," *The Negro World*, 18 July 1925.
53. Ibid.
54. Amy Jacques Garvey, "Be Prepared," Manuscript in Marcus Mosiah Garvey Memorial Collection Box 5, Folder 11, Fisk University, Nashville, TN.
55. Ibid.
56. Ibid.
57. Amy Jacques Garvey, "Liberia, the Savior of American Rubber Manufacturers—At What Price," *The Negro World*, 12 September 1925.
58. Ibid.
59. Ibid.
60. Ibid.
61. Amy Jacques Garvey, "French Debt and Black Man's Lands," *The Negro World*, 10 October 1925.
62. Ibid.
63. Jacques Garvey, "Black Men as Cannon Fodder," *The Negro World*, 11 April 1925.
64. Jacques Garvey, "French Debt and Black Man's Lands."
65. Amy Jacques Garvey, "The Germ of Armageddon," *The Negro World*, 15 May 1926.
66. Amy Jacques Garvey, "Whither Italy," *The Negro World*, 12 June 1926.
67. Amy Jacques Garvey, "What White Men Are Finding in Africa," *The Negro World*, 26 June 1926.
68. Amy Jacques Garvey, "What the World Needs You Should Produce," 4 September 1926.

69 Amy Jacque Garvey, Handwritten notation in Scrapbook, Marcus Mosiah Garvey Memorial Collection.
70 Amy Jacques Garvey, "Acquit Yourselves as Men," *The Negro World*, 30 April 1927.
71 Amy Jacques Garvey, "Italy Goes Sabre [sic] Rattling," *The Negro World*, 6 August 1927.
72 Amy Jacques Garvey, "Afghanistan and Ceylon," *The Negro World* 1 October, 1927; Jacques Garvey, "Those Who Suf1fer from India's Independence, *The Negro World*, 15 October 1927.
73 Amy Jacques Garvey, Acquit Yourselves Like Men."
74 Amy Jacques Garvey, Handwritten note in Scrapbook, Marcus Mosiah Garvey Memorial Collection, Box 12, Fisk University, Nashville, TN.
75 Amy Jacques Garvey, "New Year's Resolutions," *The Negro World*, 3 January 1925.
76 Ibid.
77 Ibid.
78 Amy Jacques Garvey, "How to Help Better the Economic Conditions of the West Indies," *The Negro World*, 10 January 1925.
79 Jacques Garvey, "Why White Men Want Africa."
80 Amy Jacques Garvey, "Is Life Worth Living?," *The Negro World*, 17 October 1925.
81 Amy Jacques Garvey, "What Have You Accomplished This Year?," *The Negro World*, 28 November 1925.
82 Ibid.
83 Amy Jacques Garvey, "Wherefore a National Urge?," *The Negro World*, 6 June 1925.
84 Ibid.
85 Amy Jacques Garvey, "Yellow and White Races."
86 Jacques Garvey, "Sweet Are the Uses of Adversity." *The Negro World*, 8 August 1925.
87 Amy Jacques Garvey, "What Have You Accomplished This Year?"
88 Jacques Garvey, "Some Handicaps."
89 Ibid.
90 Ula Y. Taylor, *The Veiled Garvey: The Life and Times of Amy Jacques Garvey* (Chapel Hill, NC: The University of North Carolina Press, 2003), 3.
91 Ibid.
92 Ibid.
93 Jacques Garvey, "Some Handicaps."
94 Ibid.
95 Ibid.

96 Ibid.
97 Amy Jacques Garvey, "Fearful of Going Black," *The Negro World*, 14 November 1925.
98 Amy Jacques Garvey, "Poverty Is Slavery," *The Negro World*, 21 August 1926.
99 Amy Jacques Garvey, "Africa Bides Her Time," *The Negro World*, 27 February 1927.
100 Ibid.
101 Ibid.
102 Jacques Garvey, "What the World Needs."
103 See, for example, Gilmore, *Gender and Jim Crow*; Giddings, *When and Where I Enter*, Gerder Lerner, *Black Women in America: A Documentary History* (New York: Vintage Press, 1973).
104 Ibid.
105 Amy Jacques Garvey, "Stop Hunting a Job and Create One," *The Negro World*, 9 October 1926.
106 Ibid.
107 Ibid.
108 Ibid.
109 Ibid.
110 Ibid.
111 Amy Jacques Garvey, "It All Depends on You," *The Negro World*, 14 May 1927.
112 Amy Jacques Garvey, "How to Help Better."
113 Ibid.
114 Ibid.
115 Ibid.
116 Jacques Garvey, "The Civilized Savage."
117 Ibid.
118 Amy Jacques Garvey, "Solving the Jewish Problem," *The Negro World*, 1 March 1924.
119 Ibid.
120 Amy Jacques Garvey, *The Negro World*, 24 May 1924.
121 Ibid.
122 Amy Jacques Garvey, "New York Jews Raise Over Six Million Dollars—What of Negroes?," *The Negro World*, 5 June 1926.
123 Amy Jacques Garvey, "Commerce and Industry Keep the World Humming," *The Negro World*, 18 September 1926.
124 Ibid.

125 Ibid.
126 Ibid.
127 Jacques Garvey, "Man's Inhumanity to Man."
128 Ibid.
129 Ibid.
130 Ibid.
131 Amy Jacques Garvey, "The High Cost of Propaganda," The Negro World 14 August 1926.
132 Ibid.
133 Amy Jacques Garvey, "World Renaissance," *The Negro World*, 3 March 1924.
134 Ibid.
135 Amy Jacques Garvey, "God Give Us Men," *The Negro World*, 2 January 1926.
136 Ibid.
137 Ibid.
138 Ibid.
139 Amy Jacques Garvey, "Acquit Yourselves Like Men."
140 Amy Jacques Garvey, "Racial Achievements," *The Negro World*, 1 November 1924.
141 Amy Jacques Garvey, "Woman's Function in Life," *The Negro World*, 19 December 1925.
142 Ibid.
143 Ibid.
144 Jacques Garvey, "Woman as Cannon Fodder."
145 Amy Jacques Garvey, "Women as Leaders Nationally and Racially," *The Negro World*, 24 October 1925.
146 Amy Jacques Garvey, "Role of Women in Liberation Struggle," Manuscript in Marcus Mosiah Garvey Memorial Collection, Box 12.
147 Amy Jacques Garvey, "Scanty Clothing Hardly," *The Negro World*, 27 November 1926.
148 Amy Jacques Garvey, "No Sex in Brains and Ability," *The Negro World*, 27 December 1926.
149 Amy Jacques Garvey, "Black Women's Resolve for 1926," *The Negro World*, 9 January 1926.
150 Ibid.
151 Jacques Garvey, "Woman as Cannon Fodder."
152 Jacques Garvey, "Women as Leaders."
153 Ibid.

Notes

154 Jacques Garvey, "Role of Women."
155 Amy Jacques Garvey, "Will the Entrance of Women in Politics Affect Home Life?," *The Negro World*, 14 June 1924.
156 Ibid.
157 Jacques Garvey, "Women as Leaders."
158 Ibid.
159 Amy Jacques Garvey, "The Home or School—Which Exercises the Greater Influence on the Lives of Children?," *The Negro World*, 26 July 1924.
160 Amy Jacques Garvey, "What the So-Called Savage Can Teach the Missionary," *The Negro World*, 2 May 1925.
161 Ibid.
162 Amy Jacques Garvey, "Lone White Woman Explore Africa—Are Negro Women Afraid?" *The Negro World*, 31 October 1925.
163 Ibid.
164 Ibid.
165 Jacques Garvey, "World Renaissance."
166 Ibid.
167 Amy Jacques Garvey, "Duty of Parents to Children."
168 Ibid.
169 Ibid.
170 Jacques Garvey, "Women as Leaders."
171 Ibid.
172 Ibid.
173 Amy Jacques Garvey, "The Negro Needs Trained Men," *The Negro World*, 3 July 1926.
174 Ibid.
175 Ibid.
176 Amy Jacques Garvey, "Listen Women," *The Negro World*, 9 April 1927.
177 Ibid.
178 Amy Jacques Garvey, "A Dearth of Husbands," *The Negro World*, 9 July 1927.
179 Ibid.
180 Amy Jacques Garvey, "It All Depends on You."
181 Ibid.
182 Franklin, *From Slavery to Freedom*, 321.
183 See, for example, Henry Louis Gates, Jr. and Terri Hume Oliver, eds., W.E.B. DuBois, *The Souls of Black Folks* (New York: W.W. Norton, 1999).
184 Quoted in Franklin, *From Slavery to Freedom*, 321.

185 For reference, see Amy Jacques Garvey, *Philosophy and Opinions of Marcus Garvey* (New York, 1923: Self).
186 For reference, see Martin, *Women in the Garvey Movement.*
187 Jacques Garvey, "World Renaissance."
188 Ibid.
189 Ibid.
190 Amy Jacques Garvey, "Is Christianity the Best Solution of the World's Ills?," *The Negro World*, 16 August 1924.
191 Ibid.
192 Ibid.
193 Amy Jacques Garvey, "Scanty Clothing Make Hardy Women."
194 Ibid.
195 Jacques Garvey, "What the So-Called Savage."
196 Amy Jacques Garvey, "Have You Written Home?," *The Negro World*, 9 August 1924.
197 Amy Jacques Garvey, *The Negro World*, 1 December 1923. (Headline Illegible.)
198 Ibid.
199 Jacques Garvey, "Have a Heart."
200 Amy Jacques Garvey, "It's Up to You."
201 Amy Jacques Garvey, "Send in Your Articles for this Page," *The Negro World*, 6 February 1926.
202 Cone, *Martin and Malcolm*, 8.

CHAPTER SIX NOTES

1 Patricia Hill Collins, *Black Feminist Thought: Knowledge, Consciousness, and the Politics of Empowerment* (New York: Routledge, Chapman and Hall, Inc., 1991), 10.
2 References to the women's home and family life are found throughout their diaries, autobiographies, and other personal papers. See, for example, Alfreda Duster, ed., *Crusade for Justice: The Autobiography of Ida B. Wells* (Chicago: The University of Chicago Press, 1990); Mary Church Terrell, *A Colored Woman in a White World* (Washington, D.C.: Ransdell, Inc., 1990); Gloria T. Hull, ed., *Give Us Each Day: The Diary of Alice Dunbar-Nelson* (New York: W. W. Norton, 1984).
3 Hull, *Give Us Each Day*, 23.
4 Darlene Clark Hine, et al. *Black Women in America: An Historical Encyclopedia*, (Bloomington, IN: Indiana University Press, 1993), 1158–1159.
5 Terrell, *A Colored Woman*, 1–2.

6	Ibid.
7	Ibid., 2.
8	Duster, *Crusade for Justice*, 10.
9	Terrell, *Colored Woman*, 22.
10	Ibid., 22–23.
11	Hull, *Give Us Each Day*, 87.
12	Wade-Gayles, "Black Women Journalist: An Approach to the Study of Black Women's History," *Callaloo*, 4:138.
13	See, for example, Jones, *Quest for Equality*, 121; Glenda Gilmore, *Gender and Jim Crow: Women and the Politics of White Supremacy in North Carolina: 1896–1920* (Chapel Hill, NC: The University of North Carolina Press, 1996), 75–76.
14	Hull, *Give Us Each Day*, 23.
15	Ibid.
16	Dorothy Sterling, ed., Introduction to *We Are Your Sisters: Black Women in the Nineteenth Century* (New York: W. W. Norton and Company, 1984), xiii.
17	Paula Giddings, *When and Where I Enter: The Impact of Women on Race and Sex in America* (New York: Morrow, 1984), 71.
18	Ibid., 71, 72.
19	Amy Jacques Garvey, "Woman's Function in Life," *The Negro World*, 19 December 1925.
20	Alice Dunbar-Nelson, "From a Woman's Point of View, *The Pittsburgh Courier*, 9 January 1926.
21	See, for example, Rosalyn Terborg-Penn, *African American Women in the Struggle for the Vote, 1850–1920* (Bloomington, IN: Indiana University Press, 1998); Rosalyn Terborg-Penn, "African American Women and the Woman Suffrage Movement," In Marjorie Spruill-Wheeler, ed., *One Woman, One Vote: Rediscovering the Woman Suffrage Movement* (Troutdale, OR: NewSage Press, 1995).
22	Beryl Satter, "Marcus Garvey, Father Divine and the Gender Politics of Race Difference and Race Neutrality," *American Quarterly*, 48.1. Satter argued that Garvey expected Jacques Garvey "to be the perfect wife, while also serving as his secretary, legal adviser, fund-raiser, editor, and full-time propagandist." Moreover, after their children were born, Jacques Garvey received "little financial or practical aid from her husband" and had to drop her political work on behalf of the UNIA "altogether in order to feed, shelter, and educate her children." Satter also pointed out that Jacques Garvey and the "race mothers" were more likely to find themselves "isolated and exhausted than active and empowered. She might even begin to feel that irresponsible black men, as much as white racism, were her primary obstacles.

23 Jacqueline Jones, *Labor of Love, Labor of Sorrow: Black Women, Work, and the Family from Slavery to the Present* (New York: Basic Books, Inc, 1985), 110.
24 Ibid.
25 Ibid.
26 See, for example, Duster, *Crusade for Justice*, 297–308, 321–334.
27 Marcus Mosiah Garvey, "The Negro's Greatest Enemy," *Current History* (1923). Cited in The Marcus Garvey and UNIA Papers Project, UCLA. Available at www.//isop.ucla./edu/mgpp/sample01.htm: INTERNET, 6.
28 Amy Jacques Garvey, "Have the Scientific Achievements of Negroes Benefited Our Race?," *The Negro World*, 18 November 1924.
29 Ibid.
30 Amy Jacques Garvey, "The High Cost of Propaganda," *The Negro World*, 14 August 1926.
31 Ibid.
32 Ibid.
33 James Cone, *Martin and Malcolm and America: A Dream or a Nightmare* (Maryknoll, NY: Orbis Books, 1991). Cone wrote that Marcus Garvey's perspectives were derived "from the bottom of the black experience" and were intended to "elevate the cultural and psychological well-being of downtrodden blacks burdened with low self-esteem in a society dominated by the violence of white hate groups, and the sophisticated racism of the Social Darwinists."
34 Amy Jacques Garvey, "Are We Proud of Our Dark Skins?" *The Negro World*, 1 August 1925.
35 Ibid.
36 Ibid.
37 Hull, *Give Us Each Day*, 266.
38 Ibid.
39 Ibid., 183.
40 Duster, *Crusade for Justice*, 329.
41 Ibid., 83; McMurry, *Keep Waters Troubled*, 183.
42 Ibid., 83.
43 Ibid., 258–261.
44 Ibid., 258
45 McMurry, *Keep Waters* Troubled, 183.
46 Duster, *Crusade for Justice*, 25, 26.
47 Ibid., 243
48 Ibid., 260.
49 Hull, *Give Us Each Day*, 87.

50 Gilmore, *Gender and Jim Crow*, 285.
51 Ibid.
52 Ibid., 151, 152.
53 Ibid., 150.
54 Giddings, *When and Where*, 6.

Bibliography

SECONDARY SOURCES

BOOKS AND ARTICLES

Aptheker, Bettina. *Woman Suffrage and the Crusade Against Lynching, 1890–1920*. Washington, D.C. The National Council of Negro Women. 1979.

Aptheker, Herbert. ed., *A Documentary History of the Negro People in the United States*. 2 vols. New York. Citadel Press. 1951. 1966.

Banner, Lois W. *Women in Modern America: A Brief History*. New York. Brace Jovanovich and Company. 1974.

Bell, Barbara L. *Black Biographical Sources: An Annotated Bibliography*. New Haven. CT. Yale University. 1970.

Bennett, Leronne. *Before the Mayflower: A History of Black America*. 4th ed. Chicago. Johnson Publishing Company. 1969.

Black, Jay, Bryant, Jennings and Thompson, Susan. *Introduction to Media Communication*. 5th edition. Boston. McGraw Hill. 1998.

Blackett, R. J. M. *Beating Against the Barriers: Biographical Essays in Nineteenth Century Afro-American History*. Baton Rouge. LA. Louisiana State University Press. 1986.

Brooks, Maxwell. *The Negro Press Re-examined*. Boston. Christopher. 1995.

Brown, Hallie Q. *Homespun Heroines and Other Women of Distinction*. Freeport. New York. Books for Libraries Press. 1971.

Brown, Warren. A *Check List of Negro Newspapers in the United States, 1827–1946*. Jefferson City. MO. Lincoln University. 1946.

Bryan, Carter R. "Negro Journalism in America Before Emancipation." *Journalism Monographs*. September. 1996.

Bryan, Violet. *The Myth of New Orleans in Literature*. Knoxville. TN. The University Tennessee Press. 1993.

Bullock, Penelope. *The Afro-American Press. 1838–1909*. Baton Rouge, LA: Louisiana State University Press. 1981.

Buni, A. *Robert L. Vann of the Pittsburgh Courier*. Pittsburgh. PA. University of Pittsburgh Press. 1974.

Campbell, Horace. In Rupert Lewis and Patrick Bryant. eds. *Garvey, His Work, and Impact*. Mona. Jamaica. Institute of Social and Economic Research. 1988.

Cook, Clark. "Ida B. Wells." Available at the Black Excellence in World History site: http://www.csusm.edu/Black_Excellence/documents/pg-i-b-wells2.html.

Cooper, Anna J. *A Voice from the South*. New York. Oxford University Press. 1988.

Daniels, S. I. *Women Builders*. Washington, D.C. Associated Publishers. 1970.

Dann, Martin E. *The Black Press: 1827–1890: The Quest for National Identity*. New York. G.P. Putnam's Sons. 1971.

Dannett, Sylvia. *Profiles of Negro Womanhood*. vol. 1. Yonkers, NY. Educational Heritage, Incorporated. 1969.

Davis, Angela Y. *Women, Race, and Class*. New York. Random House. 1989.

Davis, A.P. *From the Dark Tower: Afro-American Writers, 1900–1960*. Washington, D.C. Howard University Press. 1975.

Davis, Elizabeth L. *Lifting as They Climb: The History of the National Association of Colored Women*. Washington, D.C. National Association of Colored Women. 1933.

Davis, Lenwood G. *A History of Journalism in the Black Community: A Preliminary Survey*. Council of Planning Libraries Exchange Bibliography. #862.

Davis, Marianna. ed. *Contributions of Black Women in Media*. Columbia. SC. Kenday Press. 1982.

Bibliography

Davis, Phillip B. "Mary Church Terrell (1863–1954)," http://www.csusm.edu/Black_Excellence/documents/pg-m-c-terrell2.html.

De-Costa-Willis, Miriam. *The Memphis Diary of Ida B. Wells*. Boston. Beacon Press. 1995.

Detweiler, Frederick G. *The Negro Press in the United States*. College Park. MD. McGrath Publishing Company, 1968.

Dickens-Garcia, Hazel. *Journalistic Standards in Nineteenth-Century America*. Madison. University of Wisconsin Press. 1989.

DuBois, W.E.B. *Black Reconstruction in America*. New York. Atheneum. 1973.

Emery, Edwin and Emery, Michael. *The Press and America: An Interpretative History of the Mass Media*. 7th ed. Englewood Cliffs. NJ. Prentice Hall. 1992.

Folkerts, Jean. ed. *Media Voices: A Historical Perspective*. New York. Macmillan. 1992.

Ford-Smith, Honor. "Women and the Garvey Movement in Jamaica." In Rupert Lewis and Patrick Bryan. eds. *Garvey: His Work and Impact*. Trenton. NJ. African World Press, Inc. 1991. 78.

Franklin, John Hope and Moss, Alfred A. Jr. *From Slavery to Freedom: A History of Negro Americans*. 6th ed. New York. McGraw-Hill Publishing Company. 1988.

Garvey, Marcus Mosiah. "The Negro's Greatest Enemy." *Current History 1923*. Cited in The Marcus Garvey and UNIA Papers Project, UCLA. Available at www.isop.ucla.edu/mgpp/sample01.htm.6.

Gates, Louis Jr. and Oliver, Terri Hume. eds. W.E. B. DuBois, *The Souls of Black Folks*. New York. W.W. Norton. 1999.

Giddings, Paula. *When and Where I Enter: The Impact of Black Women on Race and Sex in America)*. New York. William Morrow and Company. Inc. 1984.

Gilmore, Glenda. *Gender and Jim Crow: Women and the Politics of White Supremacy in North Carolina, 1896–1920*. Chapel Hill. NC. The North Carolina Press. 1996.

Fuller, Juanita. *An Annotated Bibliography of Biographies and Autobiographies of Negroes, 1839–1961*. Rochester. NY. The University Press. 1965.

Hall, Nora Darlene. "On Being an African-American Woman: Gender and Race in the Writings of Six Black Women Journalists, 1849–1936." Ph.D. diss. University of Minnesota. 1998.

Hardy, Gayle. *American Women Civil Rights Activists: Biobibliographies of 68 Women Leaders, 1825–1992.* Jefferson. NC. McFarland and Company. 1993.

Harley, Sharon. Speaking Up: The Politics of Black Women's Labor History," in Higginbotham, Elizabeth and Romero, Mary. eds. *Women and Work, Exploring Race, Ethnicity and Class.* vol. 6. Thousand Oaks. CA. Sage Publications, Inc. 1997.

Harley, Sharon. and Terborg-Penn, Rosalyn. eds. *The Afro-American Woman: Struggles and Images.* New York: Kennikat Press. 1978.

Hendricks, Wanda. "Ida B Wells-Barnett." In Darlene Clack Hine. et al. *Black Women in America: An Historical Encyclopedia.* vol. 2. Bloomington. IN. Indiana University Press. 1993.

Higginbotham, Elizabeth. *Righteous Discontent: The Women's Movement in the Black Baptist Church, 1880–1920.* Cambridge. Harvard University Press. 1993.

Hill, Roy L. *Who's Who in the American Negro Press.* Dallas. TX. Royal Publishing Company. 1960.

Hine, Darlene C. Brown, Elsa and Terborg-Penn, Rosalyn. eds. *Black Women in America: An Historical Encyclopedia.* vols.1–2. Bloomington. IN. Indiana University Press. 1993.

Hine, Darlene C. *Black Women in the United States History: From Colonial Times through the Nineteenth Century.* 8 vols. Brooklyn. NY. Carlson Publishing Inc. 1990.

Hull, Gloria T. ed. *The Works of Alice Dunbar Nelson.* vol. 2. New York. Oxford University Press. 1988.

———. *Color, Sex and Poetry: Three Women Writers of the Harlem Renaissance* Bloomington. IN. Indiana University Press. 1984.

———. *All the Women Are White, All the Blacks Are Men, but Some of Us Are Brave: Black Women's Studies.* Old Westbury, N.Y. Feminist Press. 1982.

Hutton, Frankie P. "Historians Still Ignore Black Press." *Journalism Educator.* 28:48.

———. *The Early Black Press in America, 1827–1860.* Westport. CT. Greenwood Press. 1993.

Bibliography

Jones, Beverly. *Quest for Equality: The Life and Writings of Mary Eliza Church Terrell, 1863–1954*. Brooklyn. NY. Carlson Publishing. 1990.

Klots, Steve. *Ida B. Wells-Barnett: Civil Rights Leader*. New York. Chelsea House Publishers. 1994.

Koschersberger, Robert C. Jr. *More Than a Muckraker: Ida Tarbell's Life in Journalism*. Knoxville. TN. University of Tennessee Press. 1996.

Jones, Jacqueline. *Labor off Love, Labor of Sorrow: Black Women, Work, and the Family from Slavery to the Present*. New York. Basic Books, Inc. 1985.

LaBrie III, Henry L. *The Black Newspaper in America: A Guide*. 3rd ed. Kennebunkport. ME. Mercer House. 1973.

———. *Perspectives of the Black Press: 1974*. Kennebunkport. ME. Mercer House. 1974.

Lee, James Melvin. *History of American Journalism*. Boston. Houghton Mifflin. 1917.

Lerner, Gerda. *A Majority Finds Its Past*. New York. Oxford University Press. 1979.

———. *Black Women in White America: A Documentary History*. Vintage Books. 1973.

Logan, Rayford W. *The Negro in American Life and Thought: The Nadir, 1877–1901*. 1954. Re-issued as Logan, Rayford W. *The Betrayal of the Negro: From Rutherford B. Hayes to Woodrow Wilson*. New York. Collier Books. 1965.

Loewenberg, James and Bogin, Ruth. eds. 1976. *Black Women in Nineteenth-Century American Life: Their Words, Their Thoughts, Their Feelings*. University Park. PA. Pennsylvania State University Press.

Marzolf, Marion T. *Up From the Footnote: A History of Women Journalists*. New York. Hasting House Publishers. 1977.

Martin, Tony, "Women in the Garvey Movement." In Rupert Lewis and Patrick Bryan, eds. *Garvey, His Work and Impact*. Trenton. NJ. African World Press. Inc. 1991.

Matney, W. C. "Black Women in Media." In Davis, Marianna. ed. *Contributions of Black Women*. vol. 1. Columbia. SC. Kenday Press. 1982.

McMurry, Linda O. *To Keep the Waters Troubled: The Life of Ida B. Wells*. New York. Oxford University Press. 1998.

McMillen, Neil R. *Dark Journey: Black Mississippians in the Age of Jim Crow*. Chicago: University of Illinois Press. 1990.

Meier, August and Elliot Rudwick. *Negro Thought in American, 1880–1915: Racial Ideologies in the Age of Booker T. Washington*. Ann Arbor. MI. The University of Michigan Press. 1966.

Minority News Digest. 4 vols. New York. M. N. D., Inc. 1976.

Morton, Patricia. *Disfigured Images: The Historical Assault on Afro-American Women*. Westport. CT. Praeger. 1991.

Mossell, Mrs. N. F. (Gertrude). *The Work of the Afro-American Woman*. New York. Freeport. Books for Libraries Press. 1971.

Mott, Frank Luther. *American Journalism: A History, 1690–1960*. New York: The Macmillan Company. 1962.

Neverdon-Morton, Cynthia. *Afro-American Women of the South and the Advancement of the Race, 1895–1920*. Knoxville. TN. University of Tennessee Press. 1989.

Noble, Jeanne. *Beautiful, Also Are the Souls of My Black Sisters: A History of the Black Woman in America*. Englewood Cliffs. NJ. Prentice-Hall. 1978.

North Carolina Central University School of Library Science. (1978). *Newspapers and Periodicals by and about Black People: Southeastern Library Holdings*. Boston. G.K. Hall.

Penn, I. Garland. *The Afro-American Press and Its Editors*. New York. Arno Press. 1891.

Ploski, H. A. *The Negro Almanac: A Reference Work on the Afro-American*. New York. Bellwether. 1967.

Pride, Armistead and Wilson, Clint C. *A History of the Black Press*. Washington. D.C. Howard University Press. 1997.

Quarles, Benjamin. *Black Abolitionists*. New York. Oxford University Press. 1969.

Reed, Beverly. "Amy Jacques Garvey—Black, Beautiful and Free." Manuscript in Marcus Mosiah Garvey Memorial Collection, 1887–1940. Fisk University. Nashville. TN.

Reed, Beverly. "Amy Jacques-Garvey." *Ebony*. (June 1971).

Richings, G. F. *Evidence of Progress Among Colored People*. Chicago. Afro-American Press. 1969.

Bibliography

Rittenhouse, Mignon R. *The Amazing Nellie Bly*. Freeport. NY. Books for Libraries Press. 1956.

Royster, Jacqueline Jones. ed. *Southern Horrors and Other Writings: The Anti-Lynching Campaign of Ida B. Wells, 1892–1900*. Boston. Bedford Books. 1997.

Salem, Dorothy. C. "Black Women and the NAACP, 1909–1922: An Encounter with Race, Class, and Gender." In Vaz, Kim. ed. *Black Women in America*. Thousand Oaks. CA. Sage Publications. 1995.

Sanderson, Rosalie Massery. "Mary Church Terrell: A Black Woman's Crusade for Justice." Master's thesis. The University of Arkansas. 1973.

Scarborough, E. L. T. *Thomas Fortune: Militant Journalists*. Chicago. University of Chicago Press. 1972.

Semmes, Clovis E. comp. *Roots of Afrocentric Thought: A Reference Guide to Negro Digest/Black World, 1961–1976*. Westport. CT. Greenwood Press. 1998.

Shockley, Ann. *Afro-American Writers, 1746–1933: An Anthology and Critical Guide*. Boston. G. K. Hall and Company. 1988.

Simmons, Charles A. *The African American Press. With Special References to Four Newspapers, 1827–1965*. Jefferson. NC. McFarland and Company. Inc. 1998.

Sitkoff, Harvard. *A New Deal for Blacks: The Emergence of Civil Rights as a National Issue: The Depression Decade*. New York. Oxford University Press. 1978.

Skinner, Robert. "Lucy Wilmot Smith." In Jessie C. Smith. ed. *Notable Black American Women*. Detroit. Gale Research, Inc. 1992.

Smith, Jessie Smith. ed. *Notable Black American Women*. Detroit. Gale Research, Inc. 1992.

———. *Epic Lives: One Hundred Black Women Who Made a Difference*. Detroit. Visible Ink. 1993.

Solomon, Martha. *A Voice of Their Own: The Woman Suffrage Press, 1840–1910*. Tuscaloosa. University of Alabama Press. 1991.

Startt, James D. and Sloan, Wm. David. *Historical Methods in Mass Communication*. Hillsdale. NJ. Lawrence Erlbaum Associates, Inc. 1989.

Sterling, Dorothy. *Black Foremothers: Three Lives*. New York. The Feminist Press and the McGraw-Hill Book Company. 1979.

———. ed. *We Are Your Sisters: Black Women in the Nineteenth Century*. New York. W. W. Norton and Company. 1984.

Streitmatter, Rodger. *Raising Her Voice: African-American Women Journalists Who Changed History*. Lexington. KY. The University of Kentucky Press. 1994.

———. "Economic Conditions Surrounding Nineteenth-Century African-American Women Journalists: Two Case Studies." *Journalism History* 18 (1992): 33–40.

Suggs, Henry Lewis. ed. *The Black Press in the South, 1865–1979*. Westport. CT. Greenwood Press. 1983.

Taylor, Ula. "Garvey, Amy Euphemia Jacques (1896–1973)." In Hine, et al. eds. *Black Women in America: An Historical Encyclopedia*. vol.1. Bloomington. IN. Indiana University Press. 1993.

Terborg-Penn, Rosalyn. *African American Women in the Struggle for the Vote, 1850–1920*. Bloomington. IN. Indiana University Press. 1998.

———. "African American Women and the Woman Suffrage Movement." In Marjorie Spruill-Wheeler. ed. *One Woman, One Vote: Rediscovering the Woman Suffrage Movement*. Troutdale. OR. NewSage Press. 1995).

Thompson, Mildred I. *Ida B. Wells-Barnett: An Exploratory Study of an American Black Woman, 1893–1930*. Brooklyn, NY. Carlson Publishing Inc. 1990.

Thornbrough, Emma Lou. "Segregation in Indiana during the Klan Era of the 1920s," in Meier, August and Elliot Rudwick. *Negro Thought in American, 1880–1915: Racial Ideologies in the Age of Booker T. Washington*. Ann Arbor. MI. The University of Michigan Press. 1966.

Trimieu, Darryl M. *Voices of the Silenced: The Responsible Self in a Marginalized Community*. Cleveland. OH. Pilgrim Press. 1993.

Tripp, Bernell. *Origins of the Black Press: New York, 1827–1847*. Northport. AL. 1992.

Vaz, Kim M. "Organizing for Racial Justice: Black Women and the Dynamics of Race and Sex in Female Anti-Slavery Societies, 1832–1860" in *Black Women in America*. Thousand Oaks. CA. Sage Publications. 1995.

Wade-Gayles, Gloria. "Black Women Journalists in the South: 1880–1905: An Approach to the Study of Black Women's History." *Callaloo* 4 (1982).

Wesley, Charles. *The History of the National Association of Colored Women's Clubs: A Legacy of Service*. Washington, D.C. National Association of Colored Women. 1984.

Bibliography

Wheeler, Marjorie Spruill. *One Woman, One Vote: Rediscovering the Woman Suffrage Movement.* Troutdale. OR. NewSage Press. 1995.

Williams, Ruby O. "An In-Depth Portrait of Alice Dunbar-Nelson." Ph.D. Dissertation. University of California. Irvine. 1974.

Wilson, Clint C. *Black Journalists in Paradox: Historical Perspectives and Current Dilemmas.* Westport. CT. Greenwood Press. 1991.

Winks, Robin W. *The Blacks in Canada: A History.* New Haven. CT. Yale University Press. 1971.

Wolseley, Roland E. ed. *Black Achievers in American Journalism.* Nashville. TN. James C. Winston Publishing Company, Inc. 1995.

———. *The Black Press, U.S.A.* 2nd. ed. Ames, IA: Iowa State University Press. 1990.

Yee, Shirley J. "Organizing for Racial Justice: Black Women and the Dynamics of Race and Sex in Female Antislavery Societies, 1832–1860." In Vaz, Kim. ed. *Black Women in America.* Thousand Oaks. CA.1995.

Yenser, T. ed. *Who's Who in Colored America.* 6th ed. New York. Yenser Publishers. 1994.

PRIMARY SOURCES

BOOKS

Dunbar-Nelson, Alice. ed. *Masterpieces of Negro Eloquence.* ed. Harrisburg, PA. The Douglas Publishing Company. 1914.

———. *The Dunbar Speaker and Entertainer.* (Naperville, IL. J. L. Nichols and Company. 1920.

Duster, Alfreda. ed. *Crusade for Justice: The Autobiography of Ida B. Wells.* Chicago. The University of Chicago Press. 1970.

Garvey, Amy Jacques. "Contributions of Editor of Negro World." In scrapbook in Marcus Mosiah Garvey Memorial Collection, Box 12, Fisk University, Nashville, TN.

———. *Philosophy and Opinions of Marcus Garve.* New York. Self. 1923.

———. *Garvey and Garveyism.* New York. Self. 1923.

Harris, Trudier. comp. *Selected Works of Ida B. Wells-Barnett.* New York. Oxford University Press, 1991) 116–137.

Hull, Gloria T. ed. *Give Us Each Day: The Diary of Alice Dunbar-Nelson*. New York. W. W. Norton. 1984.

Terrell, Mary Church. *A Colored Woman in White America*. Washington, DC. Ransdell Inc. 1940. Reprint ed. Salem. NH. Ayer Company. 1986.

Willis, Miriam DeCosta. ed. *The Memphis Diary of Ida B. Wells*. Boston: Beacon Press. 1995.

PRIMARY SOURCES

ARTICLES

Dunbar-Nelson, Alice. "People of Color in Louisiana," Part 1. In *The Journal of Negro History*. October 1916.

———. "People of Color in Louisiana," Part 2. In *The Journal of Negro History*. January 1917.

———. "Negro Literature for Negro Pupils." *Southern Workman*. February 1922.

———. "From a Woman's Point of View." *Pittsburgh Courier*. 2 January 1926.

———. "From a Woman's Point of View." *Pittsburgh Courier*. 9 January 1926.

———. "From a Woman's Point of View." *Pittsburgh Courier*. 6 February 1926.

———. "From a Woman's Point of View." *Pittsburgh Courier*. 13 February 1926.

———. "Une Femme Dit." *Pittsburgh Courier*. 20 February 1926.

———. "Une Femme Dit." *Pittsburgh Courier*. 6 March 1926.

———. "Une Femme Dit." *Pittsburgh Courier*. 13 March 1926.

———. "Une Femme Dit." *Pittsburgh Courier*. 20 March 1926.

———. "Une Femme Dit." *Pittsburgh Courier*. 3 April 1926.

———. "Une Femme Dit." *Pittsburgh Courier*. 10 April 1926.

———. "Une Femme Dit." *Pittsburgh Courier*. 15 May 1926.

———. "Une Femme Dit." *Pittsburgh Courier*. 22 May 1926.

———. "Une Femme Dit." *Pittsburgh Courier*. 29 May 1926.

———. "Une Femme Dit." *Pittsburgh Courier*. 7 August 1926.

———. "Une Femme Dit." *Pittsburgh Courier*. 14 August 1926.

Bibliography

———. "Woman's Most Serious Problem." *The Messenger*. March 1927.

———. "The Problems of Personal Service." *The Messenger*. June 1927.

———. "Facing Life Squarely." *The Messenger*. July 1927.

———. "Woman's Most Serious Problem." *The Messenger* March 1927.

———. "The Ultimate Insult." *Washington Eagle*. 26 October 1928.

———. "As in a Looking Glass." *Washington Eagle*. 2 November 1928.

———. "As in a Looking Glass." *Washington Eagle*, 30 November 1928.

———. "As in a Looking Glass." *Washington Eagle*. 28 December 1928.

———. "As in a Looking Glass." *Washington Eagle*. 4 January 1929.

———. "As in a Looking Glass." *Washington Eagle*. 11 January 1929.

———. "As in a Looking Glass." *Washington Eagle*. 22 February 1929.

———. "As in a Looking Glass." *Washington Eagle*. 15 March 1929.

———. "As in a Looking Glass." *Washington Eagle*. 22 March 1929.

———. *The Negro World*, 1 December 1923. (Headline not legible.)

Garvey, Amy Jacques. "Will the Negro Be Re-enslaved?" *The Negro World*. 15 December 1923.

———. "Labor at the British Helm." *The Negro World*. 2 February 1924.

———. "Role of Women in Liberation Struggles. *Negro World*. 9 February 1924.

———. "The Civilized Savage." *The Negro World*. 16 February 1924.

———. "Solving the Jewish Problem." *The Negro World*. 1 March 1924.

———. "Mankind's Duty to Children." *The Negro World*. 15 March 1924

———. "World Renaissance." *The Negro World*. 22 March 1924.

———. "All the World's a Stage." *The Negro World*. 5 April 1924.

———. "Can War Be Outlawed?" *The Negro World*. 12 April 1924.

———. "Why the K.K.K. Honors Jews." *The Negro World*. 6 June 1924

———. "Will the Entrance of Women in Politics Affect Home Life?" *The Negro World*. 14 June 1924.

———. "The Joy of Living." *The Negro World*. 21 June 1924.

———. "The Home or School—Which Exercises the Greater Influence on the Lives of Children?" *The Negro World*. 26 July 1924.

———. "Have a Heart." *The Negro World*. 2 August 1924.

———. "Have You Written Home Yet?" *The Negro World*. 9 August 1924."

———. "Is Christianity the Best Solution of the World's Ills?" *The Negro World*. 16 August 1924.

———. "It's Up to You." *The Negro World*. 13 September 1924.

———. "Racial Achievements. *The Negro World*. 1 November 1924.

———. "Have the Scientific Achievements of Negroes Benefited Our Race?" .*The Negro World*. 8 November 1924.

———. "Christian or Modern Africa." *The Negro World*. 15 November 1924.

———. "It's Up to You." *The Negro World*. 13 September 1924.

———. "The White Man and Africa. *The Negro World*. 25 October 124.

———. "New Year's Resolutions." *The Negro World*. 3 January 1925.

———. "How to Help Better the Economic Conditions of the West Indies." *The Negro World*. 10 January 1925.

———. "Some Handicaps of the Negro Business Man." *The Negro World*. 7 February 1925.

———. "Wanted—Missionaries for Africa." *The Negro World*. 21 February 1925.

———. "Black Men as Cannon Fodder." *The Negro World*. 11 April 1925.

———. "Why White Men Want Africa." *The Negro World*. 18 April 1925.

———. "The Duty of Parents to Children." *The Negro World*. 2 May 1925.

———. "What the So-Called Savage Can Teach the Missionary." *The Negro World*. 2 May 1925.

———. "The Future Portends Evil for Dominant Powers." *The Negro World*. 16 May 1925.

———. "Wherefore a National Urge?" *The Negro World*. 6 June 1925.

———. "Enslave the Mind and You Enslave the Body." *The Negro World*. 20 June 1925.

Bibliography

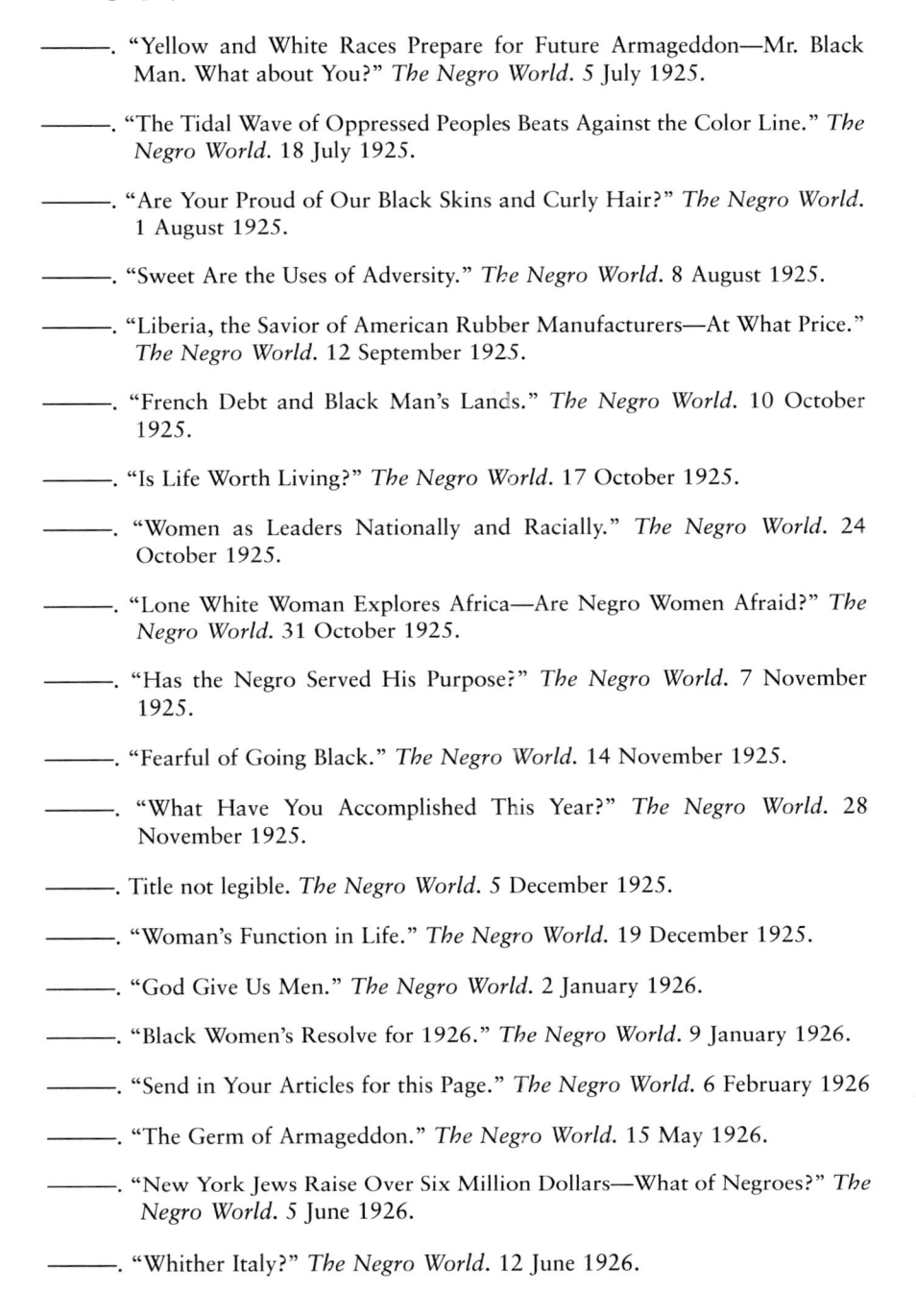

———. "Yellow and White Races Prepare for Future Armageddon—Mr. Black Man. What about You?" *The Negro World*. 5 July 1925.

———. "The Tidal Wave of Oppressed Peoples Beats Against the Color Line." *The Negro World*. 18 July 1925.

———. "Are Your Proud of Our Black Skins and Curly Hair?" *The Negro World*. 1 August 1925.

———. "Sweet Are the Uses of Adversity." *The Negro World*. 8 August 1925.

———. "Liberia, the Savior of American Rubber Manufacturers—At What Price." *The Negro World*. 12 September 1925.

———. "French Debt and Black Man's Lands." *The Negro World*. 10 October 1925.

———. "Is Life Worth Living?" *The Negro World*. 17 October 1925.

———. "Women as Leaders Nationally and Racially." *The Negro World*. 24 October 1925.

———. "Lone White Woman Explores Africa—Are Negro Women Afraid?" *The Negro World*. 31 October 1925.

———. "Has the Negro Served His Purpose?" *The Negro World*. 7 November 1925.

———. "Fearful of Going Black." *The Negro World*. 14 November 1925.

———. "What Have You Accomplished This Year?" *The Negro World*. 28 November 1925.

———. Title not legible. *The Negro World*. 5 December 1925.

———. "Woman's Function in Life." *The Negro World*. 19 December 1925.

———. "God Give Us Men." *The Negro World*. 2 January 1926.

———. "Black Women's Resolve for 1926." *The Negro World*. 9 January 1926.

———. "Send in Your Articles for this Page." *The Negro World*. 6 February 1926

———. "The Germ of Armageddon." *The Negro World*. 15 May 1926.

———. "New York Jews Raise Over Six Million Dollars—What of Negroes?" *The Negro World*. 5 June 1926.

———. "Whither Italy?" *The Negro World*. 12 June 1926.

———. "What White Men Are Finding in Africa." *The Negro World*. 26 June 1926.

———. "The Negro Race Needs Trained Men." *The Negro World*. 3 July 1926.

———. "I Am a Negro—And Beautiful." *The Negro World*. 10 July 1926.

———. "The High Cost of Propaganda." *The Negro World*. 14 August 1926.

———. "Poverty Is Slavery." *The Negro World*. 21 August 1926.

———. "What the World Needs You Should Produce." *The Negro World*. 4 September 1926.

———. "Commerce and Industry Keep the World Humming." *The Negro World*. 18 September 1926.

———. "Stop Hunting a Job and Create One." *The Negro World*. 9 October 1926.

———. "Scanty Clothing Hardly." *The Negro World*. 27 November 1926.

———. "No Sex in Brains and Ability." *The Negro World*. 27 December 1926.

———. "Man's Inhumanity to Man." *The Negro World*. 8 January 1927.

———. "Africa Bides Her Time." *The Negro World*. 27 February 1927.

———. "Listen Women." *The Negro World*. 9 April 1927.

———. "Acquit Yourselves Like Men." *The Negro World*. 30 April 1927.

———. "The Value of Propaganda." *The Negro World*. 5 May 1927.

———. "It All Depends on You." *The Negro World*. 14 May 1927.

———. "A Dearth of Husbands." *The Negro World*. 9 July 1927.

———. "Italy Goes Sabre [sic] Rattling." *The Negro World*. 6 August 1927.

———. "Afghanistan and Ceylon." *The Negro World*. 1 October 1927.

———. "Can War Be Outlawed?" *The Negro World*. 8 October 1927.

———. "Those Who Suffer from India's Independence." *The Negro World*, 15 October 1927.

———. "Be Prepared." *The Negro World*. n.d.

Terrell, Mary Church. "An Ethnologist's Injustice or Ignorance." *Ringwood's Afro-American Journal of Fashion.*"(April 1893).

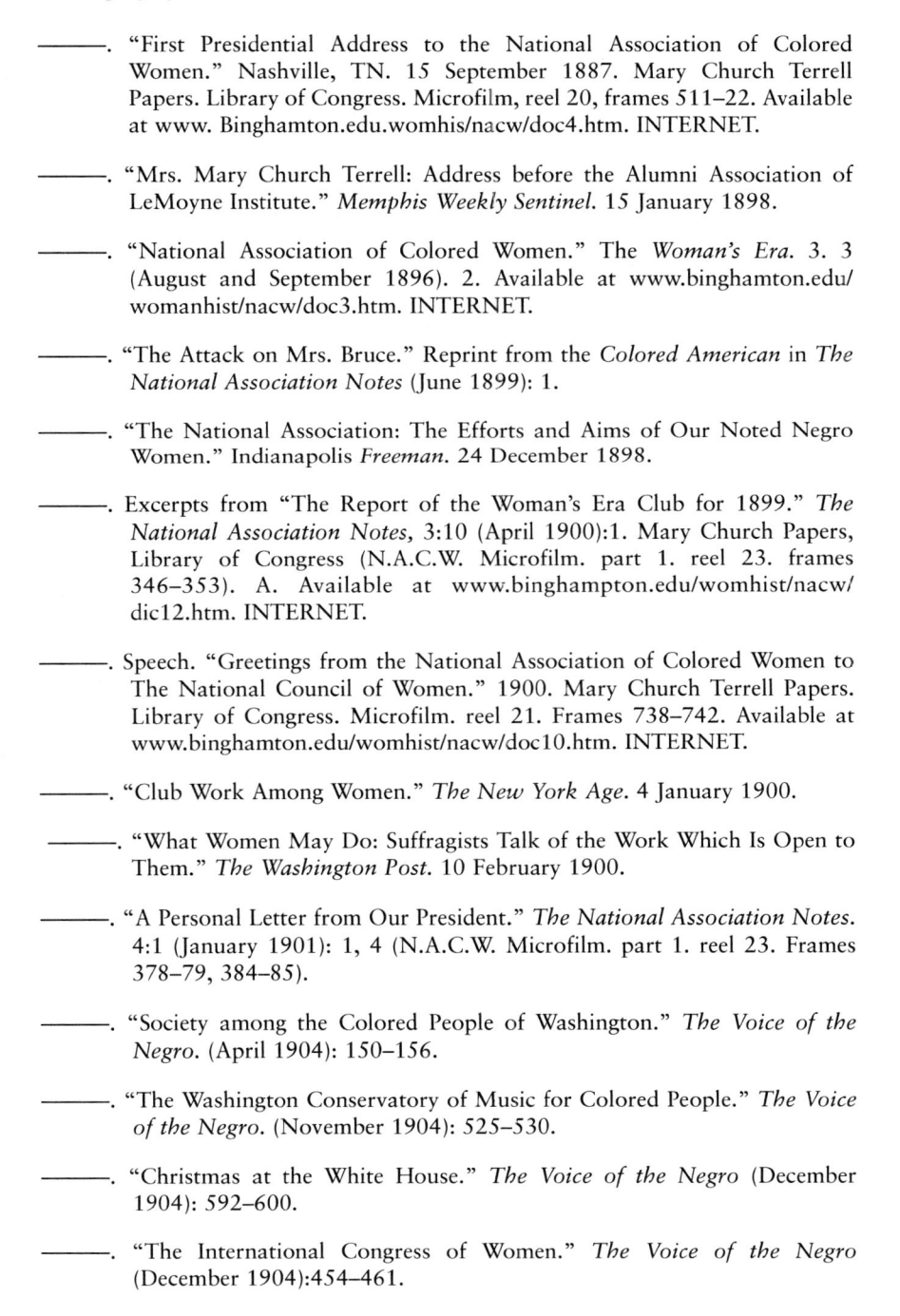

———. "First Presidential Address to the National Association of Colored Women." Nashville, TN. 15 September 1887. Mary Church Terrell Papers. Library of Congress. Microfilm, reel 20, frames 511–22. Available at www. Binghamton.edu.womhis/nacw/doc4.htm. INTERNET.

———. "Mrs. Mary Church Terrell: Address before the Alumni Association of LeMoyne Institute." *Memphis Weekly Sentinel.* 15 January 1898.

———. "National Association of Colored Women." The *Woman's Era.* 3. 3 (August and September 1896). 2. Available at www.binghamton.edu/womanhist/nacw/doc3.htm. INTERNET.

———. "The Attack on Mrs. Bruce." Reprint from the *Colored American* in *The National Association Notes* (June 1899): 1.

———. "The National Association: The Efforts and Aims of Our Noted Negro Women." Indianapolis *Freeman.* 24 December 1898.

———. Excerpts from "The Report of the Woman's Era Club for 1899." *The National Association Notes,* 3:10 (April 1900):1. Mary Church Papers, Library of Congress (N.A.C.W. Microfilm. part 1. reel 23. frames 346–353). A. Available at www.binghampton.edu/womhist/nacw/dic12.htm. INTERNET.

———. Speech. "Greetings from the National Association of Colored Women to The National Council of Women." 1900. Mary Church Terrell Papers. Library of Congress. Microfilm. reel 21. Frames 738–742. Available at www.binghamton.edu/womhist/nacw/doc10.htm. INTERNET.

———. "Club Work Among Women." *The New York Age.* 4 January 1900.

———. "What Women May Do: Suffragists Talk of the Work Which Is Open to Them." *The Washington Post.* 10 February 1900.

———. "A Personal Letter from Our President." *The National Association Notes.* 4:1 (January 1901): 1, 4 (N.A.C.W. Microfilm. part 1. reel 23. Frames 378–79, 384–85).

———. "Society among the Colored People of Washington." *The Voice of the Negro.* (April 1904): 150–156.

———. "The Washington Conservatory of Music for Colored People." *The Voice of the Negro.* (November 1904): 525–530.

———. "Christmas at the White House." *The Voice of the Negro* (December 1904): 592–600.

———. "The International Congress of Women." *The Voice of the Negro* (December 1904):454–461.

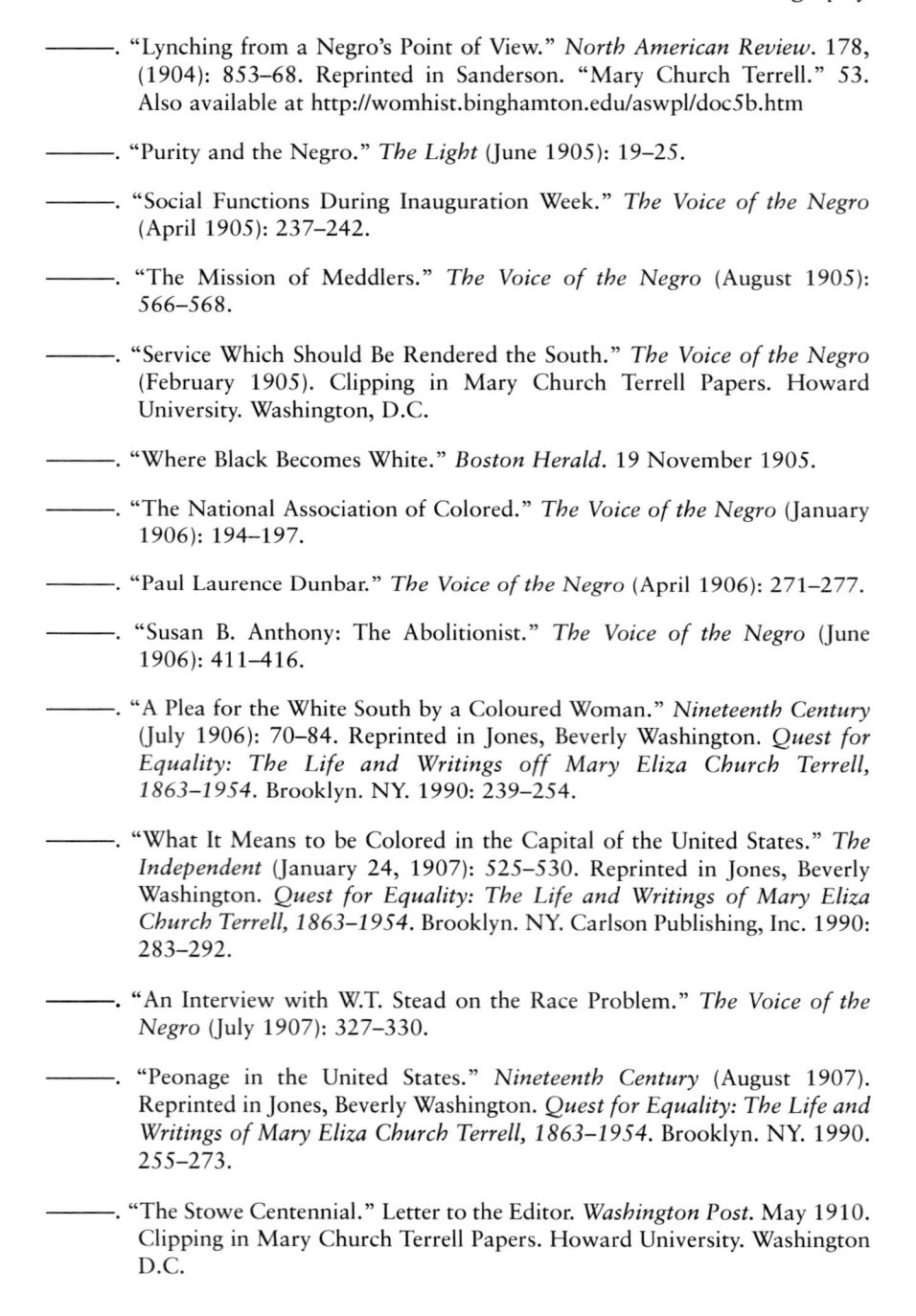

———. "Lynching from a Negro's Point of View." *North American Review*. 178, (1904): 853–68. Reprinted in Sanderson. "Mary Church Terrell." 53. Also available at http://womhist.binghamton.edu/aswpl/doc5b.htm

———. "Purity and the Negro." *The Light* (June 1905): 19–25.

———. "Social Functions During Inauguration Week." *The Voice of the Negro* (April 1905): 237–242.

———. "The Mission of Meddlers." *The Voice of the Negro* (August 1905): 566–568.

———. "Service Which Should Be Rendered the South." *The Voice of the Negro* (February 1905). Clipping in Mary Church Terrell Papers. Howard University. Washington, D.C.

———. "Where Black Becomes White." *Boston Herald*. 19 November 1905.

———. "The National Association of Colored." *The Voice of the Negro* (January 1906): 194–197.

———. "Paul Laurence Dunbar." *The Voice of the Negro* (April 1906): 271–277.

———. "Susan B. Anthony: The Abolitionist." *The Voice of the Negro* (June 1906): 411–416.

———. "A Plea for the White South by a Coloured Woman." *Nineteenth Century* (July 1906): 70–84. Reprinted in Jones, Beverly Washington. *Quest for Equality: The Life and Writings off Mary Eliza Church Terrell, 1863–1954*. Brooklyn. NY. 1990: 239–254.

———. "What It Means to be Colored in the Capital of the United States." *The Independent* (January 24, 1907): 525–530. Reprinted in Jones, Beverly Washington. *Quest for Equality: The Life and Writings of Mary Eliza Church Terrell, 1863–1954*. Brooklyn. NY. Carlson Publishing, Inc. 1990: 283–292.

———. "An Interview with W.T. Stead on the Race Problem." *The Voice of the Negro* (July 1907): 327–330.

———. "Peonage in the United States." *Nineteenth Century* (August 1907). Reprinted in Jones, Beverly Washington. *Quest for Equality: The Life and Writings of Mary Eliza Church Terrell, 1863–1954*. Brooklyn. NY. 1990. 255–273.

———. "The Stowe Centennial." Letter to the Editor. *Washington Post*. May 1910. Clipping in Mary Church Terrell Papers. Howard University. Washington D.C.

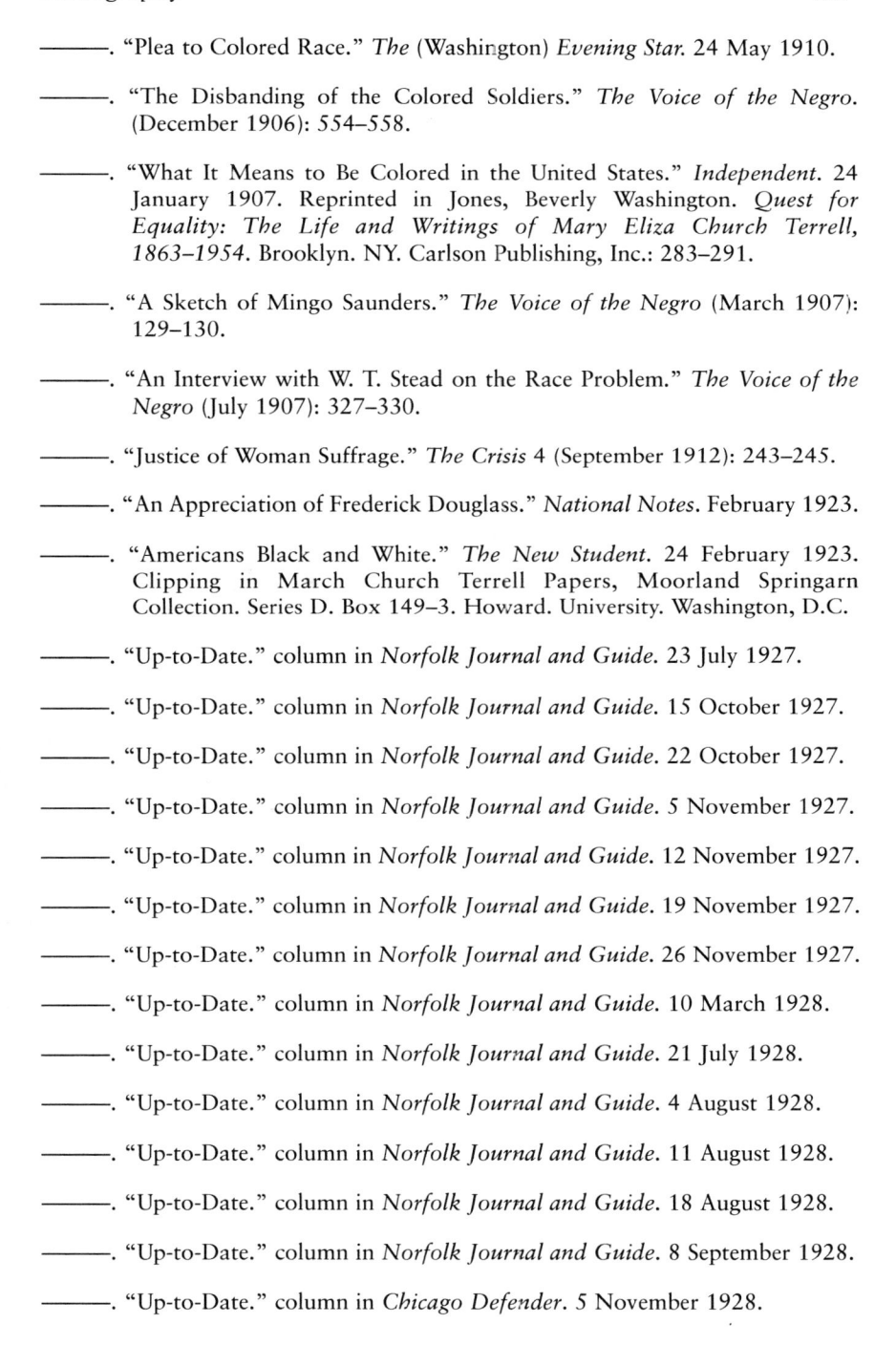

———. "Plea to Colored Race." *The* (Washington) *Evening Star.* 24 May 1910.

———. "The Disbanding of the Colored Soldiers." *The Voice of the Negro.* (December 1906): 554–558.

———. "What It Means to Be Colored in the United States." *Independent.* 24 January 1907. Reprinted in Jones, Beverly Washington. *Quest for Equality: The Life and Writings of Mary Eliza Church Terrell, 1863–1954.* Brooklyn. NY. Carlson Publishing, Inc.: 283–291.

———. "A Sketch of Mingo Saunders." *The Voice of the Negro* (March 1907): 129–130.

———. "An Interview with W. T. Stead on the Race Problem." *The Voice of the Negro* (July 1907): 327–330.

———. "Justice of Woman Suffrage." *The Crisis* 4 (September 1912): 243–245.

———. "An Appreciation of Frederick Douglass." *National Notes.* February 1923.

———. "Americans Black and White." *The New Student.* 24 February 1923. Clipping in March Church Terrell Papers, Moorland Springarn Collection. Series D. Box 149–3. Howard. University. Washington, D.C.

———. "Up-to-Date." column in *Norfolk Journal and Guide.* 23 July 1927.

———. "Up-to-Date." column in *Norfolk Journal and Guide.* 15 October 1927.

———. "Up-to-Date." column in *Norfolk Journal and Guide.* 22 October 1927.

———. "Up-to-Date." column in *Norfolk Journal and Guide.* 5 November 1927.

———. "Up-to-Date." column in *Norfolk Journal and Guide.* 12 November 1927.

———. "Up-to-Date." column in *Norfolk Journal and Guide.* 19 November 1927.

———. "Up-to-Date." column in *Norfolk Journal and Guide.* 26 November 1927.

———. "Up-to-Date." column in *Norfolk Journal and Guide.* 10 March 1928.

———. "Up-to-Date." column in *Norfolk Journal and Guide.* 21 July 1928.

———. "Up-to-Date." column in *Norfolk Journal and Guide.* 4 August 1928.

———. "Up-to-Date." column in *Norfolk Journal and Guide.* 11 August 1928.

———. "Up-to-Date." column in *Norfolk Journal and Guide.* 18 August 1928.

———. "Up-to-Date." column in *Norfolk Journal and Guide.* 8 September 1928.

———. "Up-to-Date." column in *Chicago Defender.* 5 November 1928.

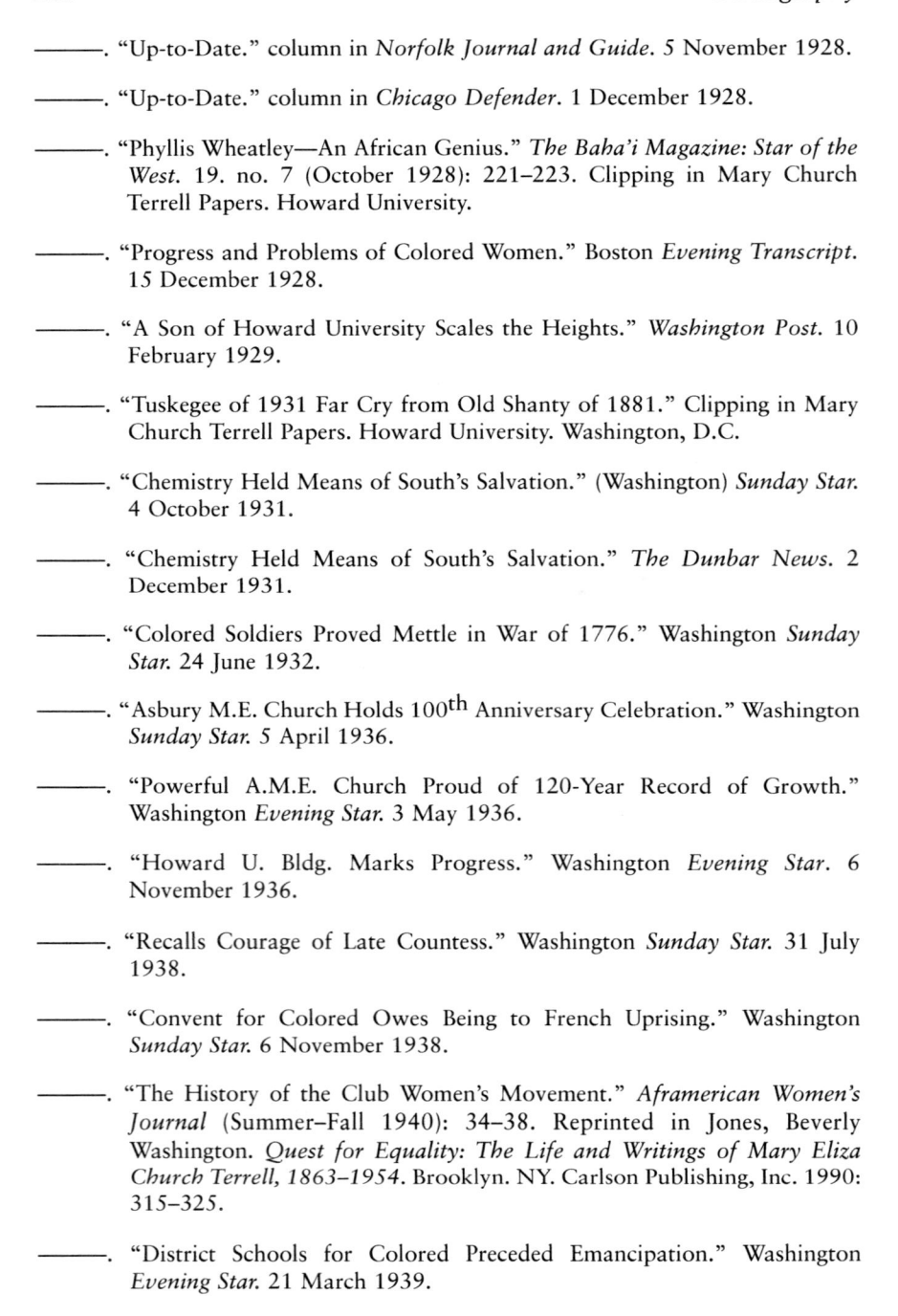

———. "Up-to-Date." column in *Norfolk Journal and Guide*. 5 November 1928.

———. "Up-to-Date." column in *Chicago Defender*. 1 December 1928.

———. "Phyllis Wheatley—An African Genius." *The Baha'i Magazine: Star of the West*. 19. no. 7 (October 1928): 221–223. Clipping in Mary Church Terrell Papers. Howard University.

———. "Progress and Problems of Colored Women." Boston *Evening Transcript*. 15 December 1928.

———. "A Son of Howard University Scales the Heights." *Washington Post*. 10 February 1929.

———. "Tuskegee of 1931 Far Cry from Old Shanty of 1881." Clipping in Mary Church Terrell Papers. Howard University. Washington, D.C.

———. "Chemistry Held Means of South's Salvation." (Washington) *Sunday Star*. 4 October 1931.

———. "Chemistry Held Means of South's Salvation." *The Dunbar News*. 2 December 1931.

———. "Colored Soldiers Proved Mettle in War of 1776." Washington *Sunday Star*. 24 June 1932.

———. "Asbury M.E. Church Holds 100th Anniversary Celebration." Washington *Sunday Star*. 5 April 1936.

———. "Powerful A.M.E. Church Proud of 120-Year Record of Growth." Washington *Evening Star*. 3 May 1936.

———. "Howard U. Bldg. Marks Progress." Washington *Evening Star*. 6 November 1936.

———. "Recalls Courage of Late Countess." Washington *Sunday Star*. 31 July 1938.

———. "Convent for Colored Owes Being to French Uprising." Washington *Sunday Star*. 6 November 1938.

———. "The History of the Club Women's Movement." *Aframerican Women's Journal* (Summer–Fall 1940): 34–38. Reprinted in Jones, Beverly Washington. *Quest for Equality: The Life and Writings of Mary Eliza Church Terrell, 1863–1954*. Brooklyn. NY. Carlson Publishing, Inc. 1990: 315–325.

———. "District Schools for Colored Preceded Emancipation." Washington *Evening Star*. 21 March 1939.

Bibliography

———. "Democracy at Work." Letter to the Editor. Washington *Star* 17 March 1941.

———. "Needed: Women Lawyers." *The Negro Digest*. September 1943.

———. "Human Relations in Transition to Peace." Speech to the National Congress of Negro Women. 13 October 1944.

———. "Outlawing 'Negro'." Letter to the Editor. *Washington Post*. 27 May 1949.

———. "Dr. Sara W. Brown." *The Journal of the College Alumni Club of Washington* 30 (Memorial Edition, April 1950).

———. "I Remember Frederick Douglas." *Ebony* (October 1953): 73–80.

———. "Phyllis Wheatlely, Slave Poetess." Clipping in Mary Church Terrell Papers. Howard University. Washington, D.C.

———. "Mrs. Mary Church-Terrell: In "Address Before the Alumni Association of LeMoyne Institute." *The (Memphis) Weekly*. Clipping in Mary Church Terrell Papers. Howard University. Washington, D.C.

———. "No Color Line Abroad." *Washington Post*. No date. Clipping in Mary Church Terrell Papers. Howard University. Washington, D.C.

———. "Noted Race Advocate Gives Interesting Reminiscences." *Chicago Defender*. No date. Clipping in Mary Church Terrell Papers. Howard University. Washington, D.C.

———. "Writes Negro Symphony." No date. Clipping in Mary Church Terrell Papers. Howard University. Washington, D.C.

———. "Efforts for His Race Bring Dr. Just Honors." No date. Clipping in Mary Church Terrell Papers. Howard University. Washington, D.C.

———. "Douglass Was No Jim-Crow Boy..." No date. Clipping in Mary Church Terrell Papers. Howard University. Washington, D.C.

———. "Scientist, Born in South Is South's Salvation." No date. Clipping in Mary Church Terrell Papers. Howard University. Washington, D.C.

———. "Miracle Among Needy Worked By Rosenwald." No date. Clipping in Mary Church Terrell Papers. Howard University. Washington, D.C.

———. "Paris Gone Wild Over Primitive African Art." No date. Clipping in Mary Church Terrell Papers. Howard University. Washington, D.C.

———. "Some Aspect of the Employment Problem, As It Concerns Colored People." Manuscript in Mary Church Terrell Papers. Moorland-Springarn Collection. Howard University. Washington, D.C.

———. "The Racial Worm Turns." Manuscript in Mary Church Terrell Papers. Howard University. Washington, D.C.

———. "The Effect of the Disfranchisement of Colored Men upon Colored women in the South." Manuscript in Mary Church Terrell Papers. Howard University. Washington, D.C.

———. "Something About Our Name." Manuscript in Mary Church Terrell Papers. Howard University. Washington, D.C.

———. "My Experiences in the Recent Political Campaign." *Howard University Record*. No date. Mary Church Terrell Papers. Howard University. Washington, D.C.

———. "Noted Race Advocate Gives Interesting Reminiscences." *The Chicago Defender*. No date. Mary Church Terrell Papers. Howard University. Washington, D.C.

———. "Solicitor General." Letter to the Editor. *The Washington Post*. No date. Mary Church Terrell Papers. Howard University. Washington, D.C.

———. "D.C. Discrimination." Letter to the Editor. *The Washington Post*. No date. Mary Church Terrell Papers. Howard University. Washington. D.C.

———. "Psychological Group's Protest." Letter to the Editor. *The Washington Star*. No date. Mary Church Terrell Papers. Howard University. Washington, D.C.

Wells, Ida B. "Lynch Law in All Its Phases." Originally published in *Our Story* (May 1893): 333–337. Reproduced in Thompson, Mildred. *An Exploratory Study of an American Black Woman, 1893–1930*. Brooklyn. NY. Carlson Publishing Inc. 1990. 171–187.

Wells, Ida B. "Iola on Discrimination." *New York Freeman*. 15 January 1887.

———. "Freedom of Political Action: A Woman's Magnificent Definition of the Political Situation." *New York Freeman*. 7 November 1885.

———. "Woman's Mission." *New York Freeman*. 26 December 1885.

———. "Functions of Leadership." Originally published in *Living Way* 12 September 1885. Reprinted in DeCosta-Willis. *The Memphis Diary of Ida B. Wells* Boston. Beacon Press. 1995. 178–179.

———. "The Model Woman: A Pen Picture of the Typical Southern Girl." *New York Freeman*. 18 February 1888.

———. "Afro-American and Africa." *A. M. E. Church Review* (July 1892).

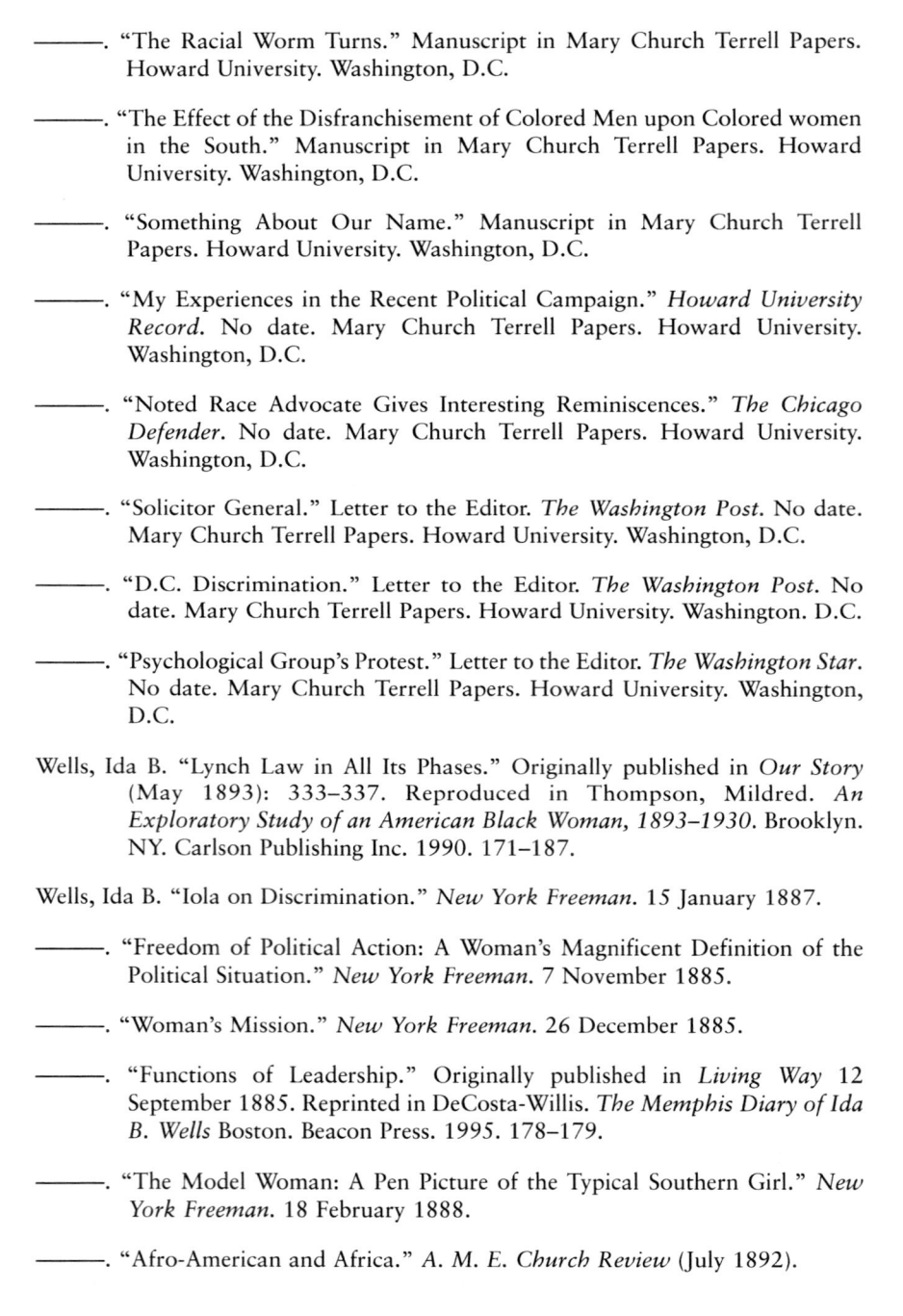

Bibliography

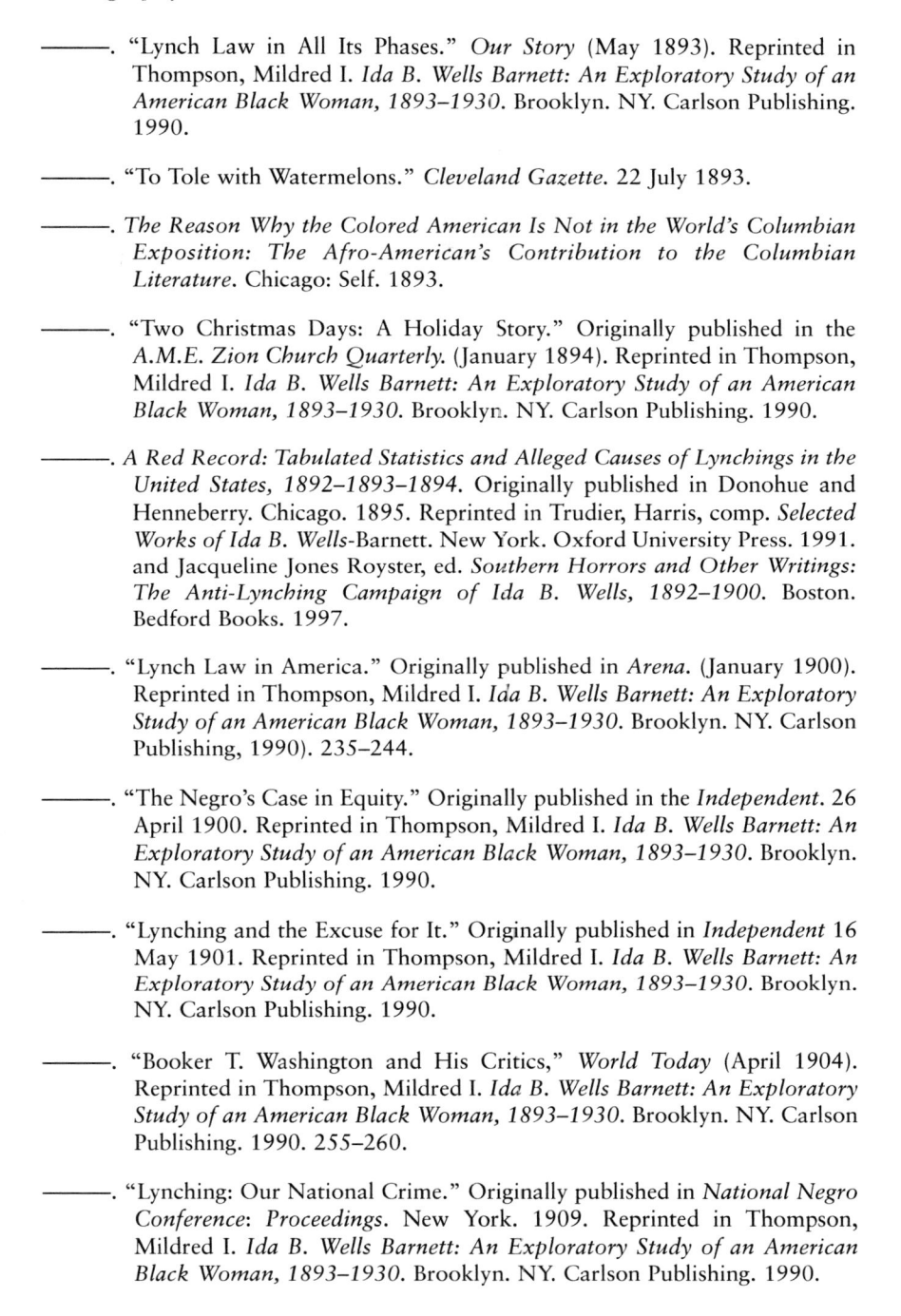

———. "Lynch Law in All Its Phases." *Our Story* (May 1893). Reprinted in Thompson, Mildred I. *Ida B. Wells Barnett: An Exploratory Study of an American Black Woman, 1893–1930.* Brooklyn. NY. Carlson Publishing. 1990.

———. "To Tole with Watermelons." *Cleveland Gazette.* 22 July 1893.

———. *The Reason Why the Colored American Is Not in the World's Columbian Exposition: The Afro-American's Contribution to the Columbian Literature.* Chicago: Self. 1893.

———. "Two Christmas Days: A Holiday Story." Originally published in the *A.M.E. Zion Church Quarterly.* (January 1894). Reprinted in Thompson, Mildred I. *Ida B. Wells Barnett: An Exploratory Study of an American Black Woman, 1893–1930.* Brooklyn. NY. Carlson Publishing. 1990.

———. *A Red Record: Tabulated Statistics and Alleged Causes of Lynchings in the United States, 1892–1893–1894.* Originally published in Donohue and Henneberry. Chicago. 1895. Reprinted in Trudier, Harris, comp. *Selected Works of Ida B. Wells*-Barnett. New York. Oxford University Press. 1991. and Jacqueline Jones Royster, ed. *Southern Horrors and Other Writings: The Anti-Lynching Campaign of Ida B. Wells, 1892–1900.* Boston. Bedford Books. 1997.

———. "Lynch Law in America." Originally published in *Arena.* (January 1900). Reprinted in Thompson, Mildred I. *Ida B. Wells Barnett: An Exploratory Study of an American Black Woman, 1893–1930.* Brooklyn. NY. Carlson Publishing, 1990). 235–244.

———. "The Negro's Case in Equity." Originally published in the *Independent.* 26 April 1900. Reprinted in Thompson, Mildred I. *Ida B. Wells Barnett: An Exploratory Study of an American Black Woman, 1893–1930.* Brooklyn. NY. Carlson Publishing. 1990.

———. "Lynching and the Excuse for It." Originally published in *Independent* 16 May 1901. Reprinted in Thompson, Mildred I. *Ida B. Wells Barnett: An Exploratory Study of an American Black Woman, 1893–1930.* Brooklyn. NY. Carlson Publishing. 1990.

———. "Booker T. Washington and His Critics," *World Today* (April 1904). Reprinted in Thompson, Mildred I. *Ida B. Wells Barnett: An Exploratory Study of an American Black Woman, 1893–1930.* Brooklyn. NY. Carlson Publishing. 1990. 255–260.

———. "Lynching: Our National Crime." Originally published in *National Negro Conference: Proceedings.* New York. 1909. Reprinted in Thompson, Mildred I. *Ida B. Wells Barnett: An Exploratory Study of an American Black Woman, 1893–1930.* Brooklyn. NY. Carlson Publishing. 1990.

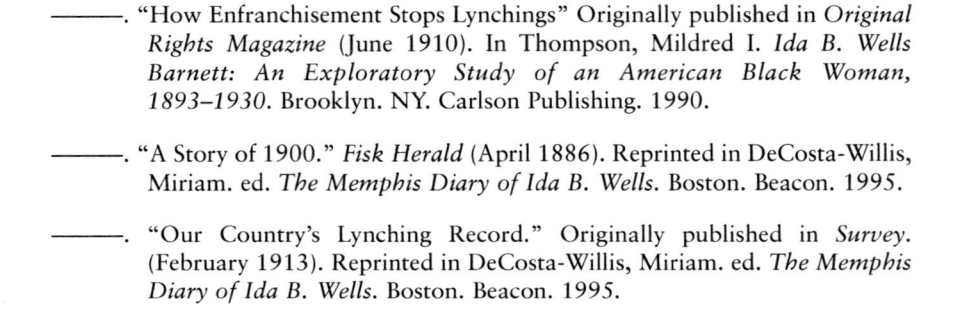

———. "How Enfranchisement Stops Lynchings" Originally published in *Original Rights Magazine* (June 1910). In Thompson, Mildred I. *Ida B. Wells Barnett: An Exploratory Study of an American Black Woman, 1893–1930*. Brooklyn. NY. Carlson Publishing. 1990.

———. "A Story of 1900." *Fisk Herald* (April 1886). Reprinted in DeCosta-Willis, Miriam. ed. *The Memphis Diary of Ida B. Wells*. Boston. Beacon. 1995.

———. "Our Country's Lynching Record." Originally published in *Survey*. (February 1913). Reprinted in DeCosta-Willis, Miriam. ed. *The Memphis Diary of Ida B. Wells*. Boston. Beacon. 1995.

UNPUBLISHED MATERIAL

Typewritten notation in Marcus Mosiah Garvey Memorial Collection, Box 12, Fisk University Library Special Collections, Nashville, Tennessee.

"Marcus Garvey and UNIA Papers Project," Fact Sheet, University of California at Los Angeles. Available at www.isop.ucla.edu/mgpp/facts.htm: INTERNET.

Amy Jacques Garvey, Handwritten notation in Scrapbook, Marcus Mosiah Garvey Memorial Collection. Fisk University Library Special Collections, Nashville. TN.

———. Notation for an August 25, 1968 television show. In Marcus Mosiah Garvey Memorial Collection. Fisk University. Nashville. TN.

———. "Be Prepared." Manuscript in Marcus Mosiah Garvey Memorial Collection. Fisk University. Nashville. TN.

"Agreement between Universal Negro Improvement Association, Inc., African Communities League, Inc., and Marcus Garvey and Amy Jacques Garvey." Marcus Mosiah Garvey Memorial Collection. Fisk University. Nashville. TN.

Amy Jacques Garvey, "Role of Women in Liberation Struggle," Manuscript in Marcus Mosiah Garvey Memorial Collection. Fisk University. Nashville. TN.

Index

African-American club women, 13–14, 30, 61–62, 73, 90, 98, 147–148
African-American women journalists
    audience, 2, 16, 19–20, 63, 90, 103
    publications for which they wrote, 1–2, 8–9, 10–17, 19–21, 34–37, 62–64, 88–90, 108
    themes, 2, 9, 14–15, 19–21, 37–52, 64–81, 100, 103, 106, 108, 143
African Methodist Episcopal Denomination, 11, 144
Age. See *New York Age*
Alpha Suffrage Club, 30

Barnett, Ferdinand L. (Ida B. Wells' husband), 47, 138
Black Star Line Steamship Company, 116, 131
Black women, 4–5, 13–14, 16–19
    club women, 13–14, 30, 61–62, 73, 90, 98, 147–148
Black women journalists
    audience, 2, 16, 19–20, 63, 90, 103
    publications for which they wrote, 1–2, 8–9, 10–17, 19–21, 34–37, 62–64, 88–90, 108
    themes, 2, 9, 14–15, 19–21, 37–52, 64–81, 100, 103, 106, 108, 143

Conservator (Chicago), 29, 34, 36
Church, Mary (Mollie), *See also* Terrell, Mary Church, 55, 57
Church, Robert, (father of Mary Church Terrell), 55–58–59, 139, 147

Douglass, Frederick, 47, 60, 78
Dunbar, Paul Laurence, 11, 86,
Dunbar-Nelson, Alice, 10–11, 83–104, 135–150
    as activist, 87, 89
    advocacy, seeds of 87–88
    biographical information, 85, 87
    birth of, 85
    death of, 87
    education, 85–86, 138
    and Dunbar, Paul Lawrence (first husband), 11
    gender, writings about, 96–99, 142
    interracial cooperation, 87–99
    and Jim Crow, 83, 84, 93, 95, 104
    journalism career
        beginnings, 11, 84, 88
        publications for which she wrote, 88–90
        themes, 90, 100, 143
        writing style, 101–103
    lynching, 87, 91, 97, 104

marriage(s) and family, 86–87, 89
race, writings about, 91–96
suffrage, 93, 97, 142
as teacher, 86
and writing style, 101–103

Fortune, T. Thomas, 26, 36, 50
Free Speech, 35–36, 38–39, 48–49
Free Speech and Headlight, 35
Freeman (*Indianapolis*), 26, 62, 72

Garvey, Amy Jacques, 11–12, 105–133, 135–150
  as activist, 105
  advocacy, seeds of, 109
  biographical information, 106–108
  birth, 106
  black men, writings about, 115, 124, 127–131
  economic independence, 108, 116–120
  education, 106, 138
  gender, writings about, 124, 127–129, 142
  and imperialism, 140
  Jews, writings about, 110, 119, 122
  journalism career
    beginnings, 1018
    publications, 108
    themes, 108
  lynching, 143
  marriage, 106–107, 130
  and Universal Negro Improvement Association (UNIA), 12, 105–106, 112, 114–118, 121–124, 130
  and white exploitation, writings about, 109–114
Garvey, Marcus Mosiah, 12, 105–107, 112, 116,122–130
Garvey Movement, 105–106, 108, 114, 123, 127131–133
Great Migration, 3, 30

Inter-Ocean (Chicago), 36–37, 51

Jacques, Charlotte, 126
Jacques, Samuel, 106
Jim Crow, 2, 15, 65, 69, 72, 83, 84, 93, 95, 104, 118, 138, 144

Lynching, 3, 8–10, 15–16, 25–27, 31, 33–34, 36, 39–44, 50–52 61, 64, 68, 87, 91, 97, 104,137, 143–145, 150

Moore, Joseph, (Alice Dunbar-Nelson's father), 85
Moore, Patricia Wright (Alice Dunbar-Nelson's mother), 85
Moss, Thomas, lynching death of, 37–38, 61,140

NAACP. *See* National Association for the Advancement of Colored People
Nadir, 2–3
National Association for the Advancement of Colored People, 30
National Association of Colored Women (NACW), 14, 30, 61, 72, 75, 147
National Press Association, 26, 35
Nelson, Robert, (husband of Alice Dunbar Nelson), 87, 89
Negro World, 11–12, 18, 105–108, 112–113, 124, 132
New York Age, 26, 34, 36, 39, 50, 62, 73, 89
Norfolk Journal and Guide, 10, 74

Reconstruction, 49, 53
Republican Party, 49, 76–79, 89, 92
Roosevelt, Theodore, 58

Smith, Lucy Wilmot, 26,
Suffrage, 10, 75–77, 93, 97, 142
Susan B. Anthony, 82

Terrell, Mary Church, 9–10, 55–82, 135–150

Index

as activist, 56, 60–61, 142, 147
advocacy, seeds of, 60
and antilynching crusade
black achievement, writings about, 77–81
biographical information, 56–58
in Europe, 58, 60
education, 9, 56–58
gender, writings about, 71–76
journalism career
  beginnings, 61
  letters to the editor, 63–65, 69
  publications for which she wrote, 62–64
  themes, 64–81
and lynching, 61, 64, 68
marriage, 58, 138
and racial identity, 58–60
race, writings about, 65–71
as speaker, 56
suffrage, 58, 60, 75–77
as teacher, 57–58
and themes, 143
Terrell, Robert, 58, 138

Universal Negro Improvement Association (UNIA), 12, 105–106, 112, 114–118, 121–124, 130

Voice of the Negro, 10, 67, 73–74, 79

Washington, Booker T., 132, 144
Wells-Barnett, Ida B., 6–9, 25–53, 135–150
  as activist, 29–30, 137, 143, 147;
  and advocacy, seeds of, 29
  anti-lynching crusade, 9, 25, 31, 61, 39–44, 61, 137, 143–144, 145, 150;
  biographical information, 27–29;
  death of, 53;
  as editor of *Free Speech*, 35–36, 38–39, 48–49;
  education, 27–28
  gender, writings about, 44–46
  journalism career, 8–37
    beginnings, 8, 31–34
    publications for which she wrote, 34–37
  lynching, writings about, 9, 31, 33–34, 36, 39–44, 50–52, 54, 145
  and marriage and family, 29, 138
  Memphis Daily Commercial, 26
  and NAACP, 30
  and National Association of Colored Women, 30, 147
  race, writings about, 46–51
  and suffrage, 30–31, 51–52
  Suit against Chesapeake and Ohio Railroad. 33
  as teacher, 28,-29, 31–32, 138, 140
  and themes, 37–52, 143
  and tour of England, 51, 145

Wells, James (Jim) (father of Ida B. Wells-Barnett), 27, 139–140
Wells, Elizabeth (Lizzie) (mother of Ida B. Wells-Barnett), 27
Wilmington Advocate, 11, 14, 84–85, 89
Wilson, Woodrow, 31